Challenges in Human Rights

Challenges in Human Rights

A Social Work Perspective

EDITED BY

ELISABETH REICHERT

Columbia University Press   *New York*

Columbia University Press
Publishers Since 1893
New York   Chichester, West Sussex
Copyright © 2007 Elisabeth Reichert
All rights reserved
Library of Congress Cataloging-in-Publication Data
Challenges in human rights : a social work perspective / edited by Elisabeth Reichert.
p.   cm.
Includes index.
ISBN 978-0-231-13720-1 (cloth : alk. paper) — ISBN 978-0-231-13721-8 (pbk.) —
ISBN 978-0-231-51034-9 (electronic)
1. Social service. 2. Human rights. 3. Cultural relativism. I. Reichert, Elisabeth. II. Title.
HV41.O84 2007
323—dc222006039529
♾
Columbia University Press books are printed on permanent and durable acid-free paper.
This book was printed on paper with recycled content.
Printed in the United States of America

Contents

Contents

Abbreviations

AMA	American Medical Association
AU	African Union
CAT	Convention Against Torture and Other Cruel, Inhuman, or Degrading Treatment or Punishment
CCWP	California Coalition of Women Prisoners
CEDAW	Convention on the Elimination of Discrimination Against Women
CERD	International Convention on the Elimination of All Forms of Racial Discrimination
CIW	Coalition of Immokalee Workers (Florida)
CORROC	Claiming our Rights/Reclaiming our Children
CRC	Convention on the Rights of the Child
CSWE	Council on Social Work Education
DESA	Department of Economic and Social Affairs
ENOC	European Network of Ombudsmen for Children
EU	European Union
GDP	gross domestic product
GNP	gross national product
GM	genetically modified
GSCC	General Social Care Council

List of Abbreviations

HDI	Human Development Index
HUD	Housing and Urban Development
IASSW	International Association of Schools of Social Work
ICCPR	International Covenants on Civil and Political Rights
ICESCR	International Covenant on Economic Social and Cultural Rights
ICESPR	International Convention on Economic, Social, and Political Rights
IFSW	International Federation of Social Workers
ILO	International Labor Organization
INS	Immigration and Naturalization Service
KCSDV	Kansas Coalition Against Domestic Violence
KWRU	Kensington Welfare Rights Union
LGBT	Lesbian, Gay, Bisexual, and Transgendered [movement]
IMF	International Monetary Fund
MAI	Multilateral Agreement on Investment
MESJ	Mormons for Economic and Social Justice (Utah)
Mhgap	Mental Health Global Action Programme
NAACP	National Association for the Advancement of Colored People
NAFTA	North Atlantic Free Trade Agreement
NASW	National Association of Social Work
NEWPIN	New Parent Infant Network [services]
NGOs	nongovernmental organizations
OAS	Organization of American States
OPVD	Office of the Prevention of Domestic Violence
PPEHRC	Poor People's Economic Human Rights Campaign
PTSD	post-traumatic stress disorder
SCLC	Southern Christian Leadership Conference
SEWA	Self-Employed Women's Association (India)
SSW&ST	School of Social Work and Social Transformation
UDHR	Universal Declaration of Human Rights
UNHCR	United Nations Human Rights Commission
UNICEF	United Nations Children's Fund
UNIFEM	United Nations Development Fund for Women
UP	University of the Poor
WEAP	Women's Economic Agenda Project (Oakland, CA)
WEDO	Women's Environment & Development Organization
WHO	World Health Organization
WTO	World Trade Organization

Introduction

Social Work Perspectives on Human Rights

ELISABETH REICHERT

Until recently the social work profession in the United States and other countries has been reluctant to integrate concepts of human rights within social work policies and practices. Although social work academics may give lip service to human rights as an important element of the social work curriculum, the reality often shows that social work has yet to fully embrace or acknowledge the significance of human rights within the profession.

One of the challenges within the social work profession, particularly in the United States, is to encourage the profession to give more than passing attention or an obligatory nod to human rights. A significant obstacle to overcoming that challenge is the lack of appropriate literature in this area. Most academic books on human rights have little to do with social work and usually shortchange discussion about economic, social, and cultural rights. Political and civil rights dominate the themes of those books, which clearly prompt social workers to question the relevance of human rights to their profession. Yet principles of economic, social, and cultural human rights permeate social work ethics, values, and principles. Therefore the objective of this book is to provide the social worker with provocative discussions to help understand the relevance of human rights to the profession.

This book, a human rights reader comprised of chapters written by educators and professionals from around the world, addresses the large gap currently existing within social work literature. The various chapters focus on one primary theme: human rights within a social work context, with emphasis on economic, social, and cultural human rights, as these areas are most relevant to social workers today. The writings in this book reflect the diversity of the authors, whose backgrounds include experiences in many different parts of the world. Thus their views on economic, social, and cultural human rights issues are perceived from different angles, including that of Western versus non-Western nations. Questions the chapters address include the following:

- How does the social work profession integrate human rights into policies and practices?
- Can the notion of cultural relativism be reconciled with a universal concept of human rights?
- Do human rights truly promote economic and social development, or are they merely a tool of rich, Western societies in their effort to dominate less economically developed countries?
- How does gender relate to the realization of human rights?

While acknowledging the complexity of human rights issues, the authors' goal is to make sense out of this complexity, and, in doing so, they necessarily challenge and confront the established thinking.

Issues

The authors address the following issues, among others, to introduce readers to specific, contemporary human rights issues within a social work context:

- Should political and civil human rights have greater priority than economic and social rights?
- Social work is a profession with the mission to help overcome injustices on a national and international level. Do wealthy nations have a duty to assist less economically developed countries?
- Cultural relativism generally refers to a culturally specific view of a particular issue. Within a human rights context, cultural relativism could be used to excuse the practice of a culturally specific theme

Introduction: Social Work Perspectives on Human Rights

even though this conflicts with human rights principles. Should cultural relativism excuse apparent human rights violations?

- What role does gender play in the practice of human rights?
- Should lower-income individuals be entitled to basic human rights, including health care?
- Can lawyers and social workers find a common cause in promoting human rights?

Chapter 1, my contribution to the volume, discusses how human rights provide the social work profession with a more global and contemporary set of guidelines that fall outside the overused category of "social justice." I emphasize that human rights are never without controversy or tension, especially within the context of cultural relativism and universality.

Lena Dominelli writes, in chapter 2, that, in theory, both the International Federation of Social Workers and the International Association of School of Social Work stress the importance of integrating human rights into theory and practice. Social workers' particular skills enable them to play a key role in ensuring that people everywhere enjoy their human rights. But to make the most of this expertise, the social work curriculum needs to provide a framework for acquiring the knowledge and skills that will assist in promoting human rights. Dominelli advocates that human rights emerge from their invisible status and become a subject explicitly covered in the academy and in practice.

The concept of "global distributive justice" is analyzed as a human right in chapter 3 by Joseph Wronka. This innovative and thought-provoking look at the encompassing problem of rich country versus poor country raises important issues for social workers everywhere. Should nations and individuals with more wealth address this inequality within the context of human rights? If this view prevails, would wealthier nations be more likely to recognize a global redistribution?

A hotly debated aspect of human rights is the relationship between culturally specific practices and universal principles. Jim Ife, in chapter 4, examines issues of universality versus cultural relativism and the tension between the two concepts. Universalism has led some to criticize human rights as part of a Western imperialist project. Ife believes that issues of universalism and cultural relativism require a careful and sophisticated analysis, that extreme views of these two positions are untenable. He also addresses shortfalls in a solely legalistic approach to human rights. The law, he contends, cannot intervene in the private domain for anything more than the most blatant of abuses, such as child abuse or domestic violence. He stresses the importance of defining human rights from below and helping people to develop their own definitions of human rights.

Turning to issues of global development, James Midgley points out, in chapter 5, that economic development brings prosperity to only a segment of the world population and that a sizable proportion of the rural population continues to live in poverty. According to Midgley, social development theory and practice have not systematically incorporated human rights, and he shows how various human rights instruments relevant to social development can be used to promote a rights-base approach to social work. By acceding to a human rights treaty, government programs dealing with education, health, nutrition, maternal well-being, and shelter are no longer discretionary but have a force of law. Despite the proverbial claim than economic, social, and cultural rights cannot legally be enforced, Midgley cites examples of the successful use of legal means to redress economic and social human rights. Known as public interest litigation, these cases are often pursued by human rights advocacy organizations working together with nongovernmental organizations engaged in social development.

Examining a topic closer to the economic and social human rights issues of the United States, authors Mary Bricker-Jenkins, Carrie Young, and Cheri Honkala, in chapter 5, describe the Kensington Welfare Rights Union, which began in the Kensington neighborhood of Philadelphia with a group of mothers on welfare meeting in a church basement to talk about how they would feed themselves and their children, given recent cuts in welfare and medical assistance. The group learned about the Universal Declaration of Human Rights and taught others about it, and now relies on it as an organizing tool. The authors also describe the community-based roots of the Poor People's Economic Human Rights Campaign (PPEHRC). The activism of the organizations involved in this campaign illustrate why social workers need to understand and study economic and social human rights. Without such knowledge, they lack an important tool in dealing with societal challenges of poverty and economic deprivation.

The author of chapter 7, Silvia Staub-Bernasconi, examines the prevalent view that, for historical and philosophical reasons, political and civil rights take priority over economic, social, and cultural rights. Part of this neglect can be traced to U.S. and European policies favoring civil and political rights over economic and social rights. Human rights are indivisible,

Introduction: Social Work Perspectives on Human Rights

however, and the realization of these rights suffers without full recognition of economic and social rights.

Janice Wood Wetzel, the author of chapter 8, examines women's rights as human rights from many different angles: women's economic rights; their rights to health, protection against violence, and reproductive health; and HIV/Aids and the law. She stresses the importance of a psychological analysis of women's universal oppression, as confirmed, for instance, in Amnesty International's conclusion that women suffer more violations of human rights than any other group worldwide, both in times of war and through traditional practices excused by culture. Wood Wetzel also argues that social justice and human rights as abstract aspirations are deficient. Human rights must be infused throughout the social work curriculum in a way that makes their implementation real. The principles must be embedded in every course of study and be central to every aspect of professional education.

In chapter 9 Katherine van Wormer examines the status of women in prison and views their circumstances in terms of human rights violations, highlighting incidents of rape, revenge, deprivation, forced nudity, pregnancies in a closed system, and forced abortions. These practices come to light in the United States in lawsuits described by Human Rights Watch and Amnesty International. Van Wormer links women's conditions in prison to Article 25 of the Universal Declaration of Human rights, which states that "everyone has the rights to a standard of living adequate for the health and well-being [of the individual]." She concludes that human rights violations in prison result from the prison system, as individual jails are poorly equipped to deal with major societal problems such as drug addiction and mental illnesses. Thus the remedy must include input from outside the prison system. Van Wormer also cautions against treating women prisoners like their male counterparts: dealing with women and men in the same way is a violation of womanhood and, in many cases, motherhood.

Rosemary Link, in chapter 10, focuses on the lives and development of children in the context of the United Nations Convention on the Rights of the Child. Link explains and connects the Convention to social work practice and demonstrates the usefulness of this policy in addressing issues of child well-being. She examines the tension between children's rights and family rights, and questions the commitment of human services in the U.S. to the rights of children, given that almost every country, except the United States, has accepted the Convention as part of its legal structure.

Elisabeth Reichert

Link believes that social workers should educate themselves in the goals and expectations of international policy instruments; alert their social work organizations and agencies to the implementation requirements; and question practices that do not meet human rights principles.

In his forward-thinking chapter, Brij Mohan incites the social work profession to focus on its potential in dealing with human tragedies. As Mohan states in chapter 11, "Social work, a quintessential human rights approach to most of the human-made tragedies, may well re-equip itself . . . if its smorgasbord is focused on universal, indivisible, and inalienable areas of the evolving structure of human rights." Although optimistic about achieving that goal, Mohan tempers that optimism by referring to his own writings about the realpolitik of the social work profession.

The book concludes with Robert McCormick's examination, in chapter 12, of human rights from both the legal and social work perspectives. After exploring the different approaches taken by lawyers and social workers, he suggests that lawyers and social workers could better promote human rights by actively working together. Although their roles may differ, both share the common goal of promoting economic, social, and cultural human rights.

These chapters, taken together, expose social workers to the challenges, and rewards, of integrating contemporary human rights into their social work practices.

Challenges in Human Rights

Human Rights in the Twenty-first Century

Creating a New Paradigm for Social Work

ELISABETH REICHERT

Where, after all, do universal human rights begin? In small places, close to home—so close and so small that they cannot be seen on any maps of the world. Yet they are the world of the individual person; the neighborhood he lives in; the school or college he attends; the factory, farm, or office where he works. Such are the places where every man, woman, and child seeks equal justice, equal opportunity, equal dignity without discrimination. Unless these rights have meaning there, they have little meaning anywhere.

—Eleanor Roosevelt, National Coordinating Committee, Universal Declaration of Human Rights 50th Anniversary, 1998

Introduction

Basic concepts underlying human rights offer little that is new to the social work profession, which, historically, advocates for education, equality, health care, housing, and fairness, all of which fit neatly under the umbrella of human rights (National Association of Social Workers [NASW], 2003; van Wormer, 2004; Wronka, 1998; Staub Bernasconi, 1998; Ife, 2001). The social work profession, by any standard, has a commonality with human rights that should guide the profession in both policy and practice.

In the United States, however, the social work profession has yet to establish a clear connection to human rights both in curricula and policy statements (Reichert, 2003). The social work literature includes only a few serious efforts to analyze and link human rights to social work, and when it does address the topic of human rights, which is rare, it is usually treated cursorily (Reichert, 2003). Thus a detailed analysis of human rights documents and principles remains in an infant stage. For social workers to truly understand the significance of human rights to the profession, a far greater emphasis on human rights education is needed. Now that the Council of Social Work Education mandates the teaching of human rights as part of the social work curricula, the option of neglecting human rights issues no longer exists (Council on Social Work Education, [CSWE] 2003).

The link between the social work profession and human rights appears more developed internationally than in the United States. The International Federation of Social Workers (IFSW) policy paper states that "social workers respect the basic human rights of individuals and groups as expressed in the United Nations Universal Declaration of Human Rights and other international conventions derived from that Declaration" (International Federation of Social Workers [IFSW], 2005). With an international policy statement in place promoting the importance of human rights to social work, the social work profession within the United States needs to view the study of human rights more seriously.

This chapter addresses the paucity of social work literature on human rights and the critical importance of correcting this lack. The social work profession can only truly fulfill its mission by adopting a more focused and analytical approach to human rights.

Why Human Rights as Part of Social Work?

A primary mission of the social work profession is to enhance human well-being and help people to meet all their basic human needs, attending particularly to the needs and empowerment of those who are vulnerable, oppressed, and living in poverty (National Association of Social Work [NASW], 1999). A historic and defining feature of social work is the profession's focus on the individual well-being of society (Reichert, 2006a).

The roles of social workers are numerous: they protect children and other vulnerable populations; they perform various counseling roles; they carry out international relief work and occupy the front lines of disaster assistance; they assist in delivering social services to all populations—in other words, without social workers, the world would enjoy a less hopeful and welcoming environment.

Yet, while the social work profession can draw upon its history and accomplishments, it must also prepare for future challenges and needs. The profession must adapt to changing social movements and respond effectively. What does this require? The short answer is a much closer alignment with human rights rather than an uncritical following of practices and policies that effectively counter the social work mission.

Social work principles are intended to ensure that a person in need never goes without shelter, food, or medical care. Labeling a person as undeserving because he or she is unemployed or lacks sufficient income to cover basic needs contradicts the very core of social work. Yet welfare laws in the United States provide minimal leeway in dealing with the economic circumstances of lower-income individuals (Reichert & McCormick, 1997, 1998; Blau & Abramovitz, 2004). Social workers often have little choice but to obey the legal guidelines that essentially determine who receives a social benefit and who does not. An important question to consider is how social workers might tailor their profession to better fit their mission when social welfare laws continually challenge that goal. One option is for the profession to embrace human rights principles and lobby politicians to include those principles in legislation. The obvious starting point in this endeavor is for the profession itself to understand the meaning of human rights. Only then can social workers move forward into the legislative sphere of assisting lawmakers to incorporate human rights principles into social welfare legislation.

Overview of Human Rights

The social work profession in the United States, as noted above, has yet to infuse specific references to human rights documents and principles into practices and policies. In its latest policy statements covering numerous social work issues, the National Association of Social Workers (NASW) refers to human rights only twice—under the international section and briefly under women's issues (NASW, 2003). The Association emphasizes the strong historical bond between human rights and social work but acknowledges that the "profession does not fully use human rights as a criterion with which to evaluate social work policies, practice, research, and program priorities" (p. 211).

The NASW Code of Ethics does not even mention human rights, and only recently has the CSWE referred to human rights within its educational standards for accreditation of schools of social work (NASW, 1999; CSWE, 2003). Although this standard only refers to human rights in passing, it does appear to require integration of human rights into social work education. A logical consequence of omitting clear and mandatory references to human rights within ethical statements or educational curricula has been the lack of impetus within the profession to incorporate human rights into policies and practices. Unless the profession advocates for human rights, it is no surprise that lawmakers may overlook human rights principles in drafting legislation.

Social Justice and Human Rights

Social work literature continually prefers the term "social justice" in analyzing core issues relevant to the profession (Swenson, 1998; Reichert, 2001, 2003). Although human rights clearly do not supersede concepts of social justice, a primary advantage of referring to human rights principles involves a clearer and more encompassing set of guidelines than those associated with social justice. NASW recognizes the limitations of social justice compared to human rights principles in the field of social work:

> Social work can be proud of its heritage. It is the only profession imbued with social justice as its fundamental value and concern. But social justice is a fairness doctrine that provides civil and political leeway in deciding what is just and unjust. Human rights, on the other hand, encompass social justice, but transcend civil and political customs, in consideration of the basic life-sustaining needs of all human beings, without distinction. (NASW, 2003, p. 211)

Human rights provide the social work profession with a global and contemporary set of guidelines, whereas social justice tends to be defined in vague terminology such as fairness versus unfairness or equality versus inequality (Reichert, 2003). This distinction gives human rights an authority that social justice lacks. Human rights can elicit discussion of common issues by people from all walks of life and every corner of the world. One example where worldwide attention to a common human rights issue has led to effective action involves violence against women (United Nations, 1981; *The Beijing Declaration and the Platform for Action*, 1995). For example, grass-roots movements and pressure on governments have increased awareness of the harm done by violence against women and have led to subsequent legislation to help prevent this type of violence. Here, by asserting that violence against women is a violation of human rights, a common link was established among social workers, and others, worldwide. A campaign organized around the words "social justice" may not have had the same effectiveness, as charging a country or a group with a human rights violation certainly sounds more forceful than a charge of violating social justice. Social justice, of course, is an important part of the social work mission, but clearly it does not have the same import as human rights in addressing issues common to social work.

What Are Human Rights?

A basic problem in teaching human rights is establishing a clear definition of what these rights are. Because social workers mostly encounter references to human rights only within the confines of politics or law, human rights may appear to have only slight relevance to social work. In restricting the term to political situations, especially in other countries, the importance of human rights to social work has been depreciated (Reichert, 2003). When U.S. politicians speak of human rights, for example, they typically do so in the context of a distant nation, one less economically developed than the United States. In stating, for instance, that a particular African country must respect human rights before the U.S. will provide aid, exactly what is meant by the term "human rights"? Clearly it is assumed that everyone understands the meaning and would readily agree that countries must respect human rights before our government will assist them.

Not only are politicians muddying the waters regarding human rights, but lawyers, too, speak of human rights in legalese that is more applicable to the courtroom or an academic treatise than to everyday life. No wonder social workers may find the topic of human rights unclear and better suited to politicians and lawyers whose explanations appear divorced from social work. But a careful study of human rights will expose this parochial view and show that social workers have at least as much claim to the exercise of human rights principles as do politicians and lawyers.

Definition of Human Rights

Human rights encompass an array of political, economic, and social arenas and, while defining needs, also present a set of individual rights that apply worldwide. The following is a general definition offered by the United Nations (1987):

> Human rights are those rights, which are inherent in our nature and without which we cannot live as human beings. Human rights and fundamental freedoms allow us to fully develop and use our human qualities, our intelligence, our talents and our conscience and to satisfy our spiritual and other needs.

One might question, however, whose nature prevails in this definition. Americans may view access to electricity and running water as an inherent right, whereas, among people in Third World nations, simply having enough to eat may be deemed sufficient to retain their dignity. Are people who have the means to obtain valuable resources more entitled to their human rights than other, lesser advantaged people? The answer is a resounding no. However, a fundamental difficulty arises in allocating resources and constructing policies by which human rights apply to all people equally and not simply to select individuals and groups (Reichert, 2003). By classifying certain rights and freedoms as *human* rights, all governments recognize the common goal of creating conditions to guarantee those rights and freedoms, despite the intricacies involved in actually ensuring that they are granted.

Another complicated issue related to the definition of human rights is its emphasis on an individual's "rights." Does a person, in order to be granted a human right, have an obligation to behave in a certain way? For example, if one refuses an opportunity to work and earn a living, should that person have a right to public assistance? Few U.S. citizens would argue that prisoners are not entitled to adequate food and medical care when in prison. Yet ordinary citizens have no guarantee that they, too, will receive adequate medical care and food. To overcome what appears to be a contradiction of human rights principles, the logical, and charitable, solution is to accept that everyone shares a common humanity and that, regardless of circumstances, every individual is entitled to live according to basic human rights principles.

Universal Declaration of Human Rights

A key starting point in understanding human rights is the Universal Declaration of Human Rights (United Nations [UN], 1948), which has been approved by every member nation of the UN (Reichert, 2001). The declaration, which provides a list of specific human rights, is not legally binding on any nation, but, at the very least, a nation's approval of the declaration indicates its commitment to satisfying the rights specified in the document.

The Universal Declaration contains three distinct sets or generations of human rights. The first, known as "negative rights," lists political and individual freedoms that most people in the United States would recognize as human rights. These include due process, freedom of speech and religion, and freedom of movement and assembly, as well as guarantees against discrimination, slavery, and torture (UN, 1948, Articles 2–15). Another set of rights, referred to as "positive rights," attempts to ensure each individual an adequate standard of living. Under this second set of human rights, everyone "has the right to a standard of living adequate for the health and well-being of himself and of his family, including food, clothing, housing and medical care and necessary social services." In addition, "motherhood and childhood are entitled to special care and assistance," and everyone has the right to a free education at the elementary level (UN, 1948, Articles 16–27).

The third generation of human rights involves collective rights among nations. Although the least developed among the three, this third set of rights indicates that solidarity among nations and individuals are a core value of the declaration. Under the 1948 declaration, everyone is entitled to a social and international order in which the "rights and freedoms" listed in the document can be fully realized (UN, 1948, Articles 28–30). Essentially the promotion of collective human rights requires intergovernmental cooperation on world issues such as environmental protection and economic development. One group of countries should not dictate conditions to another group, when these conditions would inhibit the growth or prosperity of the other group, nor should industrialized countries take advantage of less economically developed countries by exploiting resources (Reichert, 2003).

No nation today wants to be singled out as a violator of human rights, yet this aversion often promotes side-stepping or concealing human rights issues:

> Due to the activism of civil society around the world, the human rights paradigm has become such a powerful legitimizing force in national politics and international relations that no government in any part of the world today would openly reject or defy its dictates. Governments will of course deny that they have committed human rights violations or claim that they are striving to comply with those norms to the best extent permitted by their local circumstances. They will try to get the benefits of international legitimacy without the "inconvenience" of compliance with human rights standards, but that is true of constitutional rights in any domestic setting even in the most developed and stable societies. (An-Nai'im, 1995, p. 427)

Implicit in the effort of countries and individuals to avoid being labeled as failing to adhere to human rights principles is that human rights matter. Within a period of just less than sixty years, most countries recognize that human rights have evolved into a major, worldwide goal, at least a stated goal (Reichert, 2006b).

Although Americans applaud themselves for their strong commitment to the first set of human rights enumerated in the Universal Declaration, they frequently come up short with the second set. The United States, compared to many other countries, fails to fulfill its obligation to promote human rights for all (Reichert & McCormick, 1997). For instance, our failure to provide adequate health care for children and all expectant mothers violates the same Universal Declaration of Human Rights that U.S. political leaders continually call upon to denigrate China, Cuba, and Iraq, among other countries. The infant mortality rate is higher in the United States than in any other industrialized nation (Child Health USA, 2004a), and, within the U.S. itself, infant mortality rates are disparate among racial groups, with African-American infants suffering a mortality rate more than twice that of non-Hispanic whites (Child Health USA, 2004b). Although this poor ranking in infant mortality may not entirely be the result of inadequate health care, the failure of Americans to ensure adequate health care to all residents raises an important human rights issue.

In addition to the Universal Declaration of Human Rights, the UN has drafted numerous other documents addressing specific areas of human rights: the International Covenant on Economic, Social, and Cultural Rights; the Convention of the Rights of the Child; the Convention against Discrimination of Women; and the International Covenant on Civil and Political Rights. Although all member states of the UN work together to draft these documents, the enforcement of human rights generally remains within the individual countries. The United States or any other country can choose to promote a particular human right and ignore others. This lack of enforcement, or the option to pick and choose which human rights to enforce, clearly leads to hypocrisy, as demonstrated by the U.S. position on health care.

Cultural Relativism: A Necessary Element of Human Rights

There is no simple alternative to letting individual countries enforce human rights, for a major obstacle to imposing a universal enforcement is that of cultural relativism, which makes the application of human rights a balancing act.

Contradicting a founding principle that human rights are universal is the fact that individual cultures define their own values and ethics. Applying human rights universally, without deference to specific cultural principles, diminishes a nation's cultural identity—a human rights violation in itself. As stated in the UN International Covenant on Economic, Social, and Cultural Rights, "Everyone may enjoy his economic, social, and cultural rights, as well as his civil and political rights" (United Nations [UN] 1966). Culture, by necessity, often shapes the way individuals and groups view human rights, and this complicates the idea of human rights as universal.

In cultural relativism all viewpoints are equally valid, and truth is relative as it belongs only to the individual or to one's culture. Ethical, religious, and political beliefs are true only in relation to the cultural identity of the individual or the society. Still, cultural relativism is appropriate in certain aspects, for instance, it is desirable that nations retain their relative differences in language, food, clothing, art, and architecture (Pasamonik, 2004). Also, "cultural relativism maintains that there is an irreducible diversity among cultures because each culture is a unique whole with parts so intertwined that none of them can be understood or evaluated without reference to the other parts and to the cultural whole, the so-called pattern of culture" (Lawson, 1998, p. 13).

The problem, however, with blindly accepting cultural relativism is that this assumes an uncritical acceptance of the societal structure that creates the cultural norms. Because whoever determines the cultural, religious, and legal norms of a society controls the outcome, social workers should guard against an uncritical acceptance of culture relativism over universal human rights principles.

Balancing Universalism and Cultural Relativism

In the context of human rights, carefully drawn guidelines can help to identify and resolve conflicts between universal principles of human rights and specific cultural, religious, and legal norms. U.S. social policies, to take one case of cultural relativism, do not guarantee economic and social human rights such as food, shelter, and medical care (Reichert, 2003). Although assistance in these areas may be available through private donors, government, relatives, and other avenues, U.S. cultural and legal standards do not view this assistance as a human right. To analyze why this situation exists in one of the world's richest countries, consider the following guidelines:

- **Examine the history of the cultural practice.** What is the background or history of the cultural norm that conflicts with a particular human right as established by a declaration or other human rights document? What is the apparent rationale for the cultural norm to have been created?
- **Examine the powerbrokers who determined the cultural norm.** Was a democratic process instrumental in establishing the cultural norm in question? Were many voices included in the decision or was the cultural practice established by only a few segments of society?
- **Examine the cultural norm within a contemporary human rights standard.** Against which contemporary human rights standards should the cultural practice be compared? This is an important consideration, as cultural norms that have existed for many years

may, over time, appear incompatible with contemporary human rights standards.

By analyzing the historical background, relevant democratic factors, and contemporary human rights standards of a particular policy or practice, social workers can better understand the role of cultural relativism in human rights. This analysis also enables social workers to determine whether cultural relativism should control when the policy or practice conflicts with human rights (Reichert, 1998, 2006a, 2006b).

AN ANALYSIS OF CULTURAL RELATIVISM

Returning to the example concerning the U.S. position on economic and social human rights, should cultural relativism prevail in not recognizing food, shelter, and adequate medical care as human rights? Although few would question everyone's *need* for food, shelter, and medical care, the relevant question here is whether everyone is entitled to claim these needs as a human right.

- **Historical consideration.** An examination of U.S. history supports the concept of individualism where economic rights are not elevated to the status of human rights. However, that notion dates back to the time when self-sufficiency was the rule, when government barely existed in some areas of the country and support was focused on the individual and his or her community. Today the situation is different, as government now exists at all levels of society. Thus, although history may support a concept of individualism, the reality is quite different.
- **Democratic factors.** Many individuals probably agree that, in general, the government should not be the guarantor of economic and social human rights, but if a particular individual finds that he or she is without medical care or shelter, for example, would that individual then have a change of heart? Is there one elderly person who would want to be without Medicare? It seems inconceivable that politicians would dismantle Medicare without at least replacing that system with another form of guaranteed health care, but there is no legal basis to demand it. The current policy of not guaranteeing basic economic and social human rights probably has more to

do with government policies based on special interests than on specific cultural identity (Reichert, 2006a).

- **Contemporary human rights.** Many governments worldwide recognize that economic and social human rights are just as important as political human rights, and take steps to ensure that those rights are broadly delivered (UN, 1966). The United States, however, is among those countries that lag behind contemporary thinking in this area: "Twenty percent of American children live in poverty—the highest rate of any industrialized nation in the world. Millions of young Americans receive an inadequate education. Millions of young Americans are unemployed. Millions experience serious hunger. Millions lack health insurance—and, as a result, thousands of Americans die prematurely each year" (Sunstein, 2004, p. 234).

Only by distorting a nation's history, subverting democratic participation, and ignoring contemporary principles of human rights can cultural relativism prevail when analyzing the above example relating to economic and social rights in the United States.

Conflicts between universalism and cultural relativism, regardless of country or society, may be scrutinized by the guidelines given here. Often the analysis that results will disclose that cultural relativism rests upon an outmoded or oppressive foundation.

Conclusion

The social work profession in the United States could better attain its goals by encouraging the study of human rights. A foundation in human rights would provide a clearer framework with which to link the profession to economic, political, and social aims. Human rights are specific privileges and can more readily be applied to a social work situation than the often confusing notion of social or economic justice, both of which tend to bog down in needs-based theories.

Human rights elevate discussions and practices beyond the *needs* of an individual to the *rights* of an individual. In the field of human rights, governments are accountable to their residents and have cultural, economic, political, and social obligations. Governments worldwide, for instance, undoubtedly recognize that each of its residents needs adequate health care, but although the vast majority of industrialized countries legally guarantee their residents health care, the United States does not. Under the Universal Declaration of Human Rights, which the United States has approved, the U.S. should be obligated to provide health care to every legal resident.

Of additional importance to social workers in the area of human rights is the tangible connection between the individual and the broader social spectrum. For example, violence against women is not viewed, in the arena of human rights, as a problem for a particular individual but rather is seen as a structural and political problem: a woman has the right not to be battered, regardless of cultural norms or other accepted practices allowing or justifying the battering (Bunch 1991). Classifying domestic violence as a human rights issue communicates to victims of domestic violence that they are human beings entitled to protection and not simply "sick" individuals in need of treatment (Witkin, 1998). Reframing a social problem like domestic violence into a human rights issue also creates an international context in which to combat domestic violence. International pressure may induce governments to actively try to prevent domestic violence, knowing that to do otherwise could result in allegations of human rights violations.

The field of human rights is certainly not without controversy. One objection to the concept of human rights lies in the view that industrialized countries control the direction of human rights. Nations differ in the importance they place on certain rights, for example, developing countries may view freedom of speech, which is protected in the U.S. by the First Amendment, as far less important than economic progress. Generally, however, the vast majority of countries that have approved the Universal Declaration are in agreement on what constitutes a human right. Although enforcement or interpretation of those rights can vary, today the concept of human rights has achieved universal importance.

By understanding the close connection between human rights and social work, educators and social work practitioners can strengthen this association and thus enhance the stature of their profession.

References

An-Nai'im, A. (1995). Conclusion. In *Human rights in cross-cultural perspectives: A quest for consensus* (pp. 427–428). Philadelphia: University of Pennsylvania Press.

Beijing Declaration and the Platform for Action. (1995, September 4–15). Fourth World Conference on Women, Beijing, China. New York: UN Department of Public Information.

Blau, J., & Abramovitz, M. (2004). *The dynamics of social welfare policy.* New York: Oxford University Press.

Bunch, C. (1991). Women's rights as human rights: Toward a re-vision of human rights (pp. 3–18). In C. Bunch & R. Carrillo (Eds.), *Gender violence: A development and human rights issue.* New Brunswick, NJ: Center for Women's Global Leadership.

Child Health USA. (2004a). Retrieved February 15, 2006, from http://www.mchb.hrsa.gov/mchirc/chusa_04/pages/0405iimr.htm.

Child Health USA. (2004b). Retrieved February 15, 2006, from http://www.mchb.hrsa.gov/mchirc/chusa_04/pages/0406im.htm.

Council on Social Work Education (CSWE). (2003). *Handbook of accreditation standards and procedures* (5th ed.). Alexandria, VA: CSWE Press.

Ife, J. (2001). *Human rights and social work: Towards rights based practice.* Cambridge: Cambridge University Press.

International Federation of Social Workers (IFSW). (2005). Policy Paper. Retrieved February 15, 2006, from http://www.ifsw.org/en/p38000212.html.

Lawson, S. (1998). Democracy and the problem of cultural relativism: Normative issues for international politics. *Global Society: Journal of Interdisciplinary International Relations, 12*(2), 251–271.

National Association of Social Workers (NASW). (1999). *Code of ethics* (rev. ed.). Washington, DC: NASW Press.

National Association of Social Workers (NASW). (2003). *Social work speaks: National Association of Social Workers policy statements, 2003–2006* (6th ed.). Washington, DC: NASW Press.

National Coordinating Committee for UDHR50. (1998). Franklin and Eleanor Roosevelt Institute. Website: http://www.udhr50.org/history timeline.htm.

Pasamonik, B. (2004). The paradoxes of tolerance. *Social Studies, 95*(5), 206–211.

Reichert, E. (1998). Women's rights are human rights: A platform for action. *International Social Work, 15*(3), 177–185.

Reichert, E. (2001). Move from social justice to human rights provides new perspective. *Professional Development: The International Journal of Continuing Social Work Education, 4*(1), 5–13.

Reichert, E. (2003). *Social work and human rights: A foundation for policy and practice.* New York: Columbia University Press.

Reichert, E. (2006a). *Understanding human rights: An exercise book.* Thousand Oaks, CA: Sage.

Reichert, E. (2006b). Human rights: An examination of universalism and cultural relativism. *Journal of Comparative Social Welfare, 22*(1), 23–36.

Reichert, E., & McCormick, R. (1997). Different approaches to child welfare: United States and Germany. *Journal of Law and Social Work, 7*(1), 17–33.

Reichert, E., & McCormick, R. (1998). U.S. welfare law violates human rights of immigrants. *Migration World, 26*(3), 15–18.

Staub Bernasconi, S. (1998). Soziale Arbeit als Menschenrectsprofession. In A. Woehrel (Ed.), *Profession und Wissenschaft Sozialer Arbeit: Positionen in einer Phase der generellen Neuverortnung und Spezifika* (pp. 305–332). Pfaffenweiler, Germany: Cenaurus.

Sunstein, C. (2004). *The second Bill of Rights: FDR's unfinished revolution and why we need it more than ever.* New York: Basic Books.

Swenson, C. (1998). Clinical social work's contribution to a social justice perspective. *Social Work, 43*(6), 527–537.

United Nations (UN). (1948). Universal Declaration of Human Rights. Adopted December 10, 1948. GA. Res. 217 AIII. United Nations Document a/810. New York: United Nations.

United Nations. (1966). International Covenant on Economic, Social, and Cultural Rights. Adopted December 16, 1966, GA. Res. 2200 AXXI, New York: United Nations.

United Nations (1981). Convention on the Elimination of All forms of Discrimination against Women (CEDAW). G.A. Res. 34/180. U.N. GAOR, 34th Sess. Supp. No. 46 at 193 U.N. Doc. A/34–46; adopted September 3, 1981. New York: United Nations.

United Nations (1987). *Human rights: Questions and answers.* New York: Author.

U.S. Department of Health and Human Services, Center for Disease Control. (2000). Fact Sheet. Website: http://www.cdc.gov.nchs/releases/00facts/infantmo.htm.

Van Wormer, K. (2004). *Confronting oppression, restoring justice: From policy analysis to social action.* Alexandria, VA: Council on Social Work Education.

Witkin, S. (1993). A human rights approach to social work research and evaluation. *Journal of Teaching in Social Work, 8*, 239–253.

Witkin S. (1998). Human rights and social work. *Social Work, 43*, 197–201.

Wronka, J. (1998). *Human rights and social policy in the 21st century: A history of the idea of human rights and comparison of the United Nations Universal Declaration of Human Rights with United States Federal and State Constitutions* (rev. ed.). Lanham, MD: University Press of America.

Human Rights in Social Work Practice

An Invisible Part of the Social Work Curriculum?

LENA DOMINELLI

Contemporary social work claims to be rights-based and interested in delivering social justice (Ife, 2001; Reichert, 2003; Dominelli, 2004). This orientation is also clearly evident in the international definition of social work jointly agreed on by the profession's key international associations, the International Association of Schools of Social Work (IASSW) and the International Federation of Social Workers (IFSW). Thus we would expect human rights to have a high profile in social work curricula. The place of human rights teaching in the curriculum, however, except as a general commitment in social work's value base or code of ethics, is more often optional than compulsory. Law textbooks for social workers tend to ignore its human rights dimensions, even in countries with legislation carrying that title. Its absence from social work course materials and lectures contributes to the invisibility of human rights in the curriculum. Many students enter employment unaware of the potential of human rights legislation to enhance practice.

My goal in this chapter is to remedy this situation. To that end, I consider a key human rights document, the Universal Declaration of Human Rights (UDHR), both its history and provisions. I also focus on the importance of human rights in a globalizing world, consider the relevance of human rights to social work practice, and argue for making human rights a central and compulsory part of the social work curriculum. Ideally the concern to uphold human rights and secure social justice should permeate *all* discussions in classrooms where social work is taught, not just in courses labeled "human rights." Although my examples are drawn substantially from the United Kingdom (UK), the content of this chapter resonates for other countries as well, not least because all members of the United Nations subscribe to the UDHR.

The Neglect of Human Rights in Social Work Theory and Practice

Death through benign neglect seems appropriate in describing the insufficient attention given to human rights legislation and issues on qualifying programs in social work. An examination of the regulations governing qualifying training in British social work (General Social Care Council [GSCC], 2007) reveals that little explicit reference is made to human rights as a compulsory element in its regulated curriculum. Moreover, the literature relating human rights to social work practice is limited. A search of major journals such as the *British Journal of Social Work, Social Work Education, Journal of Social Work Education,* and *International Social Work,* since 2001, revealed that in the intervening period each journal has devoted only one or two articles to this subject, including those identifying specific rights such as disability or minority rights. Major texts in this field are also minimal; those we have include Jim Ife's (2001) *Human Rights and Social Work,* Elisabeth Reichert's *Social Work and Human Rights* (2003) and *Understanding Human Rights* (2006), and A. S. Kohli's *Human Rights and Social Work* (2004). Thus human rights are fairly invisible in social work teaching, and generations of students are unaware of the details of human rights legislation, instruments, and mechanisms, and their relevance for practice or application in specific situations encountered in the field. One experienced practitioner depicted the low priority of including human rights in social work practice as follows:

We discuss human rights in a general sort of way, e.g., discussing the UN report that blasted the UK's treatment of children [United Nations' Country Reports on the Convention of Rights of the Child in 1996 and

2002] when working with children and families. Otherwise, I cover human rights in relation to values, mainly in terms of discrimination against vulnerable people.

This message, first voiced in 1997, has echoed through the intervening years with only minor variations. Defining human rights as values minimizes their importance in establishing a framework of social justice enforced through legislation. In the UK this includes the Human Rights Act of 1998 that became law in 2000. This act brought European human rights legislation into Britain in addition to that embedded in UN conventions and protocols signed by the UK.

The dearth of social work educational materials on this topic was apparent earlier and prompted the IASSW and IFSW to collaborate on the production of a manual of human rights for use by social workers (United Nations, 1994). The *Manual of Children's Rights,* brought to fruition by the IFSW, recently followed. Thus the IASSW and IFSW have addressed a gap in the literature by producing materials targeting practitioners. The global ethics document that was accepted by the General Assemblies of both organizations in 2004 contains specific references to the key UN human rights instruments. These, I suggest should have well-rehearsed coverage on all social work courses, but they are rarely considered.

The IASSW and IFSW have also formed a Joint Commission on Human Rights which undertakes both advocacy in individual cases and training for practitioners and educators. Through this Commission they advocate on individual cases involving social work practitioners and educators, promote human rights teaching by providing training seminars at their congresses, and contribute to UN deliberations on the subject. The IASSW has held Board Seminars on Human Rights and, with the American Council on Social Work Education (CSWE), has introduced sessions at the Annual Program Meeting to publicize their importance and provide training. Those attending these sessions tend to be already committed to advancing the cause and new converts have been few. Although the issue of embedding human rights firmly in social work curricula remains elusive and without detailed scrutiny, a small literature is available for use in teaching the subject. This limited impact of human rights suggests that a substantial initiative is needed to shift curriculum planning to this area. None has been forthcoming thus far.

Human Rights for All: Historically a Bold if Flawed Move Forward

The idea of human rights has a long history. John Locke espoused the concept of "natural rights" as the basis for life, liberty, and property, residing with individuals. These understandings were further developed by Jean-Jacques Rousseau, who supported the idea that individuals entered civil society and exchanged the right to life, liberty, and equality for civil rights which the government protected from violation on their behalf. These notions also shaped the thinking of participants in the French and American Revolutions and gave rise, respectively, to the French Declaration of the Rights of Man and the American Declaration of Independence. These documents advanced the view that people had rights to liberty, equality, and self-determination. Adherents to these causes and their ideas often crossed the Atlantic to reach beyond the particular nation-state where they first arose (Gibney, 2003) and underpin liberal democracies today.

The Nazi atrocities in World War II, particularly the Holocaust, inspired the first efforts to internationalize human rights as a bulwark against the oppression and decimation of human beings (Gibney, 2003). Human rights thus acquired meaning as a transcendent principle aimed at valuing people and protecting individual well-being within a framework accepted by others. Although the definition of human rights is contested, this articulation makes human rights directly relevant to social work values and practice.

The concern to protect human beings from gratuitous violence culminated in the Universal Declaration of Human Rights, the product of a fledging UN organization. The UDHR symbolized an incredible achievement and signaled humanity's comprehensive attempt to deal with President Franklin D. Roosevelt's "Four Freedoms"—freedom of speech and expression; freedom of worship; freedom from want; and freedom from fear (UDHR, 2005). It also addressed Sir William Beveridge's "Five Giants"—want, disease, squalor, ignorance, and idleness—the eradication of which formed the bedrock of the British welfare state where social workers were ensconced. These remain practice issues in British social work. "Want," now termed "poverty," affects 80 percent of clients requiring social work support.

The hope of the UN that the UDHR would enshrine a new world order rooted in the dignity of the person, and a commitment to eliminate material inequalities and enable freedom, peace, and justice to flourish, was commendable. Initially proposed in 1947, it was guided through the General Assembly procedures by First Lady Eleanor Roosevelt and adopted without dissent on 10 December 1948, when forty-eight member nations of the UN General Assembly voted in favor, eight abstained, and two were absent. Given the range of regimes, political philosophies, and cultural understandings among this group, their agreement in defense of human rights was a bold move forward in the history of humanity and for the first time made human rights a universal issue.

The UDHR (2005) set the scene for the "universal respect for and observance of human rights and fundamental freedoms." It established the principle of human rights as universal, as these rights belong to all humanity by virtue of being human (Donnelly, 2003). Its principles are used to defend the human dignity and worth of every person in the world regardless of political system, ethnicity, or cultural traditions. The UDHR confirms the universality, indivisibility, and interdependence of all rights, whether political, civil, social, cultural, or economic—a view confirmed again by 171 states through the Vienna Declaration of 1993 which established the Office of the Human Rights Commissioner in Geneva and affirmed the right to development as an inalienable right and part of international human rights law. In 2006 the UN began a process of revising the administrative structures of the Human Rights Commission, aiming to replace it with a more powerful body, the Human Rights Council.

The legitimization of political rights on the international domain ultimately became useful in ensuring the emancipation of slaves and women and asserting the autonomy of colonial territories. Agreement, at least formally, of the UDHR after the end of World War II introduced a new dimension to these issues, ushering in new sites for human rights to flourish. Western powers required the implementation of human rights in what they considered repressive regimes as conditions of trade in order to promote human rights in a given country without challenging its national sovereignty. America's position over China is a classic illustration of this doctrine. Ironically this policy, however high-minded, was fostered at the same time that the U.S. was supporting other repressive regimes, for example, the Pinochet regime in Chile, despite their human rights violations.

Western powers have not been immune from charges of ignoring human rights in their own countries. Amnesty International has highlighted human rights abuses in the general treatment of terrorist suspects in the

West (Stephen, 2003). The UNHCR has documented the inadequacy of the human rights status of certain groups of individuals in specific countries through its reporting requirements. It has castigated the failure of the UK to observe conditions covered by the Convention on the Rights of the Child by allowing smacking. Social workers, in addition to using international instruments to uphold human rights, can campaign on these issues to demand improvements in services.

Despite the relevance of human rights to all countries, social work educators have failed to make this issue an explicit and central part of the social work curriculum. As a result, practitioners have a limited understanding of the provisions of the UDHR and its applicability in daily practice. Few claims concerning the inadequacy of services in meeting human need have been pursued under human rights legislation. Nor had the UN's official critiques of child care practice in the UK under the Convention on the Rights of the Child sparked widely supported advocacy and campaigns for improvements in practice, although these receive occasional mention in courses.

Key Provisions of the UDHR

The UDHR contains thirty articles which may be grouped as follows: Articles 1 and 2 lay the universal basis of human rights and guarantee these to every individual on Earth as his or her birthright and without qualification (i.e., without discrimination on the basis of status); Articles 3 to 21 identify civil and political rights, and include freedom from slavery, torture, and arbitrary arrest and the right to a fair trial, free speech, freedom of movement, and privacy; Articles 22 to 27 focus on economic, social, and cultural rights including social security, an adequate standard of living, health, education, fair remuneration for work and cultural life; Articles 28 to 30 center on the protective framework that safeguards the enjoyment of these rights and include an international order that facilitates the realization of human rights, the responsibilities of individuals and communities in affirming these rights, and the protection of these rights from destruction by others. Article 30 holds nations accountable to others for the ways in which they treat their own residents, but it is poorly enforced. This article is an amazing achievement, as it operates in the opposite direction from the principle of national sovereignty which guides interstate relations.

The UDHR has grown over its fifty-seven years of existence and currently underpins much of our international law. A major expansion in its provisions occurred in 1966 with the International Covenant on Civil and Political Rights and the International Covenant on Economic, Social, and Cultural Rights. These were further augmented by the International Convention on the Elimination of All Forms of Racial Discrimination; the Convention on the Elimination of All Forms of Discrimination against Women; the Convention against Torture and Other Cruel, Inhuman, or Degrading Treatment or Punishment; and the Convention on the Rights of the Child (CRC). Not all members of the UN have endorsed all these documents. Particularly regrettable is the failure of the U.S. to ratify the CRC, certainly crucial in interventions involving poor children and families. Arguably child poverty is a violation of Articles 1 and 2 of the UDHR, so these could be used instead. Social work students should be taught the provisions, instruments, and mechanisms of enforcement pertaining to each document for use in practice. This teaching should include the history of the documents as well as the key players and strategies used to secure agreement.

Limitations in the UN's Approach to Human Rights: Concerns for Social Work

Nation-states both guarantee and violate human rights. The UDHR has been devised as an internationally binding agreement. Its implementation lies in the hands of the nation-state, at times backed by further national or regional legislation. Even a redistribution of the resources necessary for its execution has been retained nationally. Thus a crucial limitation of the UDHR has been that the social, political, economic, and civil rights it encompasses are located in the framework of a nation-state responsible for enforcing provisions and punishing violations. Without independent compliance mechanisms, a country's failure to adhere to UDHR requirements is a serious drawback to realizing its ideals. The dependency of the international framework on nation-states for enforcement fragments interdependent realities like the links between inequitable trade conditions and poverty. This weakness is highly visible as neo-liberal approaches to economic existence spread globally. Poverty in industrializing countries can be traced directly to terms of trade that privilege rich countries and mire poor ones in increasing spirals of debt, making it impossible for the nation-states affected to raise their peoples out of poverty as required by the UDHR (Jubilee, 2000; Wichterich, 2000). Yet eliminating poverty, or "want," was a key concern of the founding signatories of the UDHR, and a concern of social work.

The aims of the UDHR are laudable, but the lack of enforcement mechanisms independent of a nation-state that may be culpable of human rights violations has diminished its potential to make a difference in people's daily lives and has made persuasion a key tool in making signatories adhere to its precepts. Reports by Amnesty International and other concerned nongovernmental organizations (NGOs) have consistently shown that recalcitrant governments are rarely held accountable for human rights violations. And, as genocide in Bosnia, Rwanda, and Darfur indicate, people continue to die in the millions. Other key criticisms of the UDHR include its focus on individual rights, and its failure to deal with the complexities of human migration and globalization.

Lodging human rights within the nation-state entitles only nationals of a particular country to the protections contained in the UDHR. National discourses on human rights have encouraged the (re)production of a binary divide between citizens and non-citizens among people who reside in a given locale and privilege the former over the latter. Applying these only to some residents jeopardizes their direct ties to being human and de-legitimates them as intrinsic characteristics of a human being situated in a society. Also, tying the realization of human rights to citizenship in a particular territory where a person has residence and claims of belonging rather than being carried wherever he or she goes denies the portability of human rights across borders. Dependency on a nation-state frames human rights as contingent on social realities beyond an individual's control and contradicts the view that dignity and human rights reside in the individual. A long-standing illustration of the violation of individual human rights is Aung Sang Suu Kyi's lengthy house arrest in Burma/Myanmar. Formal protests have yielded little change in her condition.

These issues have become crucial in discourses about refugees and asylum seekers. In Britain, a general tightening of the benefits to which these individuals were previously entitled requires that they survive on benefits set at 70 percent of income support rates, which are already considered at the poverty level, while at the same time they are denied the right to employment until after their cases are heard. Requests for help create ethical dilemmas for social workers tackling poverty among asylum seekers and refugees, because their aid cannot exceed stipulated limits. Thus asylum seekers and refugees live a hand-to-mouth existence, susceptible to exploitation in the shadow economy. Their treatment is not deemed a human rights violation, as they are excluded from benefits reserved for citizens. A major role of social workers is to advocate for the human rights of these individuals, but they seldom do. Hayes (2006, p. 193) argues that British social workers could do more to uphold these rights by refusing to assume the roles of gatekeepers and immigration agents responsible for policing the welfare state. Linda Briskman (2006, p. 215) urges Australian social work academics not to participate in the "wall of silence" the government has erected around its complicity in depriving asylum seekers of their human rights and dignity.

The focus of the UDHR on individuals led to criticism that scant attention was being given to group or collective rights, thereby promoting Western notions of human rights. The UDHR has been accused of fostering Western cultural supremacy (Parekh, 2000), a concern counteracted by claims that "Asian values" better meet the needs of those in Eastern cultural traditions (Donnelly, 2003), a worrisome view for conceding valuing human worth and dignity to the West. These challenges are thought to undermine the universality of the UDHR while ignoring the fact that it places individuals within different types of families and various social, political, religious, and cultural communities. Charges of relativity overlook the large number of regimes that have signed on to the UDHR. Rather than becoming submerged in the universality-relativity debate, it is useful to envisage the UDHR provisions as contingent on context, as the social environment and the people involved in any interaction create its meaning. Connecting the person to a social environment is familiar to social workers as "the person in their situation."

The preoccupation of the UDHR with individuals and state action in supporting recognized human rights has facilitated the neglect of corporate violations. These have become increasingly significant for the activities of large multinational businesses, some with even more resources at their disposal than national governments (Wichterich, 2000), and for the impact on the health and livelihoods of people and the planet in diverse localities, even those at a distance from decision-making locales or problematic sites. As global warming and dwindling natural resources threaten the livelihood of all humanity, human rights are becoming increasingly linked to environmental matters, and social workers are being enjoined to take these issues seriously (Ungar, 2002). Alongside these concerns, people who question the subjugation of human rights to national sovereignty and the limitation of citizenship within its territorial borders have brought the matter of global citizenship to the international agenda. Yet there is little agreement on the meaning of global citizenship or how it might be realized and enforced.

Interesting questions about the UDHR are posed by growing geographical mobility, dual nationality, and diasporic communities (Brah, 1996). What are the links between individuals and the territory where they live, possibly only transiently? Potential problems were illustrated on 29 July 2005 when Pakistan's General Pervez Musharraf declared his intention to send "home" foreign nationals studying in the country's madrassas, even if the individuals concerned were dual nationals. But the matter cannot be executed so simply. Dual citizens are the responsibility of the country where they live, from the moment they arrive. Thus dual citizens who are also Pakistani nationals must rely on Pakistan for protection while they remain within Pakistan's borders. If they encounter difficulties while in Pakistan, they cannot rely on their other nationality for formal support and intervention.

These restrictions are problematic from a human rights perspective and raise important questions: Is a government permitted to withdraw, unilaterally, a protection safeguarded by the UDHR from one of its nationals? If a person born in Pakistan holds dual nationality, can he or she be deported to the other country of citizenship? And what happens if that other country refuses admission, especially if the person is deemed a threat to national security? Who is responsible for ensuring that this individual's human rights are observed in the comings and goings that might ensue? What could a social worker do in such cases? Even if such an individual were to call on social workers and legal rights advisers from the other country, he or she might find that these professionals are bound by rules of engagement restricting them to operate only in the country where they reside, leaving them unable to intervene directly. In that scenario they could launch a campaign asking others to intercede. Minimally social workers could pressure nation-states to uphold the rights of these people as citizens of the country where they reside, and arrange legal support to enable the individual to enforce their rights.

Social workers have the crucial responsibility of ensuring that people's human rights are not violated. Seldom can they set the agenda or protest human rights violations with authority. Called on to distribute humanitarian aid, their voice seldom prevents further atrocities. Even in natural disasters the role of social workers is a remedial one. Loretta Pyles (2006) paints a poignant picture of this occurring during Hurricane Katrina, when the human rights of poor, black people in New Orleans were ignored. She argues for social workers to use human rights in a capabilities framework to assist poor people in acquiring a fair share of social resources during such times. She also suggests that American educators, under the leadership of CSWE, take the initiative in teaching students about international policy statements that endorse human rights and in this way prepare them for intervening in disaster situations.

The difficulties of protecting human rights has become more difficult in today's world, filled as it is with insecurity and uncertainty caused by increasingly frequent natural disasters, human-induced calamities including environmental degradation, and armed conflict and terrorism. After 9/11 tricky security situations became shrouded in frustration and anger at the behavior of individuals who lack respect for the dignity and rights of human beings. Such disparagement of human life has vastly complicated the task of balancing human rights and security, and, as a result, a populace is often enjoined to sacrifice human rights in the name of greater safety, at least for the short term. Unless the means for achieving an action are linked to the ends being sought, it is impossible for social workers to intervene and hold the moral high ground over those who disregard the human rights of others. In covering these issues in the social work curriculum, educators should focus on the ends versus the means, and consider the following questions:

- What does the action require?
- What are the processes whereby a particular action that supports human rights is initiated, implemented, and evaluated?
- How does the action affect those at the receiving end?

Complicating Human Rights: Multilayered and Internationalized Contexts

Respect for diversity in increasingly multicultural societies has placed human rights in new, multilayered contexts. Globalization, migration, and internationalism, once considered beyond the frontiers of the nation-state, are now near at hand. These factors interact with regional, national, and local levels, often creating problems and undermining existing responses to situations. These developments complicate the ability to realize human rights and place new demands on the nation-state if it is to treat newcomers as equals entitled to the same human and identity rights and benefits as citizens already residing in its geographical location. Taylor (1994) terms this contemporary reality "the politics of recognition" and emphasizes their centrality to the creation of a just society that embraces diversity. The impact of recognizing the new identities being forged within such spaces and the challenges of achieving their acceptance in practice cannot be underestimated. Social workers are obliged to understand multilayered, international contexts and meanings for the people they serve.

I borrow Charles Taylor's (1994) phrase about the formation of identity to suggest that human rights are "dialogically" constituted, as their composition is established through dialogue with others. Variations in meaning and in what constitutes human rights occur through these dialogical interactions and differ according to who is involved. The broader sociopolitical and socioeconomic contexts in which people operate also shape what is affirmed as human rights in practice. The relativity of human rights is created in spaces created by dialogical interactions, regardless of whether there is a universally accepted legal formulation that can be appealed to as forming them outside this relationship. We become individuals through our interactions with others, and realize our human rights through social relationships. This interactive process individuates human rights while drawing on their collective endorsement.

The freedom to practice a minority identity is enshrined in Article 27 of the UDHR. Defining people as fixed in terms of minorities and majorities misses a crucial point: identities are formed through interactions with others who are different. A majority can only exist when others are viewed as minorities. Framing the issue in a dyad such as this strengthens discourses that pit the majority against other groups and ignores the multidimensionality of even the majority group, for although the majority may be dominant in one respect, it may not be so in others. A white British man of Anglo-Saxon origins in England is a member of the dominant ethnic grouping, but, if he is gay, he is also part of a minority group regarding his sexuality.

When members of an ethnic majority are seen as privileged at the expense of minority ethnicities, the result is the demonizing of those who are ethnically different from the dominant norm, which violates the minority person's human rights. Discourses endorsing this view are currently finding expression in Europe, where migrants are cast as "undesirable" additions to the body politic, especially if they are asylum seekers or refugees. These negative discourses compound their exclusion, as they are expunged from society's midst without regard to their human rights. Such framings contribute to the judgment that the claims of asylum seekers are spurious. And if they have traveled through a "safe" third country to reach their destination, they can then be returned to the country from which they fled. Such actions are dangerous, as they can breed fascist reactions to difference and promote racist assaults (Cheles, Ferguson, & Vaughan, 1991). They also violate the provisions of the 1951 Geneva Convention which seeks to provide people in life-threatening situations with rights of protection in countries other than the one they are fleeing from. Because people convicted of hate crimes are often the clients of social workers, the social work curriculum should explore interventions that are effective in such circumstances to safeguard the human rights of both perpetrator and victim.

The right to a cultural life is enshrined in Article 5 of the International Convention on Economic, Social, and Political Rights (ICESPR). Enjoying one's culture raises a crucial question for the politics of recognition: What is the extent to which each constituent group's culture is frozen in a time warp associated with earlier expressions of identity instead of recognizing that culture and identity are fluid, constantly developing entities formed by, and modified through, interactions with others who are both similar and different? Put another way, will formal conceptualizations of identity formation incorporate agency? Without agency, the rights of individuals and collective groups to their culture and identity are in danger of becoming "ossified" (Dominelli, 2000), treated as self-contained and immutable objects independent of context, time, and space (Dominelli, 2004). Thus they are denied the right to change. Identity formation and changes in personal identification are important dimensions of social work practice. Practitioners have a vital role in helping people realize their human rights around culture and identity, ensuring that they understand the links between the local, national, and international aspects of these rights. The social work curriculum should explore these issues and provide students with the skills to address these points in practice.

Complicated identities suggest that social workers should make connections between space, people of diverse origins, and the multiple aspects of their personalities. This approach would expose the process of people developing within cultures through solidaristic, inclusive impulses rather than being separated out from others through divisive, exclusionary mechanisms. Hence each party to an interaction could acknowledge that people of different cultures share commonalities, which would facilitate their negotiating inclusion in each other's world on the basis of solidarity.

New Narratives and Reconfiguring Human Rights

A new narrative of human rights is required to take account of complex challenges and multilayered international contexts. These cover an equitable redistribution of global resources and portability of human rights. New narratives can create fresh concepts and understandings. Our actions are conceptually shaped (Hacking 1986), so new stories can teach us to enjoy the planet and share its resources more equitably. Here, social workers can bring to bear skills acquired by collecting narratives from clients and weaving these to make a story that facilitates working together (Hall, 1997).

The migration of peoples throughout human history means that we live in global diasporas (Brah, 1996) that yield new narratives. Today's Internet technology assists in their dissemination and connects us with others living beyond the geographical space we directly occupy. Technologically driven interactions can compress geography, time, and space to create new stories about our existences and form new communities and spaces. And if shared on the bases of solidarity and connections, these developments will facilitate people living in harmony with others who are different. Social workers can record and propagate these narratives in the interests of promoting acceptance of multicultural societies and harmonious relationships within them.

The human rights conventions referred to as enlarging the provisions of the UDHR have not been accepted by all governments. Some, like the United States, have refused to sign the CRC. Others have rejected certain articles of an otherwise endorsed document, for example, the right to employment which pays a decent wage and where workers are treated with respect and dignity. Still other countries distinguish between categories to exclude those they would otherwise accept, for instance, regarding the 1951 Geneva Convention on the Status of Refugees, the U.S. has declined to apply the articles concerning prisoners of war by defining them instead as "unlawful combatants" and thus not subject to the provisions of the Geneva Convention. Other nations question the relevance of the Geneva Convention to asylum seekers seeking admission and residence in another country. These nations are redefining such individuals as potential criminals seeking unlawful entry, and thus feel justified in denying their claims. According to some NGOs, including the Refugee Council in Britain and the Asylum Seekers Resource Centre in Australia, official responses on this basis constitute violations of human rights.

Staking claims to the exemption of certain actions from human rights legislation constitutes a fraying of the inalienability and indivisibility of human rights. It also negates the importance of treating people with dignity regardless of their behavior. Respecting the person while condemning his or her actions, a key social work value, is essential if we are to uphold human rights and retain our own dignity and humanity. Treating people in this way gives us the authority to hold individuals accountable for their actions and bring those who violate human rights to justice. Handling violators in ways that are consistent with upholding their human rights, even if they have denied these to others, is essential if we are not to degenerate to their level.

A global citizenship perspective regards all people as endowed with human rights by virtue of being human beings; questions negative approaches to asylum seekers and refugees; and criticizes the denial of their rights simply because they cross borders and are not considered the responsibility of the nation-state where they now reside. In Britain, Foreign Secretary Jack Straw has argued that the provisions of the Geneva Convention should be changed to deal with "bogus" asylum claims. What constitutes a false application is contentious, but it often means the absence of documents proving individual identity but that cannot be obtained without endangering lives. This stance has been supported by the then Leader of the Opposition, Michael Howard, himself the son of a former Jewish refugee. Demanding the portability of human rights poses a couple of thorny problems: Who will pay for their implementation? Who will uphold them among migratory populations? Although there is consensus about the significance of global citizenship as a concept, considerable dissent exists on its practical meaning and implementation.

Disputes about who is responsible for the cost and realization of human rights also surface over the effort to eliminate poverty throughout the world. The Make Poverty History Campaign of 2005, and the Jubilee 2000

Campaign before that, raised important concerns about human rights in an international context. How can rich countries, mainly in the West, condone high levels of poverty globally? The UN has determined that more than 2.3 billion people live on less than $U.S.2 per day, with 1.3 billion living for less than $U.S.1, signifying absolute poverty. At this poverty level, people suffer from hunger, malnutrition, illiteracy, and poor health. This reality is in sharp contrast with provisions in Articles 22 to 27 of the UDHR and undermines people's entitlement to well-being enshrined in that Declaration. Hunger should not exist in a world where current production techniques can grow all the food necessary to feed the Earth's inhabitants. But making this a reality requires political will to redistribute the necessary resources. The stalemate on this issue indicates the contested nature of human rights at the level of implementation.

Susan George (2003, p. 17) argues that Article 23 of the UDHR is relevant to poverty eradication strategies because it asserts that,

> Everyone has the right to a standard of living adequate for ... health and well-being ... including food, clothing, housing and medical care and necessary social services and the right to security in the event of unemployment, sickness, disability, widowhood, old age or other lack of livelihood.

George claims that a key barrier to realizing these human rights is globalization and its accompanying neo-liberal doctrine that privileges market priorities over people's needs. Supporting her argument that the system breeds inequalities, she shows that income and wealth distribution have become increasingly polarized so that the top 20 percent of the world's population has accumulated 86 percent of the world's wealth in the last thirty years; the lowest 20 percent controls only 1.3 percent of the world's wealth. This has resulted in a North-South differential that rose from 2 to 1 in the eighteenth century to 70 to 1 today (George, 2003, pp. 18–19). To put it more graphically, the richest three people on Earth have, between them, more than the total gross domestic product of the forty-eight poorest countries in the world. Even within countries, disparities in income and wealth have been exacerbated. An employee today, at the top rung of the corporate ladder in the West, earns two hundred to three hundred times more than the average employee, compared to forty to sixty times more in the 1960s and 1970s (George, 2003, p. 19).

Social workers could engage in these debates and argue for redistributive measures to end poverty. They need to take a more proactive role, however, than the one adopted by the British Association of Social Workers (BASW) when its members marched under its banner at the Make Poverty History Rally in Edinburgh in July 2005. A campaign, even one that address a single issue like eradicating world poverty, has to be actively sustained at many levels over time. The complexity of issues and extensive resources required for transformative action prevent small groups of social workers, as well as their national or international associations, from adopting more substantive roles.

Responding to people in need and helping them to realize their human rights is at the heart of social work. However, few social work practitioners, texts, or curricula are situated in this framework or follow human rights campaigns. Courses enabling social work students to understand poverty, its structural origins and impact on people's daily lives and lost opportunities for growth, are important elements of a curriculum based on human rights.

The Violation of Human Rights by Globalization and Multinational Corporations

Globalization is producing a considerable shift in our understanding of human rights (McGrew, 1998) and is, in part, directly undermining human rights. Globalization is linked to complex trade flows that have unequal ramifications for countries. These are implicated in rising levels of poverty and inequalities in income both within and between countries (Wichterich, 2000). People without economic resources have little chance to realize their social and economic rights, even if they enjoy political and civil rights, and states without resources cannot meet their obligations in this regard. The problem of implementing the provisions of the UDHR arose even before the document was promulgated; the desire to include an individual's right to paid employment, with holidays, as a crucial economic right was rejected early on in the negotiations, because not every country could guarantee this provision for lack of sufficient resources to do so (Evans, 1998; McGrew, 1998; Freeman, 2002).

Globalization has commodified social relations by turning people with resources into consumers who choose what they want in a market place but excludes those who lack financial resources and knowledge about how the market works (Dominelli, 2004). This development has implications for citizenship entitlements, because these have become commodified as services formerly provided by public welfare states but are now considered to be goods purchased privately by individuals acting as consumers. The shift in language from "client," "patient," or "passenger" to "customer" is indicative of the trend toward a market economy even in personal social services.

Globalization has also affected labor rights. Corporate exigencies that safeguard profit margins have compelled workers to accept lower pay rates when jobs have moved from the public sector into the private one or even to another location with lower wages (Wichterich, 2000). Companies can enact these moves with impunity, as competition among nation-states to secure jobs produces a "race to the bottom" to achieve the most conducive environment to maximize profits, for example, tax breaks, low wages, lack of union-protected labor, limited social security, and an infrastructure paid for by the public purse (Wichterich, 2000). Low wages, uncertainty, and short-term contracts rather than jobs for life and a more conservative fiscal approach to economic matters have become the norm. The overall impact has been that people are less able to take care of themselves.

Vandana Shiva (2003) tries to counteract these trends by demanding that global corporations become accountable. She accuses these corporations of destroying the environment and appropriating local agricultural knowledge in their haste to make profits. She argues that globalization is pitting the economic rights of corporations against people's human rights, and she considers the proposed Multilateral Agreement on Investment (MAI) an instrument that overrides individual human rights in favor of corporate economic rights. Shiva calls for a reversal of these developments through corporate accountability.

Shiva (2003) also points out the danger of MAI privately controlling commonly held local knowledge through the imposition of seed patents, as this will enhance monopoly control over food production and distribution; centralize intellectual capital in the hands of a few corporations; and increase the likelihood of global capital making decisions that will negatively affect people's daily lives. In her view this reality will become the norm, as MAI prevents governments from barring entry to foreign investors or interfering in the decisions they make. Under this regime Shiva fears that small independent food producers will lose their livelihoods, their right to provide for themselves and their families, and their right to live according to their own cultural traditions, which are more environmentally friendly and sensitive to the Earth's capacities for regeneration than corporate industrial methods. In fact, as she points out, the implementation of the MAI in India is now being held at bay, at least for the moment, by local citizen mobilization.

According to Shiva (2003), global agribusiness represented by companies producing genetically modified (GM) foods deleteriously affects consumers as end-users. Corporate resistance to product labeling on GM foods reduces information about their composition, making it harder for consumers to know how these products may adversely affect their health and also undermining consumers' rights to know exactly what they are purchasing. Shiva, by focusing on India, highlights how globalization has eaten away at human rights associated with democratic politics. She contends that, by thwarting people's aspirations and capacity to address injustices through democratic means, the uncertainties of globalization reinforce fascist and fundamentalist forces as people turn to narrow religious and national identities for clarity in an uncertain world. In her words: "Politics emptied of economic rights exploits fear and insecurity and builds hate as political capital. India is not alone in seeing the rise of fascist and fundamentalist forces as globalization denies people the means to defend their lives and livelihoods through democratic means" (pp. 103–104).

Stemming the erosion of people's identity and security within a globalizing world is a crucial matter to address at local, national, and international levels. Shiva (2003) posits inclusivity, interconnectedness between people, and indivisibility of human rights as helpful responses to these concerns and emphasizes the role of women in creating the appropriate conditions. This brings us to the issue of the universality of human rights and inclusivity, which encompasses both men and women in promoting a new world order that places people and the environment instead of narrow sectional corporate interests at the center of the social, economic, and political agendas. The inclusion of both genders is crucial, given men's preponderance in the decision making that creates armed conflicts which destroy people's human rights in the name of preserving them. Inclusivity is necessary, as women, excluded from decision-making processes, are increasingly finding that they must cope with the effects of "masculine" decisions that do not serve human welfare.

The realization of women's human rights has been difficult, especially those linked to women's position in the home, and their right to make their own decisions, to hold property, to be free from attack, or to participate in public life. The 1995 UN Conference on Women in Beijing redefined women's rights as human rights, and stressed their universality in order to facilitate a woman's demand for equality. Ensuring equality between men and women remains a global issue requiring urgent attention and is a social work concern.

Men also must take responsibility for changing their behaviors and attitudes, including those toward women and the environment, and their relationships with other men. Among these is resisting the desire to play zero-sum games using public resources and decision-making structures. These produce winners and losers but ultimately fail, as, in the long run, they only ensure that we will all lose. To avoid this outcome, cooperation through solidarity between diverse peoples, and between countries, must take predominance (Dominelli, 2002, 2004).

Holding governments, global corporations, and individuals to account for their actions by openly questioning powerful decision makers are essential aspects of human rights that involve the right to know. Undermining people's right to know for the sake of security only increases insecurity. People become fearful of honest debate and unable to criticize policies that can significantly disrupt or alter their lives for limited benefit. Freedom of expression and association, besides being crucial human rights, are also central underpinnings of people's capacity to act as critical citizens. These have to be supported by the right to know with access to information that assists individuals in making informed decisions about appropriate actions in a given situation. Social workers can assist citizens in acquiring the information they need and help them navigate around organizations holding this data.

Whistle-blowing supports a strategy that challenges injustice and wrongdoing. Frowned upon by powerful bodies, it must be handled with caution. The potential for a whistleblower's career and livelihood to be destroyed (Martin, 2003) makes people wary of taking this road. As demonstrated by Enron and other corporations that have misused people's money, having the right to know about an organization and its activities, whether as employees, shareholders, or members of the public, is essential if we are to eliminate the secrecy that enables corporate players to make decisions that destroy individual livelihoods in order to maintain corporate interests and self-gain, as well as transform these bodies into accountable, just economic players on the world stage. Social workers have often been involved in whistle-blowing initiatives and can help those who wish to attempt this endeavor obtain the required skills.

Globalized Terrorism, Insecurities, and State Infringements on Human Rights

Flawed decision making can be improved by transparency and accountability. In the wake of 9/11, security concerns have enhanced demands for greater secrecy within public and global corporate life as a defense against terrorists. From a human rights perspective, this raises issues about the relationship between ends and means. If a healthy body politic is epitomized by citizens acting as agents in an open society, what price do we pay when state responses to attacks are predicated on disregarding innocent lives caught in the cross-fire, and when the broader human rights which entitle people to hold the state accountable for its actions are bypassed?

Alienated individuals may be prepared to break the law to wreak vengeance on society for grievances, real or imagined, and indiscriminately destroy other peoples' right to life. If these alleged wrongs resonate among law-abiding members of a polity, this knowledge should be explored and used in finding ways that uphold moral integrity and behavior consistent with recognizing human rights in dealing with lawbreakers. Redefining terrorists as criminals facilitates responses within a framework of recognized justice, safeguards the security of all, and undermines support for those who would replace democratic ways of life with doctrinal ones. We know from historical examples like the Israeli-Palestinian dispute that military retorts do not solve political problems but instead ooze hatred and intensify armed struggle. We know from developments in Northern Ireland that bringing opposing parties into a dialogue has produced the most progress in resolving that conflict. Social workers with expertise in mediation and nonviolent resolutions to conflict can begin to transfer this knowledge to the human rights arena if the curriculum prioritizes human rights as an issue.

The increasingly authoritarian, defensive stance of Western states in such circumstances begs other questions about how best to deal with random murderers promoting their own narrow sectional interests. Do Ghandian insights offer the state the possibility of thinking differently about how to deal with this threat, or is the state stuck with responses that enhance power over relations and increase its control over a citizenry regardless of their role in this global drama? How should states proceed in delivering the peaceful and stable societies that we seek? Social workers who are accustomed to addressing complex situations have a role to play in initiating the dialogues necessary for finding appropriate solutions to these difficulties.

Ignoring the processes whereby a state responds to attacks on its national integrity can undermine its authority to act in the best interests of its populace in a way that carries the support of most of its citizens. Safeguarding the support of its citizens becomes the state's best protection against adversity in surveillance societies where there are technological means for keeping tabs on each individual and a person's right to privacy can diminish, even become meaningless. Since the state is the guarantor of personal freedoms and social life in democratic societies, the consequences of state actions on any issue can be highly significant for human rights. The role of social workers is critical in maintaining social cohesion in difficult circumstances by upholding human rights (Lorenz, 1994; Dominelli, 2004).

Migratory population flows are calling into question the restriction of human rights vested in a person to particular territorial boundaries while corporations that have achieved the status of global players can traverse borders with relative impunity. Meanwhile, individuals are finding their movements across national boundaries subjected to more technologically invasive national scrutiny, especially since the attack on the World Trade Center in New York. From that moment, the increasing emphasis on security has eroded human rights by according these a lesser priority for a protection that remains elusive, as the London bombings in 2005 indicate. Subjugating human rights to security creates profit-maximizing opportunities for companies selling the paraphernalia associated with greater security—gated communities, surveillance equipment, and technologies for tightening the law-and-order apparatus. Security becomes big business with a lesser accountability for the multinationals providing these services and unelected agencies maintaining security.

These developments devalue the currency of human rights as entitlements to freedom and dignity. Human rights are marginalized and traded off for safety in a way that presupposes the outcome. But dangerous situations are fluid, containing many unknown elements, so the guarantee of safety is only an illusion. In this context, complying with arbitrary norms acquires meanings that create the perception of ensured safety or reduced harm so that people consent to curtailed rights and freedoms, albeit grudgingly at times. Nonetheless, as long as reducing risk or minimizing harm is part of a philosophy that legitimates human rights, states can present their loss in favor of increasing security for the greatest number as consistent with upholding human rights.

Meanwhile, the state is appropriating an increasing number of violent weapons that rely on high levels of technological sophistication, and have the potential to imperil civilian lives more than the lives of soldiers in wartime (Chomsky, 2003). Hence conflicts since World War II have disproportionately affected ordinary people, primarily women and children whose human rights have been more vulnerable to loss than men's. Tony Blair's recent defense of the shooting of "suspected terrorist" Jean Charles de Menezes, an innocent twenty-seven-year-old Brazilian electrician, legally residing in the UK, who was on his way to work, by the Metropolitan Police as necessary in "uncertain" and difficult times illustrates the vulnerability of exchanging security for human rights. The freedom to walk the streets without fear of accidentally being shot is sacrificed in favor of security. Prioritizing security also carries implications for social development, as it siphons off resources for protection. Social workers can affirm the value of social development in reducing poverty and enhancing well-being by engaging in these debates.

Increasing control over the citizenry in the interests of security further undermines social development, as people become fearful of voicing dissent. Challenging decisions taken in the name of security can become extremely difficult and potentially hazardous, but, without public debate and accountability, abuses of power are more likely and freedom of expression is more readily curtailed. The four murderers who killed fifty-two innocent inhabitants of the British Isles, many nationalities represented among them, displayed their contempt for the individual's right to life and freedom from fear. Their contempt for civilian authority became absolute when they took their own lives in the process, removing themselves from the reach of temporal justice. Those in international organized crime syndicates and networks that traffic children, women, and men in order to exploit them also violate their human rights.

Links between people have been facilitated by the expansion of the new information technologies and by inexpensive airplane travel. This increasing connectedness has been paralleled by the desire of constituent units of nation-states to fragment, as has occurred in the former Soviet Union. In some cases, these fractures have been followed by violent upheavals such as in the former Yugoslavia. At other times voting has been a means to achieve change, as in Scotland, Quebec. Social workers can help people move forward by understanding these events and realizing nonviolent choices.

Promoting Human Rights in and Through the Social Work Curriculum

Human rights are central in promoting a peaceful egalitarian world conducive to world peace and human well-being. Social work students are entitled to be taught skills for the complex and difficult jobs they encounter every day. Being able to intervene while upholding human rights within a framework of social justice is integral to this goal. The social work curriculum should infuse human rights into all existing foundational courses, as well as offer specific human rights electives. Topics might include the following:

- The history of human rights
- International legislation and protocols on human rights, particularly those linked to UN structures, for instance, the International Convention on the Elimination of All Forms of Racial Discrimination; the Convention on the Elimination of All Forms of Discrimination against Women; the Convention against Torture and Other Cruel, Inhuman, or Degrading Treatment or Punishment; the Convention on the Rights of the Child; and the proposed Convention on Disability Rights
- National and regional legislation on human rights
- Key issues in and illustrations from practice, for example, women and domestic violence, women as rape victims of war, the trafficking of children, child soldiers
- Examples of human rights violations and actions that can be taken
- Ensuring that the ends and means in an action are consistent with human rights
- Processes that uphold human dignity and worth
- Questions about how to enhance human rights in practice

- Exercises involving simulations and role plays on realizing human rights
- "What if" exercises to explore the possibilities and dangers of taking action
- Projects involving cross-cultural issues and human rights
- Skills in mediation and nonviolent conflict resolution
- Advocating and campaigning for state and corporate accountability
- Whistle-blowing procedures and skills

Conclusion

The endorsement of the Universal Declaration of Human Rights at a critical juncture in the world's history brought hope of a better life to millions. Although the UDHR has successfully achieved some of its objectives, it has a long way to go as an international instrument aimed at ensuring peace, freedom, and security in the world. Certain limitations can be attributed to its overwhelming emphasis on the nation-state as both the guarantor of human rights and the judge of their violation. Modern history has shown that the state is often a perpetrator of human rights injustices, and the lack of independent, internationally enforceable mechanisms for controlling recalcitrant states has been a barrier to the practice of human rights worldwide. These limitations argue for the creation of mechanisms of enforcement in the international arena. Social workers can make a major contribution to initiating the dialogue necessary for bringing this about and servicing those who become involved.

Another key failure of the UDHR is that of eradicating widespread poverty, the prevalence of which significantly undermines all other human rights. Rooting human rights in the individual also hinders attempts at upholding these when the problem of their implementation is structurally, rather than psychologically, derived. Poverty is an example of a structurally induced social problem. People are poor not just because they lack the skills or moral fortitude to succeed, as New Right ideologues like Charles Murray (1990) insist. Rather, there are simply not enough highly paid, stimulating jobs, and high-quality education is also insufficient, as is access to social, political, and economic opportunities for all. Eradicating structural poverty calls for the construction of an entirely different social order and not simply relief action (Gutierrez, 1983). As social workers, we can use human rights to guide us on the road to justice by eliminating structural inequalities, but first we need to learn what these are.

Social workers have the skills for playing key roles in ensuring that human rights are practiced wherever people live. To make the most of their expertise, it is crucial that the social work curriculum provides the space and frameworks for acquiring the knowledge and developing the skills that will assist in their realization. Human rights must emerge from their invisible status and become an explicit topic in the academy and in practice, a considerable challenge for practitioners, academics, and service users to address. But doing so is of extreme urgency if we are to heal our nation's social and physical wounds brought on by the violation of people's dignity and worth and the degradation of our physical environment.

References

IASSW & IFSW. (1994). *Human rights and social work: A manual for schools of social work and the social work profession.* Professional Training series, no. 1. New York: United Nations.

Brah, A. (1996). *Cartographies of diaspora.* London: Routledge.

Briskman, L. (2006). Pushing ethical boundaries for children and families: Confidentiality, transparency and transformation. In R. Adams, L. Dominelli, & M. Payne, M. (Eds.), *Social work futures: Crossing boundaries, transforming practice.* London: Palgrave.

Cheles, L., Ferguson, R., & Vaughan, M. (1991). *Neo-fascism in Europe.* Harlow: Longman.

Chomsky, N. (2003). Recovering rights: A crooked path. In M. J. Gibney (Ed,), *Globalizing rights.* Oxford: Oxford University Press

Coates, J. (2003). *Ecology and social work: Toward a new paradigm.* Halifax: Fernwood.

Dominelli, L. (2000). Tackling racism in everyday realities: A task for social workers. In M. Callahan & S. Hessle (Eds.), *Valuing the field: Child welfare in an international context.* Aldershot: Ashgate.

Dominelli, L. (2002). *Anti-oppressive social work theory and practice.* London: Palgrave.

Dominelli, L. (2004). *Social work: Theory and practice for a changing profession.* Cambridge: Polity.

Donnelly, J. (2003). *Universal human rights in theory and practice* (2nd ed.). Ithaca, NY: Cornell University Press.

Evans, T, (Ed.). (1998). *Human rights fifty years on: A reappraisal.* Manchester, England: Manchester University Press.

Freeman, M, (2002), *Human rights: An interdisciplinary approach.* Cambridge: Polity.

General Social Care Council (2007). http://www.gscc.org.uk/Home/. Retrieved, January 10, 2007.

George, S. (2003). Globalizing rights? In M. J. Gibney (Ed.). *Globalizing rights.* Oxford: Oxford University Press.

Gibney, M. J. (ed). (2003). *Globalizing rights.* Oxford: Oxford University Press.

Gutierrez, G. (1983). *The power of the poor in history.* Maryknoll, NY: Orbis.

Hacking, I. (1986). Making up people. In T. C. Heller, M. Sosna, & D. E. Wellby (Eds.), *Reconstructing individualism.* Stanford: Stanford University Press.

Hall, C. (1997). *Social work as narratives: Storytelling and persuasion in professional texts.* Aldershot: Ashgate.

Hayes, D. (2006). Social work with asylum seekers and others subject to immigration control, In R. Adams, L. Dominelli, & M. Payne (Eds.), *Social work futures: Crossing boundaries, transforming practice.* London: Palgrave.

Ife, J. (2001). *Human rights and social work: Towards rights-based practice.* Cambridge: Cambridge University Press.

Jubilee. (2000). Supporting economic justice campaigns worldwide. Website: www.jubilee2000uk.org.

Kohli, A. S. (2004). *Human rights and social work: Issues, challenges and response.* New Delhi: Kanishka.

Lorenz, W. (1994). *Social work in a changing Europe.* London: Routledge.

Martin, B. (2003). Illusions of whistleblower protection. University of Technology, Sydney, *Law Review, 5,* 119–130.

McGrew, A. (1998). Human rights in a global age: Coming to terms with globalisation. In T. Evans (Ed.), *Human rights fifty years on: A reappraisal.* Manchester, England: Manchester University Press.

Murray, C. (1990). *The emerging British underclass.* London: Institute for Economic Affairs.

Parekh, B. (2000). *Rethinking multiculturalism.* London: Macmillan.

Pyles, L. (2006). Toward a post-Katrina framework: Social work as human rights and capabilities. *Journal of Comparative Social Welfare, 22(1),* 79–88.

Reichert, E. (2003). *Social work and human rights: A foundation for policy and practice.* New York: Columbia University Press.

Reichert, E. (2006). *Understanding human rights: An exercise book.* Sage, CA: Thousand Oaks.

Shiva, V. (2003). Food rights, free trade and fascism. In M. J. Gibney (Ed.), *Globalizing rights.* Oxford: Oxford University Press.

Singh, J. A. (2003). American physicians and dual obligations in the "War on Terror." *BMCBio Medical Ethics Medical Ethics 4(4),* 1–10. Website: www.biomedcentral.com/content/pdf/1472-6939-4-4.pdf.

Stephen, S. (2003, June 29). Mistrust of asylum seekers continues. *Green Left Weekly*, 8. Website: www.greenleft.org.au/back/2003/523/523/p8b.htm.

Taylor, C. (1994). The politics of recognition. In A. Gutmann (Ed.). *Multiculturalism: Examining the politics of recognition.* Princeton, NJ: Princeton University Press.

UDHR. (2005). Universal Declaration of Human Rights. New York: United Nations. Website: www.un.org/rights/50/decla.htm.

Ungar, M. (2002). A deeper, more social ecological social work practice. *Social Services Review, 76,* 480–497.

United Nations (1994). *Human rights and social work: A manual for schools of social work and the social work profession.* Professional Training Series 4. New York and Geneva: United Nations.

Wichterich, C. (2000). *Globalized woman: Reports from a future of inequality.* London: Zed Books.

[3]

Global Distributive Justice as a Human Right

Implications for the Creation of a Human Rights Culture

JOSEPH WRONKA

> It does the cause of human rights no good to inveigh against civil and political rights deviations while helping to perpetuate illiteracy, malnutrition, disease, infant mortality, and a low life expectancy among millions of human beings. All the dictators and all the aggressors throughout history, however ruthless, have not succeeded in creating as much misery and suffering as the disparities between the world's rich and poor sustain today.
>
> —Shridath Ramphal, formerly
> Commonwealth Secretary of the United Nations

The purposes of this chapter are to convey with select data the increasing seriousness of the crisis of global distributive justice; examine global distributive justice, as a solidarity right within the context of the human rights triptych; and suggest social action strategies that would have implications for the creation of a human rights culture. In brief, global distributive justice, a solidarity right, asserts ultimately that the poor countries of the world have a right to the overall prosperity of the richer countries. It calls for brotherhood, that is, fraternity,[1] among all peoples of the world, as asserted, in part, in Article 1 of the Universal Declaration of Human Rights (UDHR). It is largely a claim for a global redistribution of power, wealth, and other important values reflecting the growth of Third World nationalism and the emergence and decline of the nation-state from the latter part

---

1. Obviously sisterhood and sorority are equally important. Eleanor Roosevelt, the chairperson of the drafting committee of the Universal Declaration, wanted nonsexist language in that document, but in the end the nomenclature of the time prevailed.

of the twentieth century to the present (Human Rights, 2006). Former president Jimmy Carter, in his speech accepting the Nobel Peace Prize in Oslo (2002), poignantly expressed the urgency and increasing gravity of the violation of this important human right:

> The most serious and universal problem [today] is the growing chasm between the richest and poorest people on earth. Citizens of ten wealthiest countries are now seventy-five times richer than those who live in the ten poorest ones, and the separation is increasing every year, not only between nations but also within them. The results of this disparity are root causes of most of the world's unresolved problems, including starvation, illiteracy, environmental degradation, violent conflict, and unnecessary illnesses that range from Guinea worm to HIV/AIDS. (Carter, 2002, pp. 18–19)

Roughly 2.5 billion people in the world, constituting 40 percent of the world population, live on less than $2 per day, often making each day a struggle merely to survive. Indeed, in the mid-twentieth century the ratio of the gross domestic product of the twenty richest countries was roughly eighteen times that of the poorer countries. But at the turn of the new millennium this ratio has more than doubled to thirty-seven times. The image of a champagne glass with a large concentration of income at the top and a thin stem at the bottom roughly depicts the present situation. The ratio of income, in fact, for the world as a whole from the poorest to the richest is 1 to 103. Further reflecting the words of former president Carter, within most countries inequality has increased. The most dramatic changes occurred in formerly Communist countries transitioning to market-based economies. Russia, for example, is struggling with rising poverty, unemployment, and its corollary, violence. Yet, in the United States, increases in income inequality have risen, according to the U.S. Census Bureau, between 1968 and 2001, resulting today in the most unequal distribution of income in high income-countries (United Nations Development Program, 2005).

Obviously such disparities in income between and within nations will also result in imbalances of power, the wealthier having more access to the media to influence voters, which will eventually result in laws and policies that might not be sensitive to the voices of the disenfranchised (Worldwatch Institute, 2003). Similarly, when speaking of power, which is closely related to income, the United States, with the highest per capita income in the world (Kivel, 2004), dominates the world film industry (UN Development Program, 2004). This can easily influence both young and old to adopt the consumer lifestyles of the "rich and famous" and especially those of the United States, which has become a primary model for global policy making (Steiner & Alston, 2000). Even in international arenas like the United Nations, the five permanent members of the Security Council—China, Russia, France, Great Britain, and the United States—are generally economically richer countries, and each has a powerful privilege of veto. In fact, African countries recently demanded two permanent seats with veto power on that council, only to be rebuffed by the five current permanent members ("4 Countries Delay," 2005). Surely this global imbalance of power needs to be addressed before Erich Fromm's pithy statement, "the more the drive toward life is thwarted, the stronger is the drive toward destruction. . . . [which] is the outcome of unlived life" (cited in Gil, 1996, p. 1) results in further acts that "outrage the conscience of humanity," a fear stated in the Preamble to the Universal Declaration. Furthermore, the roughly $1.5 trillion spent on defense to keep the borders of nation-states intact, should lead, perhaps, to the conclusion that the nation-state is a questionable enterprise. Davis (1992) has even referred to the nation-state as a myth, and Nobel Prize winner Joseph Rotblatt (1997) has asserted that instead our allegiance ought to be to humanity. It appeared more sensible, therefore, to use the term *global* distributive justice" in the title of this essay instead of "*international* distributive justice" which is the more common practice, the nation-state having been born out of the Conference of Westphalia (1648), an enterprise of dubious utility.

But it is a mistake to view economic disparity and power as the only failures of the world community to distribute resources between and within nations. To be sure, other important values might be included in this right to solidarity which is still in the process of conceptual elaboration (Human Rights, 2006). Despite the relative infancy of this notion, the UN's Human Development Index (HDI)—which measures a country's overall quality of life, largely emphasizing infant mortality, schooling, and longevity rate—may serve as an effective guiding principle (Gil, 1992, 1998) to better understand the extent of this global problem and engage in appropriate social action initiatives. Briefly, the infant mortality rate in low-income countries is 13 times greater than that of high-income countries. The infant mortality rate in the U.S. is roughly 1.5 times higher for Native Americans and 2.5 times higher for African Americans than for whites (Human Rights Committee on the Elimination of Racial Discrimination, 2000). Worldwide, the average years of schooling for persons in high-income and low-income countries, respectively, are approximately 13.5 years and 7 years. Nearly half the number of adults in the U.S. can be described as functionally illiterate, a percentage comprised largely of low-income and disenfranchised groups, reflecting a lack of opportunity in education (Human Rights Committee on Civil and Political Rights, 1995). The average life expectancy gap between high-income and low-income countries is roughly nineteen years (UN Development Program, 2005). In the U.S. the death rate for African Americans from heart disease is 41 percent higher than for whites, and Native Americans are 231 percent more likely to die from diabetes than Americans as a whole. The relationship between income, education, longevity, and other concerns of President Carter, such as environmental degradation and catastrophe, violent conflict, and HIV, is complex, but one must also acknowledge that, among other factors, the average number of natural disasters in the world has skyrocketed from approximately two hundred in 1975 to seventeen hundred in 2001 (Montanari, 2005) and desertification has doubled in the last three decades (Gore, 2006). Coastal habitats, largely populated by indigenous peoples, are increasingly threatened, and women, often children, in these groups are increasingly bearing the burden of finding firewood and clean drinking water to help sustain their families. Roughly two-thirds of the indigenous who are illiterate are women, who comprise just over half the world's population. Their resulting under-representation in the formalized workforce leaves them vulnerable to contract HIV, which, in this new millennium, has increased every year since 1980. Finally, the U.S., the largest emitter of greenhouse gases, also spends roughly 47 percent of the total world income on military expenditures and more than all the top thirty countries with the largest armies (*New York Times Almanac*, 2005, p. 225), making the adage "might makes right" an ugly reality.

There are some rays of hope, but with attendant caveats. For example, the longevity rate globally between 1960 and today has increased by sixteen years in high-income countries and by six years in low-income countries. A closer examination reveals this increase occurred largely before 1980. The average income growth in low-income countries since 2000 has also increased 3.4 percent, twice the average for high-income countries. Yet that is the average, and regions like Sub-Sahara Africa, although also experiencing a slight increase (1.2 percent) have actually experienced a reversal in other indicators, such as deaths from AIDS and malaria. Although there have been gains in income in some Asian countries like China and India, these gains have not necessarily translated into improving the overall quality of life for all. Economic wealth is not necessarily a guarantee of enhancing human development. Thus Guatemala has twice the average income of Vietnam but a lower HDI ranking (UN Development Report, 2005). It appears, then, that advances, however minimal, are slowing; growth is unevenly distributed; and wealth is often not translating into fulfillment of human needs.

Such scenarios of inequality can be seen not only between and within nations but also between individuals and nations. For example, according to Sachs (2005, p. 305), "the top four hundred taxpayers [in the U.S. had] a combined income in 2000 that exceeded the combined incomes of four of the countries [visited by President Bush in 2005: Botswana, Nigeria, Senegal and Uganda]." One could also conservatively estimate that the world's 500 richest people cited in *Forbes*, whose income is equivalent to no more than 5 percent of their assets, have incomes exceeding that of the poorest 416 million people in the world (UN Development Report, 2005). The problem can also be defined by comparing corporations and nations (Danaher, 1996, 2001). "General Motors' sales," for example, "were greater in 1995 than the gross national product of 169 countries, including Saudi Arabia, South Africa, Malaysia, and Norway" (Lappe, Collins, & Rosset, 1998, p. 143). Even so, the "market capitalization of Microsoft recently passed that of General Motors" (Brown & Flavin, 1999, p. 7), and, according to Morgenson (2004), the "Chief Executive pay in the USA is approximately 531 times . . . [that of] a multiple employee average," a gap which has "yawned in recent years."

This author is continually reminded of images he saw while traveling in Asia in the late 1960s that reflect these dire situations. On a street in Izmir, Turkey, as far as the eye could see, families were begging on blankets. One woman begged feverishly for a few coins to buy water for her crying child. After receiving some coins she immediately ran to buy water, in an attempt to quench the thirst of her anguished child. The child still cried, and she begged for more. A kindly "water seller" then bent down to give the child some water, *gratis*. Not far away was what resembled a European café, where Coca-Cola and fine European wines were being sold in full view and for prices that far exceeded that for water. The café had an obvious European and North American clientele, suggesting that the profits would possibly end up in Paris or Atlanta, Georgia. Does the wisdom of the Native American sage, Chief Sitting Bill, not become a stark reality, given this global maldistribution of wealth: "The white man knows how to make everything, but he does not know how to distribute it" (Safransky, 1990, p. 74). It is doubtful that the scenario of this woman and child, and similar situations, are any different today when groundwater is depleting and it is increasingly difficult to find a good, clean cup of water.

Toward the Creation of a Human Rights Culture

If human rights are viewed as the legal mandate to fulfill human need and take seriously the notion that the only criterion of human rights is a person's humanity, then it is quite possible that this powerful idea of human rights can assist us in dealing with some of the gaps discussed above. We are speaking here of developing a human rights culture, which is a "lived awareness" of human rights principles, not only cognitively speaking but also in a person's heart, which are then dragged into one's everyday life (Wronka, 2006, 1998a). Thus it is important not only to know, for instance, that solidarity rights are human rights but for the entire global community to "feel it" in their hearts and everyday consciousness, so that the human rights of every person, everywhere, can be guaranteed. Obviously such a culture, grounded in human rights principles, would easily translate into socially just policies, a primary concern of the social work profession and of service and health professions in general.

No government today would dare say that it is against human rights, a clear about-face from the days of the Conference of Evian, in 1938, called by President Franklin D. Roosevelt to stop the abuses of the Third Reich. The consensus at that time was that no one had the right to interfere with another country's domestic affairs. Bringing the world's attention to the abuses of the Nazis would subsequently make more visible atrocities such as public lynching and genocide against Native Americans in the U.S.; officially sanctioned policies of torture by European colonies in Africa; and the horrors of the Soviet Gulag (Buergenthal, Shelton, & Stewart, 2002). The attitude of the supremacy of domestic sovereignty resulted in World War II and the wanton slaughter of at least ten million innocents, primarily Jews, but also Gypsies, Poles, gays, and others inimical to the Third Reich. From those ashes arose the United Nations and, ultimately, the Universal

Declaration of Human Rights, the authoritative definition of human rights standards drafted under the able leadership of Eleanor Roosevelt. President Roosevelt's Four Freedom's speech (1941), moreover, not only paved the way for the structuring of the UN, in general, but also, in particular, for a global rallying cry for fundamental freedoms later found in human rights documents:

In the future days, which we seek to make secure, we look forward to a world founded upon four essential human freedoms.

The first is the freedom of speech and expression everywhere in the world.

The second is the freedom of every person to worship God in his own way everywhere in the world.

The third is the freedom from want, which, translated into world terms, means economic understandings, which will secure to every nation a healthy peacetime life for its inhabitants everywhere in the world.

The fourth is freedom from fear, which, translated into world terms, means a world-wide reduction of armaments to such a point and in such a thorough fashion that no nation will be in a position to commit an act of physical aggression against any neighbor—anywhere in the world. (pp. 46–47)

Human rights are equal, interdependent, and indivisible. Most Americans are aware of the importance of civil and political rights, and the growing movement to guarantee economic and social rights, but this essay argues that solidarity rights—global distributive justice, in particular—should be of equal significance. Its importance is obvious: by distributing wealth, power, and other important values equally, the understandable resentment of much of the world that is marginalized and socially excluded from global community building could be lessened. Given that "unlived life leads to destruction," the loss of opportunity for a large majority of the world's population to develop to their capacity may ultimately result in an endless cycle of violence and counter-violence (Gil, 1995) and an increase in defense spending, channeling much needed resources to the globally disenfranchised.

Because information is power, an understanding of the "Human Rights Triptych," described below, should provide the necessary information to "arm" the social activist, the defender of human rights, with enough knowledge to move toward the creation of a human rights culture, one that espouses the indivisibility and interdependence of human rights.

The Human Rights Triptych

Renee Cassin, referred to as the "true father of human rights" (Szabo, 1982, p. 23) would compare human rights to works of art, as illustrated by painters like Peter Breughel and Hieronymus Bosch known in part for their triptychs, such as the latter's *Garden of Earthly Delights*. The central panel depicts the main theme, the descent of humanity; the right panel depicts the seven deadly sins; and the left, the Garden of Eden. Surely no metaphor is perfect, yet, in this case, the central panel, the most important in understanding human rights is the Universal Declaration. On the right are the declarations and covenants following it; on the left, the means of implementation. It is worthwhile, then, to examine these panels and discuss the historical-philosophical and experiential and social-environmental contexts that help to crystallize values into human rights, as they are increasingly understood.

The Universal Declaration

The Universal Declaration, a milestone in the long and difficult struggle of the human race, according to the late Pope John Paul II (Daughters of St. Paul, 1979), comprises the central panel of the human rights tryptich. Originally meant to be merely a hortatory document urging governments to abide by its principles, it is increasingly referred to as *customary international law* (*Filartiga v. Pena*, 1980; Wronka, 1992, 1998a, 1998b, 2002; Steiner & Alston, 2000; Weissbrodt, Fitzpatrick, & Newman, 2001; Buergenthal et al., 2002) which all countries must abide. It contains four crucial notions (Wronka, 1998a). *Human dignity and its corollary, non-discrimination,* comprise the first, and these are emphasized in Articles 1 and 2 of the Declaration. This notion comes largely from the Judeo–Christian–Islamic tradition indicative of the preponderance of Western and a few Islamic nations involved in drafting the Declaration. Thus Genesis 1:27 states, "God created man in His image," which, according to the Talmudic scholar Ben Azzai, embodies the "ultimate and supreme worth" of the individual, "the most important single verse in Scripture" (Kaplan, 1980, p. 55). Christians also accept the sanctity and dignity of the human person proclaimed in Genesis, who are also urged in the Eight Beatitudes to hunger and thirst for justice (Luke 6:20–26). Similarly the Koran asserts in Sura (6:15), "Verily, we have honored every human being." And, in the words of the Muslim scholar Riffat Hassan (1982, p. 55), "The sanctity and absolute value of human life is upheld by the Koran."

All humans have dignity, regardless of "race, color, sex, language, religion, political or other opinion, national or social origin, property, birth or other status," asserts Article 2. Keeping in mind that the Universal Declaration "is not a perfect document. . . . [o]n the whole, however, it is a good document" (UN Department of Public Information, 1950, pp. 15–16), as Eleanor Roosevelt said, we need to seriously examine further understandings of the term "other status" to include such issues as sexual orientation, medical condition, disability, family status, and culture. In fact, "culturalism," a frequent issue in social work and the field of human rights (Healy, 2001; Sachs, 2005), is one culture's feeling of superiority over another. This issue becomes complicated if the very same culture that views female genital mutilation as wrong also suffers excessively from deaths caused by anorexia nervosa. The essential point here is that the only criteria for securing one's human rights is the fact of being human.

The rallying cry during the French Revolution, "Liberté, Egalité, Fraternité," describes the next three crucial notions of the Universal Declaration. The second notion, *civil and political rights,* as asserted in Articles 3–21, is the liberty to pursue the quest for human dignity and non-discrimination free from the abuse of political authority. These freedoms, also called first-generation or negative rights, include, for example, the freedom of speech, of the press, and of religion. They correspond, by and large, to Roosevelt's first two freedoms of expression and worship mentioned above. They arose primarily in response to the abuse of tyrannical monarchs in the seventeenth and eighteenth centuries, such as the European religious wars. They resulted in such documents as the U.S. Declaration of Independence and the Bill of Rights of the U.S. Constitution. The major thrust behind these documents were Enlightenment theorists such as John Locke, who emphasized, for instance, the right to life and to freedom from arbitrary rule, and Thomas Jefferson, who wrote of the fundamental rights to "life, liberty, and the pursuit of happiness." These fundamental freedoms, ultimately, stress the need for government *not* to interfere with basic human needs. Freedom of religion, or spirituality, for example, allows people to seek the meaning of their existence in terms of their mortality as they choose.

The third crucial notion of the Document is *economic, social, and cultural rights,* that is, the government should provide *equally* for the basic necessities to ensure an existence worthy of human dignity. Articles 22–27 assert these rights which can also be called second-generation or positive rights. They roughly correspond to Roosevelt's third freedom, the freedom from want. Examples of these rights are health care, education, meaningful employment at a reasonable wage, special protections for mothers and children, security in old age, and the right to rest and leisure. Although the U.S. Constitution generally lacks the inclusion of these rights, apart from the protection of an author's interests (Wronka, 1992, 1998b), it is important to note that the U.S. delegation at the drafting of the Universal Declaration supported the inclusion of these rights in that document (Steiner & Alston, 2000). These rights arose predominantly in reaction to the abuses of industrialization that became increasingly evident in the nineteenth century resulting, for instance, in massive poverty amid great affluence. The Soviet Constitution of 1936 exemplifies these rights. Theorists, such as Gracchus Babeuf, Thomas Paine, and Karl Marx, were influential in the development of positive rights. For example, in the *Rights of Man,* Paine movingly advocates for the prevention of poverty in order that,

The hearts of the humane will not be shocked by ragged and hungry children, and persons of seventy or eighty years of age, begging for bread. The dying poor will not be dragged from place to place to breathe their last. [And] widows will have maintenance for their children and not be carted away, on the deaths of their husbands, like culprits and criminals. (Fast, 1946, pp. 255–256)

The last crucial notion of the Universal Declaration is *solidarity rights* as expressed in Articles 28–30. As noted, these rights, still in the process of conceptual elaboration, are the result primarily of the failures of colonialism and domestic sovereignty. Thus, if we are to work with one another as brothers and sisters in our struggle for a socially just world, then we must have a spirit of *fraternity* among all peoples of the world. They correspond to Roosevelt's third and fourth freedoms from want and fear. One country alone cannot effectively deal with such global inequities as distributive injustice, pollution, war, economic development, self-determination, the oppression of indigenous and other peoples, and natural and human-made disasters. These rights, therefore, emphasize a person's right to intergovernmental cooperation, the limitations of rights, and the notion that every right has a corresponding duty. Thus global cooperation and fair and just trade are necessary to ensure that income and food are distributed equitably. Individuals, furthermore, have a right to food, which must be nutritious, easily accessible, culturally appropriate, and at reasonable cost (Eide, 1987). Yet they also have a duty not to consume in excess. The philosopher Immanuel Kant, recognizing the hypocrisy of nations in his *Project for a Perpetual Peace* and asserting that "an action to have moral worth, must be done from duty" (quoted in Curtis, 1981, p. 40), seems to have paved the way for the inclusion of the idea of solidarity in human rights discussions. Gandhi, when asked by the drafting committee of the Universal Declaration the meaning of human rights, responded simply, yet profoundly, "My illiterate, but wise mother told me that all rights to be deserved come from duty well done . . . the very right to live accrued only when one also does the duty of citizenship to the world" (United Nations, 1948, p. 15).

More specifically, these rights encompass global distributive justice, peace, self-determination, humanitarian disaster relief, the right to the common heritages of humanity (e.g., space, the oceans, and cultural traditions and monuments), and a clean environment (Human Rights, 2006). Although not explicitly stated in the Universal Declaration, these rights obtain their sustenance from Article 28, which asserts the right to a "just social and international order in which the rights and freedoms set forth in this Declaration can be fully realized." The failure to spell out these rights, as well as other statuses mentioned previously, was largely owing to the social contexts of the time. Pollution, for example, was literally on the horizon, not yet necessitating a stronger statement on the right to a clean environment. There was also a preponderance of delegates from the richer, European countries of the world which may have lead to a Eurocentric bias (Alston, 2000) in the Universal Declaration and only fleeting reference to the plight of poorer countries.

These shortcomings, however, do not mean that we should dismiss the Declaration. Knowledge, like all human creations, is limited, but it is important to point out that all these crucial notions of human rights are interdependent and indivisible, that rights cannot exist without duties. The Bill of Rights to the U.S. Constitution, then, is a beautiful document rightly referred to as a "beacon of hope" for humanity, as expressed, in March 1995, when the U.S. responded to the United Nations human rights monitoring committee in its report on the Covenant on Civil and Political Rights, at which this author was present. The Bill of Rights expresses only one set of rights, however. Marx once expressed concern that talk limited to civil and political rights may be used as a "facade of capitalism" (Kolakowski, 1983, p. 85). Thus violence in the media and in advertising on children's television, when supported in terms of freedom of speech, may mask hidden agendas such as the priority of profits over human needs. If we are to do our duty to the world, it is questionable that an economic system that commodifies human need and rewards inactivity through capital gain, rather than the "sweat of one's brow" (Genesis 3:13), is not only inconsistent with the need for a just "social and international order," as stated in the Universal Declaration, but is antithetical to millennia of teaching. Consider this illustration of the interdependence of rights: the right to freedom of speech, a civil and political right, is meaningless if a person is homeless or starving, a violation of economic and social rights, or if the person lives in a world at war or an environment on the verge of catastrophe, both violations of solidarity rights. It is equally absurd to say that roughly 40 percent of the world living on less than $2 per day enjoys human rights, if they are free only to express their views and yet live in constant fear, not knowing where their next meal will come from. Echoing this call for solidarity, Rev. Martin Luther King Jr. expressed it well when he wrote: "Injustice anywhere is a threat to justice everywhere. We are caught in an inescapable network of mutuality, tied in a single garment of destiny. Whatever affects one directly, affects all indirectly" (University of Pennsylvania African Studies Center, 2006, p. 1).

Covenants and Declarations of the Universal Declaration

The six major human rights instruments of the Universal Declaration, which represent the right panel in the tryptich, and the dates they became international law, are (1) the International Covenants on Civil and Political Rights (ICCPR), 1976; (2) the International Covenant on Economic Social and Cultural Rights (ICESCR), 1976; (3) the Convention on the Rights of a Child (CRC), 1990; (4) the Convention on the Elimination of Discrimination against Women (CEDAW), 1981; (5) the Convention against Torture and Other Cruel, Inhuman, or Degrading Treatment or Punishment (CAT), 1987; and (6) the International Convention on the Elimination of All Forms of

Racial Discrimination (CERD), 1969. These conventions have the status of "treaty," and when ratified according to the Supremacy Clause of Article 6 of the U.S. Constitution, they are the "Supreme Law of the Land" and the "judges bound thereby" (Weissbrodt et al., 2001). The U.S. has ratified the ICCPR, CAT, and CERD, but with the caveat that they be "non–self-executing," that is, non-enforceable in U.S. Courts (Buergenthal et al., 2002).

Select examples of covenants and declarations following these major instruments are the following:

Convention on the Rights of People with Disabilities
Convention on Migrant Workers
Convention against Discrimination in Education
Draft Declaration on Indigenous Peoples
Declaration on the Elimination of All Forms of Intolerance and Discrimination Based on Religion or Belief
Declaration on the Elimination of Violence against Women
Standard Minimum Rules for the Treatment of Prisoners
Rule for the Protection of Juveniles Deprived of Their Liberty
Declaration of Fundamental Principles concerning the Contribution to the Mass Media to Strengthening Peace and International Understanding
Declaration on the Right to Development
Code of Conduct for Law Enforcement Officials
Convention on the Reduction of Statelessness

Occasionally documents have Optional Protocols, which generally address issues that governments felt needed further articulation, as they were addressed only briefly, if at all, in the previous document. Examples are the Optional Protocol to the ICCPR, Aiming at Abolition of the Death Penalty (1991); the Optional Protocol to the CRC, Involvement of Children in Armed Conflict; and another Optional Protocol to the CRC on the Sale of Children, Child Prostitution, and Child Pornography (2000). The U.S. has not ratified the former protocol, but has ratified the two latter ones. A list of these documents and other information can be found by clicking on "Human Rights Links" at this author's homepage: www.humanrightsculture.org.

Generally documents in this panel elaborate rights only touched on in the Universal Declaration. Thus, whereas the UDHR may say simply:

"Motherhood and childhood are entitled to special care and assistance" (Article 25), CEDAW and CRC further elaborate what this special care and assistance means. Examples from CEDAW are that this "special care and assistance" means governments ought to "encourage the provision of necessary supporting social services to enable parents to combine family obligations with work responsibilities and participation in public life, in particular through promoting the establishment and development of a network of child-care facilities" (Article 11). They should also ensure "to women appropriate services in connection with pregnancy, confinement and the post-natal period, granting free services where necessary, as well as adequate nutrition during pregnancy and lactation" (Article 12). Examples in CRC are the right of the child to "be registered immediately after birth . . . and the right from birth to a name, the right to acquire a nationality, and, as far as possible, the right to know and be cared for by his or her parents" (Article 7); to "assure to the child who is capable of forming his or her own views the right to express those views freely in all matters affecting the child, the views of the child being given due weight in accordance with the age and maturity of the child (Article 12); and "the establishment of social programmes to provide necessary support for the child and for those who have the care of the child" (Article 19).

Regarding global distributive justice, these documents in varying degrees speak of the need to narrow the imbalances, economic and otherwise, among the people of the world. ICESCR, for example, speaks of the need for state parties to "undertake steps individually and through international assistance and cooperation , especially economic and technical, to the maximum of its available resources with a view toward achieving progressively the full realization of rights" (Article 1) and "to improve methods of production, conservation and distribution of food by making full use of technical and scientific knowledge by disseminating knowledge of the principles of nutrition. . . [and] taking into account the problems of both food importing and food exporting countries, to ensure an equitable distribution of world food supplies in relation to need" (Article 11). The ICCPR states: "Everyone shall have the right to freedom of expression . . . to seek, receive and impart information and ideas of all kinds regardless of frontiers, either orally, in writing or in print, in the form of art or through any other media" (Article 19). In the CERD state parties are to "adopt immediate and effective measures, particularly in the fields of teaching, education, culture and information, with a view to combating prejudices which lead to racial discrimination and promoting understanding, tolerance, and friendship among nations and racial or ethnical groups" (Article 7).

There is currently no major document on international, albeit global, distributive justice, but the Declaration on the Right to Development (1986) comes closest. As in the other documents there is no blatant statement that "the poor countries of the world have the right to the wealth of the rich countries." Yet it seems to place an emphasis on international cooperation, indispensable to equality among nations and all people in the world. In its Preamble, for example, it calls for awareness that "efforts at the international level to promote and protect human rights should be accompanied by efforts to establish a new international economic order." Article 1 states, furthermore: "The right to development is an inalienable human right by virtue of which every human person and all peoples are entitled to participate in, contribute to, and enjoy economic, social, cultural and political development." In Article 3, we see the primary responsibility of states "for the creation of national and international conditions" as well as "the duty to cooperate with each other ensuring development and eliminating obstacles to development . . . in such a manner as to promote a new international economic order based on sovereign equality, interdependence, mutual interest and cooperation." The United States was the only country in the world to have vetoed that document largely because it considered the tone too idealistic and that would unrealistically raise the hopes of humanity (Abram, 1991). Moving from the level of the mind to the heart so that these documents are not just words but are "lived," that is, that they contribute to a human rights culture, it is necessary to examine the means of implementation.

Means of Implementation

On the left side of the triptych, then, are ways to make some of these rights a reality. To be sure, implementation is the least developed of the human rights triptych but certainly the most important. At present, such means of implementation mostly consist only of the periodic filing of reports on compliance with the six major conventions. After filing the report, the respective state engages in a "creative dialogue" (Wronka, 1995b) with members of the human rights monitoring committee who offer comments on the positive aspects of the reports as well as concerns and recommendations. The state informs the respective governmental body of the positive aspects and concerns, generally urging modifications of laws and policies in order to comply with the respective human rights instrument. These reports were difficult to obtain before the Internet. After numerous attempts to locate one of these reports in 1995, the early days of the Internet, this author's bookstore manager informed me that the Government Printing Office told her that they had never heard of the Initial Report of the USA on Compliance with the ICCPR! This was after I had attended the human rights hearing of U.S. compliance with the ICCPR. In response to the concerns of the human rights monitoring committee that NGOs were having trouble getting the report, U.S. representatives replied that they would "produce more and make them more available to the public."

Thus, after ratifying CERD, for example, the United States would respond to its progress in regard to each of the articles. Thus, for example, Article 4 reads, in part: "States shall declare an offence punishable by law . . . acts of violence or incitement to such acts against any race or group of persons of another color or ethnic origin." Article 5 reads, in part: "States [shall] eliminate racial discrimination . . . notably in the enjoyment of the . . . rights to work, to free choice of employment, to just and favorable conditions of work, to equal pay for equal work, to just and favorable remuneration . . . the right to housing . . . the right to medical care." In its Report on Compliance with the International Convention on the Elimination of All Forms of Racial Discrimination in 2001, the U.S. responded by mentioning to the monitoring committee that the Civil Rights Act of 1968 and the Fair Housing Amendments Act of 1988, which make it a federal crime to injure, intimidate, or interfere with any person because of his or her race, color, religion, sex, or disability, [were] used to prosecute the burning of crosses and other racially motivated threats and violence directed at people in their homes (para. 96). Also, while stating that "the U.S. health system provides the finest overall care in the world," the report notes numerous statutes and programs relevant to health care, such as the Hill Burton Act (1946), the Public Health Act (1994), and Medicaid and Medicare. However, it noted significant disparities in the health care system: infant mortality rates 2.5 times higher for blacks than for whites, and 1.5 times higher for Native Americans; black men over sixty-five years of age having prostate cancer roughly 2 times more than white men of the same age; and black children 3 times more likely than white children to be hospitalized for asthma (para. 376). The report also noted that the poverty rate among blacks (26.1 percent) was more than triple that of white non-Hispanics (para. 348), and the pervasiveness of child poverty is of particular concern as differences between racial and ethnic groups remain high (para. 349). The report concluded that, "over the years, the U.S. has worked hard to overcome a legacy of racism and racial discrimination, and it has done so with substantial successes. Nevertheless, significant obstacles remained and the U.S. looked forward to discussing these experiences with the Human Rights Committee" (para. 465) (Human Rights Committee on the International Convention on the Elimination of Racial Discrimination, 2000).

In response, the committee welcomed the opportunity to initiate this dialogue (para. 381), noting also the persistence of the discriminatory effects of the legacies of slavery, segregation, and destructive policies with regard to Native Americans (para. 384), and commented on both positive aspects as well as concerns relevant to the report. Concerning the former, it notes, for example, President Bill Clinton's Executive Order 13107 of December 10, 1998, which asserts that the U.S. government will fully respect and implement its obligations under the international human rights treaties to which it is a party (para. 386), and the continuous increase in the number of persons belonging to, in particular, the African-American and Hispanic communities in fields of employment previously predominantly occupied by whites (para. 389). The committee, however, expressed particular concern according to which the prohibition of dissemination of all ideas based on racial superiority or hatred is compatible with the right to freedom of opinion and expression, given that a citizen's exercise of this right carried special responsibilities (para. 391). It also noted with concern the incidents of police violence and brutality, including cases of deaths as the result of excessive use of force by law enforcement officials, which particularly affect minority groups (para. 394); a disturbing correlation between race, both victim and the defendant, and the imposition of the death penalty (para. 396); political disenfranchisement of a large segment of the ethnic minority population who are denied the right to vote (para. 397); and, among other matters, persistent disparities in the enjoyment of the right to adequate housing, equal opportunities for education and employment, and access to health care (para. 398).

Of course, there are other reports beyond the scope of this chapter. Yet, it is important to note, at least regarding Native Americans, who appear substantively affected by policies of genocide, as evidenced by numerous criteria of the Genocide Convention such as prohibitions against forced removal of children, that the 2005 U.S. report to the human rights committee under ICCPR (United States of America, 2005) did mention issues pertaining to Native Americans more substantively than the previous CERD report. It further mentioned, for instance, that a federal government–Indian trust relationship dates back more than a century (para. 11); the Secretary of the Interior may collect income from tribal properties held in trust (para. 11); and tribes have sued the government claiming that the U.S. had failed to provide adequate accounting and asset management of such lands (para. 14). The committee responded in part by urging that that the U.S. take steps to ensure that previously recognized aboriginal Native American rights cannot be extinguished (para. 15); that a full judicial review takes place regarding the determinations of federal recognition of tribes (para.16); and that the U.S. strengthen programs to continue to fight the high incidence of poverty, sickness, and alcoholism among Native Americans (para.17).

Regarding global distributive justice, it is noteworthy that these committees monitoring human rights have at least, with respect to the ICESCR, commented upon the amount of aid a particular country gives to poorer countries. As stated earlier, the U.S., unfortunately, has not ratified that document and therefore need not respond to the committee's concerns on that and other matters. For example, the ICESCR monitoring committee, in 2004, praised Italy's commitment to raising the level of official development from the current .23 percent of GDP (gross domestic product) to .33 percent by 2006 but was concerned that the level of development assistance still falls short of the UN target of .7 percent of GDP (para. 13). The committee, in 2005, also appreciated Norway's commitment to international cooperation as reflected in the volume of official development assistance at .92 percent of its gross national product (GNP) (para. 2). These reports are available on the Internet at www.unhchr.ch/tbs/doc.nsf/newhv docsbytreaty?OpenView.

There are other means of implementation, of course, such as having the UN appoint special "Charter-based" rapporteurs, referring to the UN Charter, rather than "Treaty-based" mechanisms just discussed. Among other things, the Charter calls for "solutions of international economic, social, health, and related problems" (Article 55). These rapporteurs report on such issues as extreme poverty, violence against women, racism, pollution of the environment, and religious intolerance, or on a situation of a particular country. Regarding global distributive justice, special rapporteur Leandro Déspouy, in his report "Human Rights and Extreme Poverty," spoke also of the increasing spread of extreme poverty in the world, calling it the "new face of apartheid" on a global scale (1996, p. 37). There are also world conferences that deal with human rights issues, for example, the Earth Summit (Rio, 1992); the Summit for Social Development (Copenhagen, 1995); and Disaster Reduction (Hyogo, Japan, 2005); as well as other major initiatives like the Millennium Development Goals. These goals aim to (1) eradicate extreme poverty and hunger; (2) achieve universal primary education; (3) promote gender equality and empower women; (4) reduce child mortality; (5) improve maternal health; (6) combat HIV/AIDS, malaria, and other diseases; (7) ensure environmental sustainability; and (8) develop global partnership for development (UN Development Program, 2005). Finally, other major human rights documents and implementation mechanisms exist, now known as human rights "regimes," that are not within the scope of this essay; these include the Organization of American States (OAS), the African Union (AU), and the European Union (EU). Briefly, the Protocol of San Salvador on Economic, Social, and Cultural Rights (1988) of the OAS, which the U.S. has not ratified, asserts in its Preamble: "That the different categories of rights constitute an indivisible whole based on the recognition of the dignity of the human person." The challenge then becomes how to compel governments and other powerful entities to listen to the results of these implementation mechanisms and then act on them.

Suggested Social Action Strategies

The foregoing discussion leads to the following overlapping, yet relatively distinct, social action strategies. To lessen the inequities of wealth, power, and other important values throughout the world, therefore, and to use human rights as "guiding principles" to assist in the development of a human rights culture, which will result in socially just policies, *we must first acknowledge, in any forum, that only chosen values endure.* No one can force such a culture on anyone. The word "culture" derives from the Latin word *cultura*, meaning "tilling, cultivation." Human rights discourse, then, ought to serve as a perfect means to provide a solid grounding for a culture where all humans can flourish to their fullest capacities. People must see that being decent to one another, as defined in large measure by human rights principles, is a viable strategy to create a socially just world. A person can learn human rights principles, their interdependency and indivisibility, from documents and reports, but such changes will be temporary at best unless there is a change of heart, or in the poignant words of Dorothy Day (2005, p. 1), founder of the Catholic Worker movement, a "revolution of the heart."

Second, *we must have a major impetus for human rights education from grammar school to postsecondary levels.* With the end of the People's Decade for Human Rights Education in 2004, the UN has recently initiated a World Program on Human Rights Education which emphasizes the right to know one's rights (Human Rights Education Associates, 2005). Curricula needs to be continually developed to teach others about human rights in order to bring to fruition Eleanor Roosevelt's wish that children know as much about the Universal Declaration of Human Rights as they do about the Bill of Rights. Students need to be aware of the Supremacy Clause of the U.S. Constitution as well as major provisions of human rights documents that have the status of treaty. Although education is essential to the development of such a culture, spreading knowledge about human rights does not always have to occur in a formal setting. There can be "sound bites," even MTV skits. In France, for instance, this author recalls a brief television skit where people danced as they recited word by word Article 1 of the Universal Declaration. The skit ended with all shouting in unison: "Think about it"! The magazine of the airline Air France had the entire Universal Declaration of Human Rights on the front page during the 1998 Human Rights Defenders Conference in Paris, commemorating the fiftieth anniversary of the UN's endorsement of the Universal Declaration! Certainly teaching about the interdependence of rights would require an integration of solidarity rights, especially the right to global distributive justice. Human rights violations, as argued here, are seen, for example, not only in transgressions at Guantánamo Bay in the face of the Patriot's Act, which has predominated public discourse, but also in the struggles of peoples throughout the world to eke out an existence worthy of human dignity. Surely the message must be that every person, everywhere, is guaranteed human rights. This is no small feat, of course, but obviously creating a human rights culture is itself a struggle.

Third, in ensuring human rights for all, it is important to note that the National Association of Social Work (NASW)

> endorses the fundamental principles set forth in the human rights documents of the United Nations . . . [and] [s]upports the concept that human rights be adopted as a foundation[al] principle upon which all of social work theory and applied knowledge rests. . . . [And] [s]*upports the two fundamental Covenants of the United Nations* . . . which confirm the civil and political rights of all people, as well as their economic, social and cultural rights. The profession also endorses *the treaties and conventions as they have evolved* [which] establish that the rights of people take precedent over social customs when those customs infringe on human rights. (Falk, 1999, p. 17; emphasis added)

Consequently *social work ought to integrate in its profession fundamental human rights principles, which will have implications for practice.* If human rights are for all, and indeed social work "from its inception is a human rights profession" (International Federation of Social Work, cited in United Nations, 1994, p. 1), then we must find ways to have the human rights principles speak to practice situations. Thus we could note not only principles like human dignity as ways to assist in our relations with our clients but also speak of our interconnectedness in the environment broadly defined to include the entire human race, and the economic and social arrangements that have led to artificial state boundaries and military spending at the expense of the fulfillment of human needs (Ife, 2001; Reichert, 2003, 2006; Wronka, 2002, 2004). Clearly more courses in international social work should be forthcoming. Being attuned to human rights and dignity also means that "macro" strategies to help those in poorer countries necessitate an ability to share in their struggle rather than perceiving of them as "children that they must save," to quote Jean-Claude Tonme (2005, p. 21) commenting on global rock concerts intended to help Africans. Perhaps the greatest challenge for social work, in fact for all service professions, is to offer assistance in ways that are not demeaning so that others do not to experience the indignity of handouts but retain a sense of self-respect as they earn a living to support their families.

In viewing human rights as the cornerstone of social justice, a major commitment of social work, it may be helpful to examine the etymological roots of the term "social justice." The word "social," from the Latin *socius,* means "friend, ally, partner" and, in another context, "sharing, accompanying, and acting together"; "justice." from the Latin *Justus*, means "just, equitable, fair, mainly of persons" (Wronka, forthcoming). Thus, when we speak of social justice, we mean working with others as equals, as partners in the struggle for a socially just world, not poor people in need of the wonderful things we can provide for them as helping professionals. The well-known work of Muhammad Yunnus, founder of the first micro credit bank, the Grameen Bank, which provides low-interest loans to people in poverty, is one example where people may be able to live with respect and as partners in a shared journey.

Fourth, *social work must engage in dialogue across disciplines and with other service and health professions that have similar human rights commitments.* The American Sociological Association (ASA), for example, "urges all governments . . . to uphold the spirit and the substance of the articles of the Universal Declaration of Human Rights and other international agreements that [assert] the importance of full equality of all peoples and cultures" (ASA, 2005, 2). The first principle in the Medical Ethics that guides the American Medical Association (AMA) states: "A physician shall be dedicated to providing competent medical care, with compassion and respect for human dignity and rights." The American Psychological Association, in its Ethics Code, speaks of the dignity and worth of all people; the American Public Health Association speaks, in its Public Health Code of Ethics, about the interdependency of humans and human dignity values found in human rights documents; the Ethics of the American Nurses Association urges the protection and promotion of the advancement of human rights. Human rights, then, can provide a common ground to engage in coalition building across disciplines and with the helping and health professions in general (Wronka, forthcoming). These professional associations also have sections dedicated to international issues that include obvious unfair distributions of items humans need for survival.

Fifth, *groups interested in human rights can sponsor bills such as the "Human Rights for All: Massachusetts Initiative to Infuse Human Rights Standards and Values into State Law,"* spearheaded largely by the Massachusetts Chapter of the Women's International League for Peace and Freedom.[2] Known as House Bill 706, this act would "establish a special commission to inves-

---

2. To sponsor such bills, contact the Massachusetts CEDAW Project at masscedaw@yahoo .com.

tigate the integration of international human rights standards into Massachusetts state law and policies." Not coincidentally the first president of this group was Jane Addams, the Nobel Peace Prize recipient and proponent of world citizenship, "world duty [and] world consciousness" (cited in Healy, 2001, p. 1) and sometimes referred to as the "Mother of Social Work." This idea of human rights is so powerful that, by the time of the Senate hearing, House Bill 706 had a coalition of roughly fifty organizations ranging over the entire political spectrum and including such groups as Physicians for Human Rights, Amnesty International, the Massachusetts Welfare Rights Union, and Arise for Social Justice. At the writing of this essay, the bill is still in committee, but it is worthwhile to point out that a similar bill, the Curry Resolution, was passed largely through the efforts of the Pennsylvania Chapter of NASW, the Kensington Welfare Rights Union, and the Poor People's Economic Human Rights Campaign" (Stoesen, 2002, p. 1). A bill such as House Bill 706, therefore, would monitor, among other things, executive, judicial, and legislative movements toward compliance with international human rights standards. Recent research has found, for example, that economic, social, and cultural rights are almost entirely absent in the U.S. Constitution, apart from the protection of an author's interests. Regarding the excluded rights, states have failed to act as "laboratories of democracy," to quote Supreme Court Justice Louis Brandeis, to extend rights not found in the Constitution; indeed, the only major economic and social right in the majority of state constitutions is the right to education (Wronka, 1992, 1998b). Global distributive justice as a right to solidarity is in none of them, but noteworthy is the Proposed Constitution for the State of New Columbia, presently, the District of Columbia, which in its Preamble states:

> We the people of the free and sovereign State of New Columbia, seek to secure and provide for each person: health, safety and welfare; a peaceful and orderly life, and the right to legal, social and economic justice and equality. . . [and] *we reach out to all the peoples of the world in a spirit of friendship and cooperation, certain that together we can build a future of peace and harmony.* (cited in Wronka, 1992, pp. 240–241; emphasis added)

Sixth, given that much of the success in pushing back poverty globally occurred in the 1980s and early 1990s (Human Development Report, 2005) it is quite possible that multilateral agreements such as the North

Atlantic Free Trade Agreement (NAFTA) are not working, nor is the situation being helped by the rise in power and influence of corporations and organizations like the World Trade Organization (WTO), the International Monetary Fund (IMF) and the World Bank. The Chiapas rebellion in Mexico, for one, occurred the same day that NAFTA was enacted, January 1, 1994, a foreboding perhaps of increasing global distributive injustice. *We need to find ways to engage in dialogue about the efficacy of such multilateral policies and of such organizations like the WTO and IMF while persuasively using this powerful idea of human rights.* For example, we can agree that the goals of the Universal Declaration of Human Rights are worthwhile and gauge the effects of policies of such institutions on the qualities of life for everyone, everywhere. We can then issue reports that "bear witness" to the world of the effects of their policies, to show how such policies are progressing toward or retreating from compliance with human rights documents. Groups, such as Global Trade Watch, Alliance for Global Justice, Global Exchange, People's Global Action, and the Jubilee USA Network may assist in our endeavors (Prokosch & Raymond, 2002). Jubilee supporters, for example, recently convinced the World Bank, after tens of thousands of e-mails and phone calls, to speed up debt cancellation freeing up much needed money for social needs like education, health care, and clean water in some of the poorest countries. They are now mobilizing for a Sabbath 2007 to raise their "voices publicly for a bold and prophetic Jubilee cancellation of [all] debts" ("Drop the Debt," 2006, p. 4).

Seventh, *we need a major global consensus to support international initiatives in general, such as world conferences and the Millennium Development Goals.* We must emphatically take heed of the interdependency of rights, so that, for instance, a conference on women considers men's issues as well, or, regarding the Millennium Development Goals, that one goal, such as improving maternal health, is directly related to environmental sustainability and the development of global partnerships. Such initiatives could also help the world community deal with "the obvious," such as providing forums, say, to set up collections for mosquito nets to prevent malaria, or for computers so that poor farmers are in a better position to determine the values of their crops in the global community. There are also other groups like Oxfam, which works with poor communities throughout the world, and Grassroots International, which has numerous progressive partners in Africa, the Middle East, Latin America, and the Caribbean.

Eighth, *we need a domestic agency that would coordinate international hu-*

man rights initiatives with domestic policies, such as a Human Rights Cabinet. Such a cabinet would, for example, assist in developing a strategy to have the U.S. ratify all major human rights conventions. It would also not only draw up human rights reports but be responsible to ensure the implementation of human rights committee recommendations, such as giving .7 percent of the GNP to the poorest countries. Inversely, it could also help, perhaps, to ensure that international agencies work cooperatively to deal with problems pertaining to global distributive injustice. To be sure, the lack of coordination of international agencies is also blocking much needed aid to poorer countries (Jencks, 2005). The recent development of the Human Rights Council at the UN, which answers essentially to the General Assembly, rather than relying on the Economic and Social Council, is also a positive step, especially regarding global distributive justice. This is because every country in the General Assembly, whether rich or poor, gets one vote concerning a major human rights initiative. Such a cabinet could easily have a solid connection with the Human Rights Council, which, in turn, could translate into policies that lessen the gap between the rich and poor nations of the world.

Ninth, *we need to overturn the U.S. veto of the Declaration on the Right to Development and work toward an International Convention on Global Distributive Justice.* As expected, however, there is now much resistance in Geneva to such a convention, primarily by the richer nations. It is up to us to pressure our government to make such a convention a reality. Whereas an immediate response might be that even the rich countries have their share of problems, ensuring a just social and international order could easily translate into less defense spending, which arguably protects the wealth and interests of the richer countries worldwide. Certainly the current ratio of GDP of 103 to 1 between the richest and poorest countries is unacceptable. With a mounting concern about the injustice of the growing gaps between CEO and average worker pay, perhaps we could move toward a global consensus to lessen the ratio between the rich and poor countries. Imagine, for the time being, a world where the ratio between the richest and poorest country is 6 to 1, numbers chosen arbitrarily! Surely, what is going on now, "shocks the conscience of humanity," to quote the Preamble to the Universal Declaration! Today, some ask: How could the genocide of Native Americans have happened, or the Trans-Atlantic Slave Trade, or the Holocaust? Given the present global distribution of wealth, will the world ask the same questions in years hence?

Tenth, *we need global distributive justice to become what is known as a "justiciable," rather than "aspirational" right.* In other words, global distributive justice need not merely be an ideal or aspiration. International organs such as the World Court may be able to help achieve this goal. Presently, for example, a country may file a suit in that court against another country for violations such as Nicaragua's actions against the U.S. for its purported bombing of Nicaragua's harbors during the Reagan administration. Only three decades ago it was inconceivable that, for example, tobacco companies could be sued for causing cancer. But today it is an increasingly accepted reality. Perhaps countries, corporations, maybe even individuals will eventually be brought to a judicial forum, such as the World Court, for their roles in causing the unjust, global distributions of wealth and power. Let us always be mindful of Gandhi's famous maxim: "First, they ignore you; then they laugh at you; then they fight you; and then you win."

Eleventh, *regional organizations like the African Union, the Organization of American States, and the European Union need to work in concert with the UN to move toward a concerted strategy to eradicate global distributive injustice.* Despite the growing pains of the new European currency, the Euro, it still appears to have lessened the possibility of war in a land historically torn apart by acts of aggression. One suggestion would be to have a world currency, perhaps the "Mondo," toward which all the regional organizations could play a major role. Whereas one could say that, arguably, the U.S. dollar is a world currency, given its ever growing ubiquity, it may be that this currency is more reflective, at least currently, of consumerism, defense spending, and an emphasis on extolling the virtues of privatization. Another currency constructed perhaps from more cooperative efforts, an ethic of sharing and the promulgation of peace, might help pave the way for an allegiance to humanity, let alone free up much needed time and energy to alleviate poverty, exhausted partly on efforts to exchange a myriad of state currencies.

Twelfth, recognizing the struggle for social justice, *particular attention ought to be given to the situation of Indigenous Peoples,* who often live in remote areas and are disproportionately affected by the fallout (quite literally) of global distributive injustice, such as desertification and water pollution, which also affect their cultural subsistence lifestyles. This author recalls, for instance, while living in Alaska, stories of dentists not needing to take x-rays of Inuit patients' teeth. The fallout from A-bomb tests in New Mexico had landed on lichen in the Arctic, which was then eaten by the caribou, and then by Inuit. It is no surprise, perhaps, that richer nations like the

U.S. and New Zealand, also with sizable indigenous populations, expressed concern that the notion of "self-determination" in the Draft Declaration of Indigenous Peoples, endorsed by the General Assembly in 2006, was too strong a term, preferring the words "management of resources." However, these words, according to the Mohawk legal scholar Patricia Monture, are similar to indigenous notions of "law" and "justice," meaning "living together nicely." Indeed, this right does not mean conquest or the seizure of institutional power often characteristic of European wars but simply the freedom to live well and enjoy the rights that all human beings should be guaranteed. Governments have nothing to fear from this concept. The issue regarding self-determination is merely that Indigenous Peoples actually feel that they have choices about their way of life and feel secure in making them (Daes, 2001).

Indigenous Peoples do not, by and large, identify with notions of "ethnicity" or "race" but rather are, as their name states, indigenous, a notion also recognized in the CRC. Certainly the principles of the recent Draft Declaration should become an internationally binding convention, ensuring respect of issues specific to Indigenous Peoples. These include:

1. Full guarantees against genocide, which calls for an end to the removal of indigenous children under pretext and an end to relocation without full informed consent;

2. Redress for deprivations of cultural values and identities which shall include the right to repatriation of human remains and compensation for being deprived of the means of subsistence;

3. The right to control the education of indigenous children which shall include the right to be educated in one's language in a manner appropriate to cultural methods of teaching and learning;

4. The right to establish indigenous media, which shall be in indigenous language but with access to non-indigenous media and also reflect indigenous cultural diversity;

5. The right to traditional medicines and health practices which shall include the protection of vital medicinal plants, animals, and minerals;

6. The right to maintain and strengthen distinctive spiritual and material relationships with lands, waters, seas, and other resources traditionally owned, including sea ice, flora, and fauna; and

7. Full recognition of cultural and intellectual property, which shall include special measures as necessary to control, develop, and protect human and other genetic resources, seeds, medicines, and knowledge of cultural traditions.

It is obvious that the previous reports to the human rights committees only barely touched upon such issues.

Finally, *we need compassion, vision, courage, and hope*. The great spiritual leader of the Oglala Sioux, Tashunkewitko, more commonly known as Crazy Horse, said it well: "A very great vision is needed and the man [sic] who has it must follow it as the eagle seeks the deepest blue of the sky" (Indigenous Peoples' Literature, 2006, p. 1). Eagles are notorious for flying straight into the storm, searching relentlessly for food for their families. Indeed, the Spirit of Crazy Horse has become known as compassion for the unfortunate in a spirit of humility; a vision that every person, everywhere, can have every human right; courage to get out of our comfort zones to make that happen; never giving up hope; and a heart of "peace, understanding, and everlasting love" (Geocities, 2006, p. 1). Certainly this Spirit of Crazy Horse may serve us well as we struggle for a socially just world, built upon a culture of human rights.

References

Abram, M. (1991, February 11). Forty-seventh Session of the UN Commission on Human Rights by the United States Representative to the United Nations in Geneva on Item B, The Right to Development. Geneva: United States Mission Office of Public Affairs.

American Sociological Association. (2005). Statement on human rights on the occasion of the American Sociological Association's Centenary. Retrieved September 27, 2005, from www.asanet.org/page.ww?section=Issue+Statements&name=Statement+on+Human.

Brown, L., & Flavin, C. (1999). A new economy for a new century. In Worldwatch Institute, *State of the world millennial edition* (pp. 4–21). New York: W. W. Norton.

Buergenthal, T., Shelton, D., & Stewart, D. (2002). *International human rights in a nutshell* (3rd ed.). St. Paul, MN: West.

Carter, J. (2002). *The Nobel Peace Prize Lecture: Delivered in Oslo on the 10th of December 2002.* New York: Simon & Schuster.

Curtis, M. (1981). *The great political theories* (Vol. 1). New York: Avon.

Daes, E. (2001). Striving for self-determination for indigenous peoples. In Y. Kly & D. Kly (Eds.), *In pursuit of the right to self-determination* (pp. 50–62). Atlanta, GA: Clarity.

Danaher, K. (1996). *Corporations are gonna get your Mama: Globalization and the downsizing of the American dream.* Monroe, ME: Common Courage.

Danaher, K. (2001). *Ten reasons to abolish the IMF & the World Bank.* New York: Seven Stories.

Daughters of St. Paul. (1979). *USA: The message of justice, peace and love: John Paul II.* Boston: St. Paul Editions.

Davis, G. (1992). *Passport to freedom: A guide for world citizens.* Cabin John, MD: Seven Locks.

Day, D. (2005). The Catholic Worker movement. Retrieved July 9, 2005, from www .catholicworker.org/dorothyday/index.cfm.

Despouy, L. (1996). *Final report on human rights and extreme poverty* (E/CN.4/ Sub.2/1996/13). New York: United Nations.

Drop the Debt. (2006, summer). Jubilee supporters convince World Bank to change policy as plans advance for 2007 Sabbath year. *News and Action from Jubilee Network,* 1–4.

Economic and Social Council. (2005). *Concluding observations of the Committee on Economic, Social, and Cultural Rights: Norway* (E/C.12/1Add.109). New York: United Nations.

Economic and Social Council. (2004). *Concluding observations of the Committee on Economic, Social, and Cultural Rights: Italy* (E/ C.12/1Add.103). New York: United Nations.

Economic and Social Council. (2001). *Concluding observations of the Committee on the Elimination of All Forms of Racial Discrimination.* New York: United Nations.

Eide, A. (1987). UN Commission on Human Rights. *Report on the right to adequate food as a human right* (E/CN.4/Sub.2/1987/23). New York: United Nations.

Falk, D. (1999, March). International policy on human rights. *NASW News, 44* (3), 17.

Fast, H. (1946). *The selected works of Tom Paine and citizen Tom Paine.* New York: Random House.

Fialrtiga v. Pena-Irala. 630 F. 2d 876 (1980).

4 Countries Delay in Pursuing New UN Role. (2005, July 18). *New York Times,* p. A6.

Geocities. (2006). *In the Spirit of Crazy Horse.* Retrieved: July 18, 2006, from www .geocities.com/CapitolHill/2638/?200618.

Gil, D. (1992). *Unraveling social policy* (5th rev. ed.). Rochester, VT: Schenkman.

Gil, D. (1995). Preventing violence in a structurally violent society: Mission impossible. *American Journal of Orthopsychiatry, 44*(1), 77–84.

Gil, D. (1998). *Confronting injustice and oppression: Concepts and strategies for social workers.* New York: Columbia University Press.

Gore, A. (2006). *An inconvenient truth.* New York: Rodale.

Hassan, R. (1982). On human rights and the Qur'anic perspective. In A. Swindler (Ed.), *Human rights in religious traditions* (pp., 51–65). New York: Pilgrim.

Healy, L. (2001). *International social work: Professional action in an interdependent world.* New York: Oxford University Press.

Human Rights. (2006). *Encyclopedia Britannica Online.* Retrieved July 18, 2006, from http://search.eb.com/eb/article-9106289.

Human Rights Committee on the International Covenant on Civil and Political Rights. (1994). Consideration of reports submitted by states parties under article 40 of the Covenant: The United States of America. New York: United Nations.

Human Rights Committee on the International Convention on the Elimination of Racial Discrimination. (2000). Consideration of reports submitted by states parties under Article 9 of the Convention. New York: United Nations.

Human Rights Education Associates. (2005). Available: www.hrea.org. Retrieved: June 20, 2005.

Ife, J. (2001). *Human rights and social work: Towards rights based practice.* New York: Cambridge University Press.

Indigenous Peoples Literature. (2006). Retrieved: July 12, 2006, from www.indians .org/welker/crazyhor.htm.

Kaplan, A. (1980). Human relations and human rights in Judaism. In A. Rosenbaum (Ed.), *The philosophy of human rights* (pp. 53–85). Westport, CT: Greenwood.

Kivel, P. (2004). *You call this democracy? Who benefits, who pays, and who really decides.* New York: Apex.

Kolakowski, P. (1983). Marxism and human rights. *Daedalus, 112*(4), 81–92.

Lappe, F., Collins, J., Rosset, P. (1998). *World hunger: 12 myths* (2nd rev. ed.). New York: Grove.

Montanari, S. (2005, September/October). Global climate change linked to increasing world hunger. *Worldwatch: Vision for a sustainable world, 18*(5), 6.

Morgenson, G. (2004, January 25). Explaining why the boss is paid so much. *New York Times,* sec. 3, p. 1.

New York Times Almanac. (2005). Global military expenditures. New York: World Almanac Books.

Prokosch, M., & Raymond, L. (2002). *The global activist's manual: Local ways to change the world.* New York: Thunder's Mouth.

Reichert, E. (2003). *Social work and human rights: A foundation for policy and practice*. New York: Columbia University Press.

Reichert, E. (2006). *Understanding human rights: An exercise book*. Thousand Oaks, CA: Sage.

Roosevelt, F. D. (1941). "Four Freedoms" Speech, 87-I Cong. Rec. 4, 46–47.

Rotblatt, J. (Ed.). (1997). *World citizenship: Allegiance to humanity*. New York: St. Martin's.

Roy, A., & Vecchiolla, F. (Eds.). (2004). *Thoughts on advanced generalist education: Models, readings and essays*. Peosta, IO: Eddie Bowers.

Sachs, J. (2005). *The end of poverty: Economic possibilities for our time*. New York: Penguin.

Safransky, S. (Ed.). (1990). *Sunbeams: A book of quotations*. Berkeley, CA: North Atlantic Books.

Steiner, H., & Alston, P. (2000). *International human rights in context: Law, politics, and morals* (2nd ed.). New York: Oxford University Press.

Stoesen, L. (2002, October.). Human rights measure passes in Pennsylvania House. *NASW News*, I.

Szabo, I. (1982). Historical foundations of human rights and subsequent developments. In K. Vasak (Ed.), *The international dimensions of human rights* (Vol. I) (pp. II–41). Westport, CT: Greenwood.

Tonme, J. (2005, July 15). All rock, no action. *New York Times*, p. A2I.

United Nations (UN). (1948). The final debates. *United Nations Weekly Bulletin*, I–50.

United Nations (UN). (1994). *Human rights and social work: A manual for schools of social work and the social work profession*. New York: Author.

United Nations Department of Public Information. (1950). *These rights and freedoms*. New York: Author.

United Nations Development Program. (2005). *Human development report: International cooperation at the crossroads: Aid, trade, and security in an unequal world*. New York: United Nations.

United States of America. (2005). Consideration of reports submitted by states parties to the International Covenant on Civil and Political Rights (ICCPR). New York: UN Human Rights Committee.

University of Pennsylvania African Studies Center. (2006). Letter from a Birmingham Jail, April 16, 1963. Retrieved: July 18, 2006, from www.africa.upenn.edu/Articles_Gen/Letter_Birmingham.html.

Worldwatch Institute. (2003). *Vital signs: The trends that are shaping our future*. New York: Norton.

Weissbrodt, D., Fitzpatrick, J., & Newman, F. (2001). *International human rights: Law, policy, and process* (3rd ed.). Cincinnati: Anderson.

Wronka, J. (in press). *Human rights and social justice: Action and service for the helping and health professions*. Thousand Oaks, CA: Sage.

Wronka, J. (2006). Toward the creation of a human rights culture. Retrieved: July 10, 2006, from www.humanrightsculture.org.

Wronka, J. (2004). Human rights and advanced generalist practice. In A. Roy & F. Vecchiolla (Eds.), *Thoughts on advanced generalist practice* (pp. 223–241). Peosta, IO: Eddie Bowers.

Wronka, J. (2002). *The Dr. Ambedkar lectures on the theme: Creating a Human Rights Culture*. Bhubanaswar, India: National Institute of Social Work and the Social Sciences.

Wronka, J. (1998a, summer). A little humility, please: Human rights and social policy in the United States. *Harvard International Review*, 72–75.

Wronka, J. (1998b). *Human rights and social policy in the 21st century: A history of the idea of human rights and comparison of the United Nations Universal Declaration of Human Rights with United States federal and state constitutions* (rev. ed.). Lanham, MD: University Press of America.

Wronka, J. (1995a). Human rights. In R. Edwards (Ed.), *Encyclopedia of social work* (pp. 1404–1418). Washington, DC: National Association of Social Work.

Wronka, J. (1995b). On the human rights committee's consideration of the initial report of the USA on the International Covenant on Civil and Political Rights, *Human rights interest group newsletter of the American Society of International Law*, 3, 14–16.

Wronka, J. (1992). *Human rights and social policy in the 21st century: A history of the idea of human rights and comparison of the United Nations Universal Declaration of Human Rights with United States federal and state constitutions*. Lanham, MD: University Press of America.

[4]

Cultural Relativism and Community Activism

JIM IFE

The problem of universalism versus cultural relativism is central to understanding human rights, and poses difficult questions for researchers, theoreticians, and practitioners. It is one of the first problems raised by anyone interested in human rights, and is associated with an extensive literature (Douzinas, 2000; Bell, Nathan, & Peleg, 2001; Meijer, 2001; Bauer & Bell, 1999; Van Ness, 1999; Lyons & Mayall, 2003; Caney & Jones, 2001).

Human rights that are understood simply as "universal," or self-evident, do not consider cultural difference, and therefore will be applied in the same way regardless of context. This simplistic approach has led to the criticism that human rights are merely part of a Western, imperialist project, and reflect discourses that are predominantly Western, patriarchal, modernist, and individualist (Pereira, 1997; Gibney, 2003). The origins of the human rights movement in Western Enlightenment thinking only serve to reinforce this criticism (Hayden, 2001; Herbert, 2002; Ishay, 2004). On the other hand, the argument that human rights are culturally relative, and that human rights will mean different things in different contexts, lead to a reluctance to intervene in perceived cases of human rights violation for fear of disrespecting other cultures. This erosion of human rights, in the name of cultural sensitivity, has at times been cynically used by some national leaders to negate criticisms of their human rights records and to silence their critics by labeling them as colonialist.

Clearly, then, uncritical universalism may lead to colonialist practice, and uncritical relativism may lead to disempowerment. Perhaps the most commonly discussed problem this raises concerns female circumcision, which is practiced in communities often associated with Islam. Many people, including many Muslims, regard the practice as an unacceptable mutilation of women's bodies, deeply enmeshed in issues of male power and control, and a violation of women's rights. Should one take a stand against this practice and impose "Western" cultural values on others, or should one condone this apparently barbaric behavior? Stating the question as a black-and-white choice grossly oversimplifies a complex issue, and it casts the problem within a particular version of Western thought and Western intellectual hegemony. Yet, too often this is the way this kind of problem is viewed, not only in the media but also in the professional literature.

Clearly the problem of universalism versus relativism requires a more careful and sophisticated analysis. This chapter argues that the two extreme positions, when set against each other in a dualistic framework, pose an insoluble conflict. A less dualistic view of relativism and universalism is required if we are to move beyond the simple view of seeing the two values as necessarily in opposition.

Colonialism, Culturalism, and Cultural Sensitivity

A naïve universalism views universal human rights as a constant in every context, and ignores the importance of culture and cultural diversity in how people construct their lives and derive meaning from their experiences. It assumes that human rights somehow "exist" in an objective positivistic sense, external to the experience of the actors involved. Not only is this philosophically dubious—resting as it does on a positivist worldview that has been largely discredited by all but the most single-minded empiricists (Ife, 1997), but it is also dangerous. The acceptance of absolute universal knowledge, in the Enlightenment tradition, has led to the imposition of Western values and ideologies on other cultural groups, and has also allowed the cultural bias built up in those values to remain hidden behind a veil of pseudo-objectivity and science. Inevitably it has been associated with colonialist practice in social work as well as in other professions, so that colonialism may remain the inevitable consequence of such naïve universalism.

If naïve universalism raises the danger of colonialism, naïve relativism and the belief in the sanctity of culture implies that interfering in another's culture is always detrimental (Booth, 1999). "If it is cultural, it is good" is a view that denies the validity of any external moral reference point for making judgments about cultural practices.

Given the problems of both naïve universalism and naïve relativism, it is important to find a way that is not merely a "middle course" but transcends simplistic dualisms. The first approach to resolve the problem is to move to a more sophisticated understanding of culture and cultural contexts. It is important to emphasize that cultures are not monolithic. Again using the example of female circumcision, that this is a cultural practice does not mean that everyone in a particular cultural group either supports or practices it. Another example is that if a particular sport is an important part of American culture, this does not imply that all Americans are avid sports fans. Cultures are not static; they constantly adapt to new circumstances, and no culture will be the same now as it was fifty years ago. This is the common experience of emigrants who return to visit their country of origin after spending several decades elsewhere; they are often surprised to find that the culture they remember and cherish has changed in significant ways. Realizing that cultures are pluralist and dynamic, rather than monolithic and static, goes a long way toward overcoming the problem of culturalism, where anything that is seen as "cultural" becomes untouchable. Rather, it is legitimate and appropriate to hold cultural practices up to scrutiny, to realize that they are often undergoing change, and are likely to be challenged by people within that culture. Female circumcision, for example, is challenged by many people who live within the cultures where it is practiced. It is also challenged by many Muslims who argue that it is not a necessary part of practicing the religion of Islam. Human rights provide an important framework from which such critique can emerge.

This does not mean that one can ignore cultural sensitivity. If a human rights issue, such as female circumcision, is to be addressed, it must be done in a culturally appropriate way and draw on the resources of people from within the relevant cultural groups. The struggle for the liberation of women takes place across cultural boundaries, and takes different forms in different cultures. In this particular case, it is also necessary to understand the importance of the cultural practice and its significance for the people involved, and to enter into dialogue rather than impose a conflicting view from "outside." Dialogue is important in community-based human rights work and is discussed in more detail later in the chapter.

It is also important to be prepared to accept scrutiny of one's own cultural group and cultural practices, both from within and from outside. Before seeking to criticize practices in another culture in the name of human rights, one should ask how we might feel if people from other cultures questioned practices within our own cultural community. Americans who may wish to question human rights abuses in other countries, for example, need to accept people from other countries questioning the use of the death penalty in America, or the torture either passively sanctioned or actively carried out by American military and security forces in Iraq and Afghanistan. Similarly Australians must accept criticism of Australia's treatment of asylum seekers and of the human rights abuses of Aboriginal Australians, if they are to have any credibility in criticizing human rights abuses in other countries.

Beyond the Dichotomy of Universalism/Relativism

Cultural context must be more carefully considered before making any strong statements about the application of human rights concepts. But this is only a first step toward analyzing the universalism/relativism problem. Breaking down the universal/relative dualism suggests that it is not a case of "either/or" but rather of thinking about ways that we can consider them a case of "both/and." There are several ways this might be achieved.

The first is to consider that there are two categories of human rights: one for universally applicable rights and the other for rights in specific contexts. The former would be at a fairly general level and not specified in detail, such as the right to freedom, the right to dignity, the right to education, and the right to health care. This limited list of rights could be agreed to apply universally, but they would necessarily be kept vague as statements of principle or intent rather than upheld by laws or constitutional guarantees. Other rights would then be understood as varying from one cultural context to another, and, though not "universal," they may be significant in particular contexts. This approach to human rights—developing an "A list" and a "B list"—does not advance the argument very far, but at least it departs from human rights being either exclusively universal or exclusively relative.

Another way to think about universalism and relativism is to consider a range of universal rights, but with cultural, historical, political, and economic factors leading different rights to the forefront in different places and at different times. For example, the right to freedom of speech might be regarded as a universal right, but in some cultural traditions it is relatively unimportant for most people, whereas in other traditions it may provide the very basis of the political system. Similarly a certain right might be particularly significant at certain times, as in times of war when there is often media censorship, and less so at other times. Thus, although human rights are seen as universal, their significance will vary with the context.

Another approach is to consider the relationship between rights and needs. It is commonly assumed that there are universal human needs from which we can derive ideas of human rights. However, the position argued here is that this should be reversed. We can think of human rights as universal, with needs derived from our understanding of rights. Even an apparently "basic human need" such as the need for food only makes sense if we accept the idea of the human right to live; if the right to live is denied, then a normative "need" for food cannot be so readily justified. The imperative of "human needs" rests on the assumption of human rights, and, indeed, any statement of need that a social worker may make—the needs of a community, a family's need for support, a parent's need for child care, a person's need for a mobility—rests on the implicit assumption of the *rights* of the person, family, or community concerned. Thus, instead of basic needs implying derived rights, basic rights imply derived needs. This provides a useful way of thinking about universalism/relativism: while assuming human *rights* are universal, *needs* derived from these rights will vary with cultural context. The universal right to education, for example, varies with educational needs; in one context it might mean teachers and school buildings, in another it is access to radios or computers, and in still another it may be educational materials for families. We can understand human rights and human needs, then, as representing the two aspects of universalism/relativism: rights are universal, but they give rise to very different culturally determined needs.

A third way of thinking about the universalism/relativism dilemma is to realize that human rights are universal *aspirations,* not *empirical* universals. Human rights do not exist in an objective positivist sense. They are constructed to represent our ideas about the important features that make us "human" and that we have in common with humanity. In this sense human rights are not static; they are not "handed down in tablets of stone" from the United Nations. Rather, they are constantly reconstructed as our ideas and values change. When I make a statement of "human rights," therefore, I am not delivering an empirical truth but stating a value that I believe ought to apply to all humanity. The universalism lies in my wishing that this right would apply to all human beings, not in my assertion that in fact it does. A member of another culture will probably construct human rights somewhat differently—our views are, inevitably, culturally determined, and a different cultural context is likely to produce different constructions of "human rights." Both my view and that other person's view are "universal" in that we each have articulated values that we would wish to apply to all people. Nevertheless, they are different. In this sense, there can be various "universals," with cultural difference providing differing understandings of what our "common humanity" might comprise. This is a very fruitful approach, as it opens the possibility of dialogue; if another person and I have different ideas of what should constitute our common humanity, or human rights, then we can listen to and learn from each other, and have a significant dialogue from which more shared understandings can develop. It should also be noted, however, that the construction of the "human," and of what it means to be "human," involves complex philosophical issues, and such dialogue is a good way to engage with others. This complexity is no reason to avoid the topic, as it is necessary to address these issues if one is to use the idea of "human rights" appropriately. A definition of "human" is too often taken as so obvious as to be non-problematic. In fact, the definition is highly problematic and has been the subject of considerable philosophical discussion (see, e.g., Caroll, 2004).

A fourth way of thinking about universalism and relativism is to understand them not as a dichotomy but as mutually interdependent, and to realize that we need both universals and specifics in order to make sense of what is meant by human rights. Universal statements of human rights will only be reasonable within our own cultural context; any statement about, for example, freedom of speech, freedom from abuse, or the right to health care can be understandable only if we relate it to our own experience. In other words, any universal statement needs a context to give it meaning. Similarly any statement about our own context can only be made if we have some other, larger-scale, more "universal" understanding. We could only describe American culture as "materialistic," for instance, if we have some broader understanding of other cultures and can compare American customs to more universal norms. Thus contextual statements need universal understandings to give them meaning, just as universal statements need context to give them meaning. From this perspective, we cannot talk about universalism and cultural relativism as if each existed in contradistinction to the other. Rather, we need to understand that each needs the other, and that the two belong together. It is true that one or the other will sometimes be in the forefront, but every statement of human rights will contain and rely on both universal and relativist understandings. In this sense the dichotomy disappears; any statement of human rights is simultaneously a universal statement and a contextual statement, and we need to understand and explore both the universal and contextual aspects of all human rights. A fuller account of universalism and relativism can be found in Douzinas (2000).

With regard to social work practice, the idea of working across cultural boundaries based on universal human rights, as simplistically understood, might be seen as impeding the goals of social work, as the universal view denies differences and devalues cultural context. However, a more sophisticated analysis of the issue reveals the opposite; human rights can provide a framework within which the tensions of working across cultural difference can be overcome.

Human Rights and the Law

One of the problems with the conventional framing of human rights is that it is too readily equated with law. Lawyers are seen as the dominant human rights professionals, and human rights issues are often defined in legal terms. From a legal perspective, human rights can be obtained only if they are justiciable, if they can be realized or protected through legislation and legal processes. Certainly the law has been critically important in human rights, and lawyers have much to contribute to the wording of human rights conventions and the legal processes that safeguard people's rights. It is a mistake, however, to see lawyers as the only human rights profession-als, and to see human rights as nothing more than a branch of the law. To do so is to limit the idea and scope of human rights, and devalue the contri-butions of other professional groups.

Constructing human rights as law leads to undercutting rights that may not be readily justiciable, and confines human rights to those that are best guaranteed by the courts. These tend to be negative rights, namely, rights that need to be protected, rather than positive rights such as health, educa-tion and housing that require active provision by the civil society. Negative rights are largely civil and political rights, as opposed to economic, social, or cultural rights, and this has led to the privileged status of civil and po-litical rights over others in public discourse. For example, when the media suggest that a nation has a "poor human rights record" they almost cer-tainly are referring to a tyrannical government with a corrupt legal system, a country where torture is used to extract confessions, where there is cen-sorship of public expression and restrictions on freedom of movement or assembly. The media are unlikely to mean a country with a poor health ser-vice, an inadequate housing or educational system; yet these are also hu-man rights violations, though they are violations of economic, social, and cultural rights less readily guaranteed by the law.

Another problem with equating human rights with law is that it un-dervalues other ways our rights may be protected (in the case of negative rights) or realized (with regard to positive rights). It is not only through the law that our human rights are achieved. The right to be free from ha-rassment or discrimination, for example, is inadequately protected by the law. Laws can protect from the more blatant and demonstrable cases of discrimination or harassment but are inadequate to deal with "low grade" harassment or discrimination, especially if it persists over a long period and can amount to a gross violation of human rights. Just as outlawing racial discrimination does not eliminate racism, legal measures against hu-man rights abuse of all kinds can only ever be partially successful. This is particularly so in the private or domestic domain, which, for many people, especially women and children, is where their human rights are regularly violated. The law is unable to intervene in the private domain for anything more than the most blatant of abuses, such as serious and demonstrable child abuse or domestic violence, and even then it is often not effective. It is totally unable to deal with cases of "low-level" harassment, even though they may be long-lasting. If we expand our understanding of human rights to include the domestic sphere, the right to freedom of expression becomes as important within the family as it does in civil society, and the right to be free from harassment or bullying becomes as significant in the household as it is in the workplace. Yet if the law attempted to regulate these rights in the family to the same degree that it does in the public arena, serious issues would arise of the violation of the right to privacy and of the state interfering in the private lives of citizens. Similarly we can think about the right of access to resources within a family, the right to freedom of religion within a family, the right to reasonable leisure for all family members, and so on. Such human rights issues in the private domain are important for social workers—as important as human rights violations in the public domain— but they are inadequately protected or realized if we rely only, or primarily, on legal mechanisms. The law is important, but it is not the only means for achieving human rights, and the danger of giving primacy to the law in human rights work is that other forms of practice are devalued, and human rights issues in the domestic sphere will remain largely unaddressed.

Another problem with an exclusively legal understanding is that it is consistent with the idea of human rights somehow "existing" in an objective, positivist, and decontextualized sense, as discussed earlier in relation to universalism. Legally defined human rights can easily become reified so that it is assumed simply that they "exist" in their own right, having been handed down "in tablets of stone" from some higher authority. This positivist understanding of human rights is consistent with the positivist tradition of the law, but it is a narrow and disempowering way to understand our human rights. Rather, human rights must be seen not as existing objectively but as social constructions. We are constantly constructing, deconstructing, and reconstructing human rights, because human rights are an expression of our common humanity, and "common humanity" is a complex, contested, and changing idea. It will change with cultural context, and over time. For example, the Universal Declaration of Human Rights, while a magnificent and inspiring document, represents issues that were seen as important by its drafters in 1948; more than fifty years later it now seems dated, failing to include matters that many people view now as important, for example, freedom from discrimination on the grounds of sexual preference. Indeed, it might be argued that the idea of a "common humanity" is so bound up with the Western humanist tradition that it cannot be freed from the bounds of that worldview, and so will always devalue other philosophies of the human. Others may argue that the humanist tradition is a necessary, unifying worldview in the era of globalization, and that seeing human rights as part of it is necessary if we are to achieve global peace, justice, and sustainability. In other words, if we are globalizing the economy and the culture, it is important that we also globalize people's rights (Gibney, 2003). Still others would argue that the idea of human rights can be found in many different religious and philosophical traditions, and that human rights is far more than simply a child of the Western Enlightenment. There is insufficient space here to examine these arguments in detail, but they are explored in a substantial human rights literature (Hayden, 2001; Campbell, Ewing, & Tomkins, 2001; Bell, Nathan, & Peleg, 2001; Douzinas, 2000; Gaita, 1999; Herbert, 2002). The point for our purposes here is simply to reduce the importance of the objective positivist assumptions about human rights that are inherent in the legal tradition.

The legal tradition is essentially one of human rights "from above," rights that are defined by an elite group, usually lawyers, politicians, academics, opinion leaders, and a small group from human rights nongovernmental organizations (NGOs). The rights are often couched in difficult legal language when converted into conventions and laws, which is necessary for the effective operation of the law; in other words, it is done *for the benefit of the legal system* rather than for the intended recipients of the rights. It is therefore seen as more important for lawyers to be able to use the conventions than for people to be able to understand them, so that the grand vision of human rights becomes sacrificed to legal rationality and removed from the understanding of the very people it seeks to protect. In this way, a sense of ownership of human rights is lost, and, like so much else (e.g., the economy), human rights become something that we leave to the "experts," as if rights are too important to be entrusted to the people themselves. It has long been argued by philosophers of social science (e.g. Fay, 1975) that such technical rationality and effective disenfranchisement is an inevitable outcome of a positivist worldview, and this is as true of human rights as it is of economics, law, social policy, and social work.

The view of human rights "from above" leads to an essentially deductive model of social work practice (Ife, 2001), practice where human rights are accepted as "given," and human rights conventions and declarations are seen as the ultimate authority and are quoted uncritically, with the virtual status of holy writ. Practice then becomes simply a process of applying those rights to particular situations and contexts, using statements of rights, uncritically accepted, to advocate and ensure that people's rights are protected and realized. While much valuable work can be done from within this perspective, leading to significant outcomes for those whom social workers serve, it is also a limited and uncritical approach to human rights leading to a limited, uncritical approach to social work. The remainder of this chapter explores an alternative, more inductive approach, based on the idea of human rights emanating "from below."

Human Rights from Below

If we accept the idea of human rights as constructed, rather than existing in an objective sense, then the important question to ask is who does the constructing. Earlier criticisms were that human rights were defined by white men, and so reflected an uncritically accepted white male worldview. This was never fully true; Eleanor Roosevelt, for example, played a major role in the establishment of the United Nations Universal Declaration of Human Rights, as did UN delegations from non-Western countries. More realistic, however, is that human rights discourse was unduly influenced by patriarchal and Western worldviews that effectively silenced other voices. More recently this has changed, and even a cursory examination of the human rights literature indicates that women's voices and those from non-Western traditions have very significant roles in framing the discourse (Van Ness, 1999; Meijer, 2001; Nirmal, 2000; Davis, 1995; Moussalli, 2001; Rendel, 1997). Feminist and postcolonial theorizing has been prominent and, indeed, seen as necessary for an academic understanding of the human rights field, and women's voices and non-Western voices are prominent in UN conferences where human rights declarations are drawn up. But although the voices that frame the human rights discourse are no longer predominantly the voices of white men, they are still almost exclusively the voices of privilege. As noted earlier, human rights are defined largely by lawyers, politicians, academics, and privileged activists. The voices may no longer be exclusively white and male, but they still represent a narrow elite, one from which the overwhelming majority is excluded. In this sense, continuing debate over issues of gender and race/ethnicity in human rights, which obviously are important in themselves, can blind us to a major contradiction: responsibility for defining human rights and our common humanity is assumed by a small minority; and those most likely to suffer from the denial or abuse of human rights (the most disadvantaged) are excluded. It becomes, therefore, a discourse of the powerful about the powerless. In these terms, human rights "from above" itself represents a form of human rights abuse, a denial of people's right to a role in defining their rights.

Thus, developing an alternative, that is, human rights "from below," must involve ways of helping people to define human rights for themselves, in their particular context, and developing a *culture of human rights* where human rights are part of everyday, lived experience. This sits squarely within the agenda of community work (Ife, 2002), which has long been concerned with helping people and communities define their own needs—rather than having those needs imposed on them by others—and then take action to have those needs met, whether externally (through advocacy, lobbying, etc.) or internally (through development, self-reliance, etc.). Human rights are inextricably connected to human needs. Indeed, as discussed earlier in this chapter, the definition of needs is one way in which universal rights can be put in context. By helping people define their needs, community workers are also engaging in a process of helping people define their rights. So it is important that community workers seek to use "rights language" as well as "needs language" in working with community groups, to bring to the fore the rights issues implied by perceived or assessed needs. Framing a need in terms of an implicit right can be a much more robust position leading to strong advocacy, as rights language tends to carry a stronger imperative to action than needs language.

Defining Rights

Helping people define their rights, from their own perspective, does not imply that human rights declarations and conventions are ignored. It can be useful to incorporate such documents as the Universal Declaration of Human Rights, or conventions on specific rights such as the Convention on the Rights of the Child, but not uncritically. Rather, they can be presented as one view of human rights or as a text for critique and deconstruction or for presenting ideas worth talking about, rather than as unquestioned wisdom. A discussion comparing the rights people themselves feel are important to rights as defined in the Universal Declaration can be an effective way to help people think more broadly about human rights and what they mean. Also, in discussing human rights at this level, it is important to emphasize that the idea of *human* rights includes rights we want not only for ourselves but also for all humanity. Thus the discussion also can include a reflection on what it means to be human and what it is that we value in our own humanity and that of others.

An essential component of this form of practice is dialogue. Many forces in modern Western societies work against dialogue, an art that has been at least partly lost. Dialogue requires us to listen as much as we talk, and to learn as much as to persuade. It requires acknowledging that the other participant in the dialogue has at least as much wisdom and knowledge as we do, and that we can learn from each other. It requires each of us to admit that we do not have all the answers but that together we will be able to understand and achieve more than we could alone. This contrasts with the more common form of exchange, which is debate not dialogue. In debate, one side seeks to "win," to defeat the other rather than to learn. The idea of winners and losers, and of discussion being some kind of competition rather than a mutual exploration, is so ingrained in Western ways of thinking that we do not recognize its pervasiveness. Dialogue means opening up to the other rather than seeing the other as a competitor. And it means not favoring our knowledge and wisdom over the knowledge and wisdom of another, even if the knowledge and wisdom belong to the professional social worker, as opposed to the lived experience and folk wisdom of our clients. This is a form of practice that respects the rights of others, and their right to define their own rights themselves. It resonates with the traditional social work value of the right to self-determination, which has been so eroded in this era of specified outcomes, evidence-based practice, and managerialism, but surely needs to remain at the center of social work values.

Securing Rights

Working with people to define their rights is only a first step in human rights–based practice. Once rights have been articulated, the next phase is moving toward protecting those rights (in the case of negative rights) or realizing them (in the case of positive rights). The reality of social work practice is that this will usually involve some form of advocacy or activism, possibly by a social worker or the people or community concerned. For a social worker to move unthinkingly to advocacy without first considering the capacity of the people concerned to advocate for themselves is to risk denying people their rights to self-expression, and hence to risk disempowerment. On the other hand, for social workers to refuse to be advocates on the grounds that it is disempowering can be equally dangerous. Sometimes there may be a risk associated with advocacy or activism, which the social worker has no mandate to impose on another person. And sometimes, for example, when a person has a severe intellectual disability, advocacy by the social worker is essential. This emphasizes the importance of careful judgment by social workers, in dialogue with the people with whom they are working, about the best way to proceed with advocacy/activism, and the need for social workers to have the necessary political and ethical background to help make such judgments.

It must be remembered, however, that social workers acting in what they see as in the best interests of others has resulted in practice amounting to human rights abuse. An example is the forced removal of Indigenous children from their families in Australia, Canada, and the United States. Any time social workers act on their own initiative with the justification that it is "in the best interests" of another, there is a danger of human rights abuse. Sometimes, of course, it is necessary, but it must only be undertaken with careful reflection about the possible harm that might be done, and the best way to protect the rights of the people concerned. Social workers should always undertake this work with doubt and self-searching, never with arrogant professional certainty.

The problems and issues of activism and advocacy are beyond the scope of this chapter. The important point here is that the perspective of human rights "from below" leads naturally to such activism for social work. People and communities, especially those with whom social workers cooperate, often cannot have their rights realized, guaranteed, or protected without engaging in struggle, and social work that is concerned with human rights needs to support such struggles. If those struggles are couched in the language of rights, and not in the language of needs, the impact is likely to be greater, as a discourse of rights includes claims that those rights *must* be met as a matter of *obligation or justice*, whereas reference to needs implies that they *might* be met as a matter of *charity*, and only if resources are available.

Exercising Rights

There is no point having rights unless they are exercised. The right to free expression, for example, is meaningless unless people actively exercise it, and the same can be said of many other human rights. From this we might conclude that we have a certain obligation not only to secure our rights but to exercise them.

This is further reinforced by a perceived debt owed to those who struggled in the past to secure human rights. Many of the rights we may take for granted were hard won, only after the struggles of others who in many cases suffered and even died to secure those rights. Those who do not take those rights seriously do a disservice to those who struggled for them, and this also implies a responsibility for us to exercise our rights, or at least to take them seriously. The right to vote, for example, was hard won, and those of us who hold that right owe a debt to those who fought for it in the past. This implies either that we should exercise that right or, if we choose not to, that we do so from a carefully considered position rather than simply from apathy.

A society that values human rights, therefore, is an active participatory society, where citizens take their rights seriously and exercise them. Encouraging citizen participation is therefore an important component of working toward human rights, and this again places human rights firmly within the agenda of community development. Encouraging citizen participation has long been a feature of community development practice, and there are many techniques to facilitate such participation outlined in community development texts (Ife, 2002).

Human Rights in Everyday Life

Another way of thinking about human rights "from below" is to think about the way we constantly construct and reconstruct rights and responsibilities in our everyday life. In all our interactions with others, particularly with those we do not know, we act on the assumption of rights and responsibilities. To use an example from Western cultures, when we wait in line at a bank, post office, or supermarket checkout, we make an assumption about the rights of others, namely, that those in front of us are served first. But if there is a person in line whose mobility is seriously impaired, we are likely to let that person go to the head of the line out of recognition of their rights. When we are served, we treat salespersons with politeness, understanding their right to be treated with dignity, and we also expect them to provide us with efficient and courteous service, which is our right as customers. However, we do not stop to talk to them at length about the weather or football, out of our recognition of the rights of those behind us in line. In other aspects of our daily lives in public spaces—in workplaces, shopping centers, driving, catching a bus, at the beach, in a classroom, or in a place of worship—we are constantly acting on a set of largely unconscious assumptions about our rights, the rights of others, and the responsibilities that we and they therefore have. Because we do not know these people personally, these are rights derived not from personal familiarity or any special status but simply because they are other human beings—and hence these are human rights. Sometimes, of course, those understandings will not be shared, resulting in conflicts such as road rage or arguments about who should be served first. But the important point is that our daily lives proceed on the basis of assumptions of the rights of ourselves and others, and thus human rights are at the core of our daily lived experience, even if we do not recognize them as such.

This notion of human rights being a part of everyday lives is particularly significant for human rights education and practice. It means that there are opportunities to identify and discuss the way we treat other people as demonstrating our understandings of human rights, and it represents the opposite extreme from the notion of human rights defined by a small elite attending UN conferences. Rather, it suggests that we are all engaged in the process of constructing and reconstructing human rights, and that far from being a creation of the UN, they are created by all of us. It brings human rights to an essentially human scale, making them understandable for all. And because of this it represents a good starting point for the process of defining human rights, as discussed earlier.

This view of human rights also relates to the universalism/relativism debate. Such socially constructed human rights are not the same everywhere but of course will vary with cultures. Queuing practices, to continue the previous example, vary from culture to culture. And so a micro-level definition of human rights will not be universal in that the rights will apply the same way everywhere; but, as we have seen, the notion of universalism is naïve, not viable in a world of cultural diversity. However, the principles on which those constructions are based, which might be understood in terms of respecting another, may reflect values that are held universally, although contextualized differently.

Human Rights and Community Development

The link between human rights and community development has been a recurring theme in this chapter, which has shown how this broader understanding of human rights "beyond the legal" and of "human rights from below" sets human rights squarely within the community development agenda. However, human rights and community development are connected in a more fundamental way, which can be seen from the necessarily collective nature of human rights.

For an individual to claim rights in isolation is nonsense. The individual on a desert island effectively has no rights, because there is no one to meet the responsibilities that go with those rights. Because the rights of one necessarily involve the responsibilities of another—my rights become your responsibilities, and your rights become my responsibilities—human rights connect us to our fellow humans in a profound way. They imply a society where we are concerned for each other, where we feel responsible for the other, and where we share our rights in common. Therefore to understand human rights in the conventional individual framing of "my rights" is misleading. Human rights do not imply a rugged individualism as some people have suggested but imply a form of collectivism, where it is not "my right" but rather "our right" that is important. This suggests that human rights require some form of human community in which they can be located or, to use the term of the American philosopher Alan Gewirth (1996), a "community of rights." Human rights, implying as they do obligations to one another, are at the heart of human community, and hence strong human rights require strong human communities. In this sense, community development can be seen as human rights work. In the above paragraphs, it was suggested that a society valuing human rights is an active, participatory society, and so to establish human rights it can be argued that we need human community.

Similarly we can argue that community development needs human rights. Community development must be understood and practiced from a position that values human rights, or else it could have dangerous consequences. For example, in the absence of human rights, one of the most successful community development programs could be said to have been the Hitler Youth: it achieved a high level of community participation, gave young people a sense of identity and achievement, provided a clear direction and sense of purpose, and raised the self-esteem of the young people involved. Yet it was part of a program that, historically, is one of the worst violators of human rights, on a massive scale. A strong human rights framework is essential for community development practice, if it is not to repeat the Nazi experience even at a less extreme level.

Human rights and community development, therefore, need each other, and each implies the other. Indeed, one could argue that they are similar, or parallel, processes, if one takes a "human rights from below" perspective. This can be seen simply in the language used in both discourses. Human rights, it is often said, is concerned with establishing our *common humanity*, whereas community development is concerned with establishing *human community*. The words are the same, and in this sense we might argue that the two are pursuing a common agenda. Similarly, if one looks at what "human rights workers" do, and what "community workers" do, there is little difference. Although the language used may be different, the skills of activism, advocacy, dialogue, inclusiveness, participation, consultation, and so on, are the same, as is the value base used by practitioners. This suggests not only that community workers have something to *learn* from the human rights field to enrich their practice but also that they have something to *contribute* to the human rights field.

There are other ways in which human rights and community development can be seen to have commonalities, which are outside the scope of this essay. And a similar argument can be made for social work practice more generally. Social work is a profession that bases its values in human rights, and there are real parallels between human rights and social work practice at all levels (see Ife, 2001).

Conclusion

The approach to human rights from below, as developed in the second half of this chapter, is important in addressing some of the issues of universalism and relativism posed earlier. One of the major criticisms of mainstream human rights discourse has been that it is based in Western indi-vidualism and does not take account of more collective or communitarian norms found in other cultural traditions. However, the argument in the second part of this chapter suggests that human rights, far from being in-dividualist, require a more collective and organic understanding. From this perspective it is the Western individual tradition that is more at odds with ideas of human rights, and this poses human rights as a possible *alternative* to the exploitation, inequality, and moral bankruptcy of Western liberal individualism, rather than as an outcome of that tradition. Indeed, it is no coincidence that the cause of human rights has been taken up by many who oppose the dominant order, such as the anti-globalization movement, as a central reference point. In the absence of any other "legitimate" alter-native to the ravages of global capitalism, the idea of human rights emerges as perhaps the only legitimate alternative discourse for those seeking sig-nificant social, economic, and political change.

Addressing issues of diversity remains one of the greatest challenges facing Western society, as the Western modernist Enlightenment tradition has found it difficult to deal with difference, without classifying one group as superior to another; this has been at the heart of racism, sexism, and dis-crimination against people with disabilities, gays and lesbians, and other groups seen as "different." Modernity has been unable to accept that differ-ence need not be hierarchical; rather, any classification of people into two or more groups seems to require a judgment that one is somehow superior and others inferior. Human rights, when understood from within a mod-ernist perspective, is confronted by the same difficulty, in that anything other than the uniformity of an imposed universalism leads to value judg-ments about different cultural practices. To move beyond this, the challenge is to develop an approach to the universalism of human rights that, while emphasizing our common "humanity" and seeking to articulate what that humanity means, at the same time acknowledges different cultural tradi-tions as providing different contexts within which that humanity is con-structed. Universalism need not mean uniformity, and difference need not mean hierarchy, though these distinctions are often difficult for the West-ern modernist to grasp. Community development faces similar dilemmas, though it has a longer history of working with ideas of change from below. Bringing community development and human rights together provides not only a fertile ground for moving beyond the problems of universalism and cultural difference, but it also provides a powerful framework for social work practice based on human rights.

References

Bauer, J., & Bell, D. (Eds.). (1999). *The East Asian challenge for human rights.* Cambridge: Cambridge University Press.

Bell, L., Nathan, A., & Peleg, I. (Eds.). (2001). *Negotiating culture and human rights.* New York: Columbia University Press.

Booth, K. (1999). Three tyrannies. In T. Dunne & N. Wheeler (Eds.), *Human rights in global politics* (pp. 31–70). Cambridge: Cambridge University Press.

Campbell, T., Ewing, K. D., & Tomkins, A. (Eds.). (2001). *Sceptical essays on human rights.* Oxford: Oxford University Press.

Caney, S., & Jones, P. (Eds.). (2001). *Human rights and global diversity.* London: Frank Cass.

Caroll, J. (2004). *The wreck of Western culture: Humanism revisited.* Victoria, Australia: Scribe.

Davis, M. (Ed.). (1995). *Human rights and Chinese values: Legal, philosophical and political perspectives.* Hong Kong: Oxford University Press.

Douzinas, C. (2000). *The end of human rights: Critical legal thought at the turn of the century.* Oxford: Hart.

Fay, B. (1975). *Social theory and political practce.* London: Allen & Unwin.

Gaita, R. (1999). *A common humanity: Thinking about love, truth and justice.* Melbourne: Text Publishing.

Gewirth, A. (1996). *The community of rights,* Chicago: University of Chicago Press.

Gibney, M. (Ed.). (2003). *Globalizing rights.* Oxford: Oxford University Press.

Hayden, P. (Ed.). (2001). *The philosophy of human rights.* St Paul, MN: Paragon.

Herbert, G. (2002). *A philosophical history of rights.* New Brunswick, NJ: Transaction.

Ife, J. (2002). *Community development: Community-based alternatives in an age of globalisation* (2nd ed.). Sydney: Pearson.

Ife, J. (2001). *Human rights and social work: Towards rights-based practice.* Cambridge: Cambridge University Press.

Ife, J. (1997). *Rethinking social work: Towards critical practice.* Melbourne: Longman.

Ishay, M. (2004). *The history of human rights: From ancient times to the globalization era.* Berkeley: University of California Press.

Lyons, G., & Mayall, J. (Eds.). 2003. *International human rights in the 21st century: Protecting the rights of groups.* Lanham, MD: Rowman & Littlefield.

Meijer, M. (Ed.). (2001(. *Dealing with human rights: Asian and Western views on the value of human rights.* Utrecht: HOM.

Moussalli, A. (2001). *The Islamic quest for democracy, pluralism and human rights.* Gainesville: University Press of Florida.

Nirmal, C. (2000). *Human rights in India: Historical, social and political perspectives.* New Delhi: Oxford University Press.

Pereira, W. (1997). *Inhuman rights: The Western system and global human rights abuse.* Mapusa: The Other India Press.

Rendell, M. (1997). *Whose human rights?* Staffordshire, UK: Trentham Books.

Van Ness, P. (Ed.). (1999). *Debating human rights: Critical essays from the United States and Asia.* London: Routledge.

5

Development, Social Development, and Human Rights

JAMES MIDGLEY

Development—widely defined as the economic and social changes driven by industrialization—has been a prominent concern in the social sciences and in the world of public policy for more than a century. Defining "development" in this way, of course, is based on the historical experience of the Western countries that underwent economic modernization in the nineteenth and twentieth centuries. The ramifications of development have also inspired governments in many developing countries in Africa, Asia, and Central and South America as they have sought to foster economic growth and raise standards of living.

A major problem is that economic development often benefits only a small part of the population. Although development has indeed brought prosperity to many regions of the world, a relatively small fraction of the population in many developing countries has been drawn into modern wage employment, while improvements in living standards are largely concentrated in urban areas. In many countries a sizable proportion of the rural population continues to live in poverty and conditions of appalling deprivation, and urban slums and squatter settlements are prevalent in many developing countries. In many parts of the Global South, economic modernization has led to distorted development, where economic growth has not been accompanied by corresponding degrees of social progress.

Recognizing the need for social policies and programs that can address these problems, the term "social development" (or "human development" as it is sometimes known), has been employed to connote efforts to challenge the problems of poverty and deprivation directly by harmonizing social policies with economic development. Social development is comprised of an amalgam of projects, programs, and interventions undertaken by governments, international development agencies, nongovernmental organizations (NGOs), and local community groups. These activities are primarily focused on material welfare goals such as poverty eradication and raising living standards, but social development is also concerned with inequality and social injustice, which are widely regarded as inseparable from the promotion of material well-being for all.

Although human rights have been widely debated in political, journalistic, and academic circles, they have not been systematically incorporated in social development theory and practice. Given the legalistic nature of human rights discourse, it is perhaps not surprising that development scholars and practitioners have paid relatively little attention to human rights issues. However, a number of social development writers and practitioners have recently argued that human rights should be integrated into social development activities. Many have been inspired by grass-roots human rights efforts and by the advocacy activities of developmental organizations that have effectively adopted human rights approaches. Over the last decade, the term "rights-based development" has been popularized to connote these efforts.

This chapter describes various human rights instruments that are relevant to social development, and points up how they can be used to promote a rights-based approach to such development. The numerous international human rights conventions and treaties that address social and economic concerns are discussed and suggestions are made for how these instruments can harness the capacity of economic growth to bring about significant improvements in living standards for all. But before discussing the way human rights can be implemented in social development through the adoption of a rights-based approach, the fields of development and social development, and their historical evolution and central tenets, are briefly described.

Development and Social Development

Although the above definition of development is based on the historical experience of the Western industrial nations, it reflects older ideas about social change and social progress. As Arndt (1978) suggests, modern conceptions of development are rooted in optimistic Enlightenment beliefs that extol the role of rational knowledge, technological invention, and human agency in fostering social change. These ideas soon found expression in economic planning and in the widespread adoption of Keynesian economic policies in the Western capitalist nations as well as in centralized state planning in the Soviet Union in the middle decades of the twentieth century.

Economic planning was also adopted by many previously colonized developing countries that had secured independence from European imperial rule in the years World War II. Many governments in the Global South created central planning ministries that sought to transform predominantly agrarian societies into modern, industrial states. Economic planning was designed to promote rapid industrialization and create employment opportunities that would draw labor out of the agrarian subsistence sector, and raise incomes and living standards for the population as a whole.

The Economic Development Enterprise

In addition to the Keynesian influence, economic development planning was inspired by a growing body of academic scholarship focused on the needs of the developing countries. A new field of development economics emerged, and this was augmented by the creation of the new subject of development studies. At the time, the economies of the developing countries were conceptualized in terms of a dualistic model that contrasted the large traditional and impoverished subsistence sector with the small modern sector that had emerged during the colonial era (Boeke, 1953; Higgins, 1956). If wage employment opportunities in the modern sector could be expanded, surplus labor could be transferred from the traditional to the modern sector, thus raising incomes and living standards. Arthur Lewis (1955), the influential Caribbean economist and subsequent Nobel Prize winner, formalized these ideas by stressing the need for capital investment in manufacturing industry, which he believed would stimulate rapid economic growth and create wage employment on a large scale. Lewis's ideas were widely disseminated and embellished by other development scholars. His view that the agrarian societies of the Global South could be transformed through rapid industrialization was also adopted by the planning agencies of many newly independent countries.

To foster rapid industrial development, most governments of the developing countries adopted an import substitution approach that restricted foreign imports, protected nascent industrial expansion, and stimulated and met demand for local manufacture in domestic markets. Of course, the expansion of the modern sector through rapid industrial development required massive injections of capital that were obtained primarily through international borrowing. Because few developing countries had sufficient domestic resources to create a vibrant industrial sector, most sought investment capital from the Western nations or from international development agencies such as the World Bank. In addition, since interest rates were comparatively low, many governments borrowed extensively on commercial markets. It was assumed, of course, that rapid industrial development would facilitate the speedy repayment of these loans.

The overall results of the industrial import substitution development model were mixed. On the one hand, many developing countries recorded high rates of annual economic growth, and this reflected the success of policies designed to expand the modern industrial sector and create wage employment. In some countries, growth rates were unprecedented and a significant degree of industrial development occurred. For example, growth rates in Brazil in the 1960s were so high that the country was internationally touted as the new "economic development miracle." On the other hand, industrialization clearly was not absorbing labor from the rural subsistence sector at a rate that would significantly reduce the incidence of absolute poverty. A study in Kenya by the International Labour Organization (1972) showed that only a small proportion of the large numbers of people migrating to the cities had found regular jobs. The study also found that most migrants were eking out a living for themselves and their families in what became known as the informal sector (Bromley & Gerry, 1979). For most in the informal sector, livelihoods were characterized by squalor, poverty, and deprivation.

There were a few places, in fact, where the industrial development model seemed to be producing positive results. In several East Asian countries, for example, massive capital investments in modern industry had produced high growth rates, and wage employment had increased substantially, but, instead of adopting the conventional import substitution approach, these countries produced inexpensive manufactured commodities for export to the United States and other Western nations. Emulating the experience of Japan and some other Western countries, such as Sweden and Switzerland, export-led industrial development was accompanied by substantial investments in education, health care and housing, resulting in the emergence of a highly skilled labor force capable of participating in a modern, technological economy.

Although attempts were subsequently made to adopt the export-led industrial development strategy in other parts of the world, events in the 1970s created serious problems for the development enterprise. The oil shocks of the 1970s significantly raised the costs of industrial development, and the new phenomena of rapid inflation accompanied by economic stagnation in the Western, industrial nations resulted in significant increases in interest rates as governments sought to bring inflation under control. Consequently many developing countries that had borrowed heavily on international markets were now faced with huge debts. Many were compelled to turn to the International Monetary Fund (IMF) and the World Bank for help, and, as a condition for aid, many were required to adopt structural adjustment programs that severely curtailed government intervention in the economy. In some parts of the world, particularly Africa and South Asia, social conditions deteriorated and the incidence of poverty and deprivation increased.

Over the last fifty years the process of development has produced significant gains, but, with some notable exceptions, the hope that it would transform the impoverished colonized societies of the developing world into modern industrial states has not been realized. Although many have benefited because of the expansion of the modern economy, many others have been left behind. The result is a process of distorted development in which the rapid rates of economic growth recorded in many parts of the world have not been accompanied by widespread prosperity. The persistence of poverty in the midst of economic affluence remains the central paradox of the development enterprise and presents a huge challenge for the future.

The Social Development Alternative

Social development advocates believe that the problem of distorted development can best be remedied through combining economic growth and social welfare policies. They do not deny that industrial development has made a significant contribution by creating wage employment and raising incomes, but they reject the idea that well-being for all will automatically accompany economic growth. Instead, they argue for the adoption of social development policies and programs that specifically address the problems of poverty and deprivation associated with economic development(Midgley, 1995).

Social welfare activities known as "social development" were first introduced by imaginative expatriate social workers in Ghana and other British colonies in West Africa. They implemented community-level projects to address people's economic and social needs and, at the same time, contribute to national development efforts. These formative social development programs included the promotion of small-scale agriculture and small-family enterprises, the development of crafts and village technologies, the construction of economic and social infrastructure, including feeder roads, community water supplies, village sanitation, health and day care centers, and schools and other community facilities (Midgley, 1994).

These early social development programs were replicated in many other parts of the developing world, initially through the directives of the British imperial authorities, and then through the involvement of the United Nations. The popularization of the term "social development" as a distinctly "Third Worldist" approach to social welfare owed much to the efforts of the United Nations and its affiliated agencies. In the 1960s and 1970s other international organizations, such as the World Bank and the International Labor Organization, also contributed to the adoption of social development.

Different strategies were advocated to achieve social development goals and were characterized by novel terminologies giving social development a formative conceptual flavor (Midgley, 2003). In the 1950s the United Nations encouraged the adoption of community-level social development programs and urged the creation of nationwide participatory mechanisms to ensure that ordinary people were actively involved in all aspects of development. In the 1960s the United Nations promoted state-sponsored interventions such as "unified socioeconomic planning," which urged national planning authorities to transcend their conventional focus on promoting manufacturing and economic infrastructure to include a concern with the social sectors. The hope was that development planning would achieve social goals as well as narrowly defined economic aims (United Nations, 1971).

The World Bank was also active in formulating innovative social development strategies. During the years of the McNamara presidency in the 1970s, the World Bank gave high priority to poverty alleviation. The Bank also addressed the issue of inequality in development, contending that poverty and inequality were inextricably linked. Guided by its chief economist, Hollis Chennery, the Bank embraced the controversial idea that it is possible to combine economic growth and redistributive strategies (Chennery, Ahluwalia, Bell, Duloy, & Jolly, 1974). By using its lending programs to shape policy in many developing countries, the Bank was particularly instrumental in fostering the adoption of social development in the Global South.

In the 1970s the International Labour Organization challenged the conventional view that development policy should be primarily concerned with the creation of employment in the formal sector of the economy. Recognizing that a sizable proportion of the population was engaged in subsistence agriculture or working in the informal urban sector, the organization argued that the overriding goal of economic development efforts should be to meet people's basic needs for security, livelihoods, education, and health, shelter, and clean water. The labor group urged governments to refocus their development efforts so that the priority that had previously been given to industrial development would now be given to meeting basic needs (International Labour Office, 1976; Streeten & Burki, 1978).

Although the basic needs approach did not preclude extensive involvement of NGOs in social service delivery, it was essentially statist in character, and by the 1980s the anti-statist tide of neo-liberalism, as well as populist disenchantment with many governments, undermined the basic needs approach in development circles. Populist approaches that rephrased earlier notions of community development gained currency in social development circles primarily through the rapid expansion of nongovernmental development organizations and the provision of international aid to these bodies. In addition, some international development organizations such as UNICEF and the World Health Organization (WHO) advocated vigorously for "community participation" as the best means of promoting "health for all," and for children and mothers in particular. These themes are now widely emphasized by the many NGOs that implement social development programs around the world today.

Although these developments contributed to the formulation of social development as a distinctive approach for promoting human welfare, social development still lacks a coherent conceptual framework to guide social development efforts. Social development is still loosely defined, and it is unclear about what social development entails. It cannot be claimed, moreover, that social development policies have been effectively implemented in all parts of the world or that social development has adequately addressed the pressing problems of poverty, deprivation, inequality, and oppression that continue to characterize the human condition.

Nevertheless, by 1995, when the United Nations convened the World Summit on Social Development in Copenhagen, it could be claimed that social development had reached a new level of maturity and sophistication (United Nations, 1996). Subsequent efforts to promote social development globally through the Millennium Development Goals (United Nations, 2005; United Nations Development Program, 2003) and other initiatives have created an agenda for action, and focused media and public attention in the industrial nations on the need for renewed social development efforts. This has, in turn, energized public opinion in support of increased development aid, the reform of neo-liberal lending policies, and the abrogation of developing country debt. In this context, notions of human rights can make a particularly important contribution. As will be shown, the infusion of a rights-based approach in development can help to mobilize support for social development and renew efforts to meet the challenge of global poverty and deprivation.

Human Rights and Development

Contemporary human rights discourse is based on a rich legacy of ideas and beliefs expressing the simple idea that human beings have rights that require recognition, respect, and observance. This latter notion gives human rights a formalistic character that translates the abstract ideas of human rights theory into concrete programs of action. It strengthens the notion of entitlement in human rights discourse and provides a legal basis for ensuring compliance. Ideally, therefore, human rights are justiciable in that those who believe their rights have been violated may secure redress through the legal system.

Although human rights involve many complex and abstract issues, this chapter focuses on formal human rights instruments that give human rights concrete, distinctive, legalistic status. Formal human rights instruments of this kind include national constitutions, statutes and case law, as well as regional human rights instruments that include the European Convention for the Protection of Human Rights and Fundamental Freedoms of 1950, the American Convention on Human Rights of 1969, and the African Charter on Human and People's Rights of 1981. Perhaps most important are the many international instruments adopted by the UN and its affiliated agencies. Also relevant are a plethora of reports and the declarations and proclamations adopted at major international social development conferences, as well as the work of specialized commissions, experts, and advisory groups. While these documents and national and regional instruments are relevant to human rights debates, this chapter deals with international instruments that the United Nations and its affiliated agencies have sponsored over the last fifty years that have direct implications for social development.

Key Human Rights Instruments

The most important international human rights declarations, covenants, and conventions adopted over the recent decades to address social development issues are the Universal Declaration of Human Rights (1948), and the two subsequent Covenants that translated the principles in the Declaration into legally binding treaties: the United Nations International Covenant on Civil and Political Rights (1966) and the United Nations International Covenant on Economic, Social, and Cultural Rights (1966). Both Covenants and the Declaration itself are fundamentally important to social development. Other relevant instruments include the United Nations Convention on the Elimination of All Forms of Racial Discrimination (1965), the United Nations Convention on the Elimination of All Forms of Discrimination against Women (1979), the United Nations Declaration on the Right to Development (1986), the United Nations Convention of the Rights of the Child (1989), and the Convention against Torture and other Cruel, Inhuman, and Degrading Punishments (1984).

The Universal Declaration of Human Rights is arguably the most important human rights document in history, as it enshrines a large number of human rights. The first part of the Declaration focuses on civil and political rights including the prohibition on arbitrary arrest, detention, or exile (Article 8), the right to a fair trial by an independent and impartial court (Article 10), and the right to participate in the political process and to choose political representatives (Article 21). Economic, social, and cultural rights are covered in the latter part of the Declaration and include the right to social security and access to medical care and social services (Articles 22 and 25), the right to employment with equal pay for equal work (Article 23), the right to education, which shall be free at least at the elementary level (Article 26), the right to a standard of living adequate for the well-being of individuals and their families (Article 25), and the right to enjoy rest and leisure, and to participate in the cultural life of the community and enjoy the arts and share in scientific advancement and its benefits (Article 27).

Although it is standard practice for a declaration to contain formalized principles ratified through a treaty, the implementation of the Universal Declaration of Human Rights was delayed for political reasons. An influential minority of the organization's member states, including the Soviet Union, Czechoslovakia, Poland, and Yugoslavia, abstained from the General Assembly vote on the Declaration. Two non-communist members, Saudi Arabia and South Africa, also abstained. The abstention of the communist member states reflected the way the emerging ideological struggles of the Cold War later affected the evolution of international human rights discourse.

The Western member states favored a view of human rights that emphasized individual civil and political rights, whereas the communist states stressed the importance of social and economic rights. Both camps frequently accused each other of violating human rights. In this confrontational climate, it proved difficult to formulate a legally binding international treaty that would enforce the provisions of the Declaration. In fact, it was only in 1966 that the goal of creating a treaty of this kind was realized, and this resulted in not one but two separate treaties: the International Covenant on Civil and Political Rights and the International Covenant on Economic, Social, and Cultural Rights, mentioned earlier. Both Covenants came into force in 1976, after they had been ratified by the required minimum 35 member states of the United Nations. By the end of the century more than 140 member states had ratified both Covenants (Freeman, 2002).

Although both Covenants have been widely ratified, civil and political rights are generally accorded higher priority and recognition than economic, social, and cultural rights. This reveals the dominance of Western liberal interpretations of human rights, and the way human rights are popularly defined. References to human rights in the media usually focus on civil and political rights, and popular opinion generally reflects this preference. In addition, scholarly writings on human rights often categorize them into distinct "generations." Conventionally, civil and political rights are viewed as comprising first-generation "liberty" rights, whereas economic, social, and cultural or "equality" rights are viewed as comprising the second-generation rights. In more recent years a third generation known as "solidarity" rights have emerged (Freeman, 2002). The right to development is usually included in this third generation.

The preference for civil and political rights is also reflected in the idea that these rights are justiciable, whereas economic, social, and cultural rights are not. The adoption of the International Convention on Civil and Political Rights was accompanied by the establishment of an optional protocol that permits the Covenant's monitoring body to hear complaints about alleged violations. No provisions of this kind accompanied the adoption of the International Covenant on Economic, Social, and Cultural Rights. Also, the Covenant on Economic, Social, and Cultural Rights recognizes that the achievement of economic and social rights depends on the availability of resources to meet social needs. It also recognizes that states which have approved the covenant will "progressively" achieve the rights outlined in the Covenant. On the other hand, the rights identified in the Covenant on Civil and Political Rights were to be enforced immediately.

Although it is common to classify and implicitly rank human rights in this way, many human rights scholars believe that human rights are indivisible in that they have equal validity and universal application (Merali & Oosterveld, 2001). This is not a new idea. At the time the Universal Declaration was drafted, the UN General Assembly resolved that civil and political rights and economic and social rights were "interconnected and independent" (Puta-Chekwe & Flood, 2001, p. 40). This belief was subsequently reaffirmed at the International Conference on Human Rights held in Teheran in 1968, and at the World Conference on Human Rights held in Vienna in 1993. The view that human rights are indivisible has also been widely accepted in social development circles.

Ideological struggles over human rights in the 1950s and 1960s were compounded by the organization's non-aligned member states, which championed self-determination, cultural rights, and development. Most of these states were from the Global South and offered a distinctive "Third

World" view on human rights reflecting their anti-colonial struggles and asserting their independence from Superpower control. The right to national self-determination and the right to express indigenous cultural values in the context of universal principles were emphasized by the delegations of the non-aligned member states and eloquently articulated in speeches before the General Assembly by Third World leaders such as Kwame Nkrumah, Julius Nyereye, Leopold Senghor, and Che Guevara (Ishay, 2004).

Early attempts by the non-aligned member states to assert their own perspective on human rights found expression in their support of instruments that addressed social injustice. One example was their commitment to the 1965 UN Convention on the Elimination of All Forms of Racial Discrimination. Although this Convention was endorsed by both the Western and communist nations, the non-aligned nations were particularly active in advocating its adoption, as it expressed their struggles against colonialism and the racism inherent in colonial domination. Earlier references to non-discrimination before the law, and the role of education in promoting tolerance and understanding between national, racial, and religious groups in the Universal Declaration of Human Rights, were now more systematically articulated to expressly prohibit discrimination on racial grounds. This sentiment also reflected the anger non-aligned member states (particularly those that secured independence from European imperial rule) felt toward the continuation of what they regarded as the colonialist and racist practices of the South African and Israeli governments. Many non-aligned nations viewed both apartheid and Zionism as forms of racism even though attempts to link Zionism with racism were vigorously denounced by the United States and other Western member states. On the other hand, apartheid was universally condemned. The International Convention specifically referenced apartheid but not Zionism. The Convention was ratified by many member states, including Israel, within a relatively short time. For obvious reasons, it was ratified by South Africa only in 1998.

Efforts to address racism through human rights instruments were accompanied by attempts to deal with the ubiquitous challenge of gender oppression. Although the Universal Declaration of Human Rights referred to the civil and political rights of women, advocates for women's rights campaigned for the adoption of instruments that addressed these rights in a more systematic way. Their efforts resulted in the adoption of the 1952 Convention of the Political Rights of Women, which protects the rights of women to vote and be elected to political office, and the 1957 Convention on the Nationality of Married Women requiring that marriage shall not affect a woman's nationality. However, the most important instrument relating to women's rights is the 1979 Convention on the Elimination of All Forms of Discrimination against Women. The Convention, which was enforced in 1981, contains thirty articles, including women's right to vote and serve as elected officials, have equal access to educational opportunities, and enjoy equal access to health care and other social services. It affirms the reproductive rights of women and their rights under marriage. States Parties to the Convention undertake to eliminate discrimination against women in all spheres of life. The Convention has now been ratified by 180 UN member states. However, it has still not been ratified by the United States.

A related human rights instrument is the 1989 Convention on the Rights of the Child, which contains fifty-four articles dealing with an array of children's rights. These extend many of the rights contained in previous human rights instruments to children, including the right to education, health care, and nutrition, and the children's right to protection against discrimination and exploitation. They also provide for children's right to participate in cultural activities and enjoy a full family life. In particular, State Parties are required to support parents both in their efforts to provide for children, and, when necessary, to provide parents with material assistance and services. The Convention also contains numerous articles dealing with the way the social services should serve and protect children. Among the 192 countries that have now ratified the Convention, the only exceptions are Somalia and the United States.

The Right to Development

As noted earlier, the non-aligned nations were particularly committed to mobilizing support for human rights instruments concerned with poverty, deprivation, international exploitation, global debt, and other developmental issues. These concerns eventually coalesced under the notion of the right to development. Proponents of the right to development drew inspiration from Article 28 of the Universal Declaration, which states that "Everyone is entitled to a social and international order in which the rights and freedoms set forth in this Declaration can be fully realized," and from Article 1 of the International Covenant on Economic, Social, and Cultural Rights, which states that "All peoples have the right of self-determination.

By virtue of that right they freely determine their political status and freely pursue their economic, social, and cultural development." Both provided the basis for their campaign to embrace the notions of self-determination and development in one comprehensive human rights instrument.

The primary inspiration for the right to development originated in a lecture by Judge Keba M'Baye of Senegal at the 1972 International Institute of Human Rights (Freeman, 2002). Judge M'Baye, who was chairman of the United Nations Human Rights Commission at the time, argued that development should be a right. In view of the tendency to equate human rights with civil and political rights, this was a highly original, even provocative idea that remains controversial today. Nevertheless, M'Baye was able to secure the adoption of a General Assembly resolution in 1977, which authorized a study of the issue and resulted in the adoption, in 1986, of the United Nations Declaration on the Right to Development.

The adoption of the 1986 Declaration was part of a concerted effort to promote greater collaboration on international development between the industrialized and developing nations. In the 1970s the UN championed the creation of a New International Economic Order intended to produce greater cooperation and equity between the world's nations. This idea was subsequently reinforced by the Brandt Commission in 1980 (Independent Commission on International Development Issues, 1980), which urged greater North-South collaboration and numerous subsequent multilateral efforts to address debt, global poverty, and the negative effects of neo-liberal globalization policies. The Right to Development has also been informed by the growing concern about environmental issues and the need to promote sustainable development. Major international meetings have reinforced these efforts. They include the 1972 United Nations Conference on Environment and Development in Stockholm, the 1992 Rio Earth Summit, as well as the work of the Brutland Commission (World Commission on Environment and Development, 1987).

The Declaration is relatively short, with only ten articles. At the core of the Declaration is that the right to development is an inalienable human right that includes the right to self-determination. It requires states to promote national development and ensure that their citizens benefit from development. It also asserts that states are obliged to cooperate in formulating international policies to promote the rapid growth of the developing countries. The Declaration also requires states to take steps to eliminate the violations of human rights arising from racism, colonialism, foreign domination or occupation, and other forms of oppression.

Not surprisingly, the Declaration has been opposed by the United States and several other Western nations, and consequently has not been formalized as a binding Convention. The Western member states are particularly critical of the idea that the economically developed nations should be required, through a binding legal instrument, to modify their trade and related international policies to address the needs of the world's poor nations. Although efforts have been made to find a consensus that will permit the implementation of the principles contained in the Declaration, progress has been limited. Nevertheless, efforts to translate the Declaration into a binding Convention continue (Centre for Development and Human Rights, 2004).

Toward a Rights-Based Approach to Social Development

Framed by the Universal Declaration of Human Rights, and supported by the Declaration on the Right to Development, the various international human rights instruments described earlier provide for a rights-based approach to development that has major implications for social development. These instruments are augmented by many other international, regional, and national human rights instruments, and they are also supported by reports and declarations from international conferences, as well as the work of special commissions and bodies. Recognizing the indivisibility and universality of human rights, the rights-based approach gives expression to a number of instruments and human rights activities, and is not exclusively dependent on the Declaration on the Right to Development. Although still loosely defined, the rights-based approach is based on the belief that human rights can inform and enhance social development efforts. This can be achieved in several interrelated ways.

The rights-based approach can infuse social development with the language of human rights and with a new way of thinking that explicitly incorporates and employs human rights discourse in social development practice. Although human rights and development have long been treated as separate domains, there is growing support for the view that human rights should be integrated more systematically into social development thinking.

Also, a rights-based approach can help define the goals of social development and identify preconditions for successful social development efforts. Finally, a rights-based approach can inform and facilitate the implementation of social development policies and programs.

Infusing Social Development Thinking with the Language of Human Rights

Advocates of the rights-based approach seek to infuse social development with the language and mind-set of human rights. Social development, as noted earlier, has been concerned largely with material welfare and meeting basic human needs. This certainly is a desirable goal, but proponents of the rights-based approach argue that it does not sufficiently address wider issues of inequality and oppression. Nor, they believe, does it adequately express the belief that the eradication of poverty and the enjoyment of health, education, and shelter are inalienable human rights, not the result of compassion or charity. Some proponents of a rights-based approach have been critical of the needs-based approach (Molyneux & Lazar, 2003), claiming that it is paternalistic, reducing people with unmet needs to the status of passive recipients. Because basic needs and the setting of social development targets through the millennium implicitly evoke rights, this criticism may be unfair, but the infusion of a human rights discourse into social development would make this commitment explicit. Similarly, although social development has long been concerned with inequality and social injustice, a rights-based approach can solidify these commitments.

Infusing social development with a rights-based approach can also support efforts to define the field more coherently and provide it with a more systematic conceptual framework. It has already been noted that social development is poorly defined, and this ambiguity suggests various practical interventions. Despite attempts to address the problem, social development still lacks an overarching framework that integrates and provides a sound conceptual basis for these interventions (Midgley, 2003). The language of human rights may facilitate this task. As an important briefing paper published by the Overseas Development Institute (1999) suggested, the discourse of human rights could serve as the "scaffolding" for social development policy.

Although there is a tendency to associate social development with human rights instruments that deal specifically with economic, social, and cultural rights, or with the right to development, the advocates of a rights-based approach insist that *all* human rights are relevant and should be incorporated into social development discourse. It may seem that human rights instruments dealing with issues such as torture have little direct bearing on social development, but it is clear that improvements in living standards for a population as a whole are more likely to occur in politically democratic environments where individual civil rights and freedoms are guaranteed.

Defining the Goals of Social Development

Several social development scholars have pointed out that social development goals are vague, abstract, idealistic, and hortatory. G. A. Lloyd as long ago as 1982, expressed frustration at the failure of social development theorists to provide concrete definitions of social development goals or to clearly prescribe ways to attain them. Much of the literature, he claimed, is a "set of values, aspirations and heuristic notions" (p. 44) lacking specificity. Although Lloyd's criticism was valid, it was addressed primarily to the academic community and did not refer to the efforts of social development practitioners to solidify social development efforts. One such effort was the basic-needs approach that gave an operational definition of the goals of social development as the attainment of fundamental human needs such as survival, security, nutrition, shelter, health, education, and so on (International Labour Organization, 1976; Streeten & Burki, 1978). Although this approach provided social development with a set of tangible tasks that could be assessed in terms of specific outcome measures, it was narrowly focused on meeting needs and neglected other important social development dimensions. In an attempt to address this concern, Midgley (1995) offered a definition of the goal of social development as the attainment of human welfare. Focusing primarily on the material aspects of the concept, he defined a condition of social welfare, or well-being, as a condition in which social problems are managed, needs are met, and opportunities for advancement are provided (p. 14).

Although broader than the basic-needs approach, Midgley's definition fails to address wider issues of inequality and oppression and has been criticized as being narrowly concerned with "welfarist" goals (Green, 2002). On the other hand, definitions that allude to oppression and inequality are

also at risk of being nebulous, hortatory, and failing to provide tangible pre-
scriptions for social development practice. The concept of empowerment
is notoriously imprecise but has been used by activists of both the political
Left and Right to characterize interventions they believe gain their respective ideological ends.

On the other hand, human rights documents provide a clear and tangible statement of the entitlements that obligate compliance by States Parties,
and it is the very formalism of these documents that can inform efforts to
attain social development goals operationally. The Universal Declaration of
Human Rights and the treaties that have been adopted to put its principles
into effect, offer a clear statement about these goals. They reveal that social
development goals are made concrete by expressing them as human rights
including the right to life; to security; to freedom; to an adequate living
standard; to employment; to education; to health, nutrition, and shelter;
to social security; to participation in the cultural life of the community;
to self-determination, and to development itself. The discourse of human
rights, therefore, defines the attainment of human rights as the ultimate
goal of development effort (Overseas Development Institute, 1999). In
terms of this approach, a "developed" society may be viewed as one that
has achieved human rights for all.

Making the goals of social development tangible through the adoption
of a rights-based approach also facilitates the measurement of social development outcomes. Although difficulties may arise in the collection, analysis, and presentation of data, human rights attainments can be pursued operationally. The United Nations Development Program (2000) has played
a major role in measuring social development and has also contributed to
measuring human rights performance. The program links human rights
measures to the Human Development Index, or HDI, which is an aggre-
gate indicator of social development attainment. The target setting in the
program has been used in some countries to link social development goals
with human rights. For example, the government of Thailand's central
planning agency, the National Economic and Social Development Board,
has established specific social development targets based on the 1989 Covenant on the Rights of the Child, which relate to a reduction in maternal
and infant mortality, the access to basic education, and improvements in
nutritional status. These efforts are compatible with current global efforts
to set social development targets through the adoption of the Millennium

Development Goals (United Nations, 2005; United Nations Development Program, 2003).

Establishing Preconditions for Successful Social Development

In addition to targeting human rights as the ultimate goal of social development, it is also possible to view the provision of human rights as a precondition for successful social development efforts. This may seem paradoxical but it reflects the belief that social development policies and programs can be most successfully implemented in conditions of political stability, freedom, peace, and security. Although relatively little attention has been paid to these issues, development performance is affected by the wider social and political context. Obviously social development efforts are inhibited by civil conflicts, institutionalized corruption, entrenched hierarchical inequalities, insufficient opportunities, high crime rates, political oppression, and the denial of basic freedoms.

Widespread violence, perhaps, has the most devastating impact on social development policies and programs. Many economies, including those of Lebanon, the former Yugoslavia, and Palestine, have been devastated by armed conflicts and military occupation. It often takes years for countries affected by violence on those scales to recover. Vietnam's economy is now experiencing rapid growth, but this has required enormous efforts over several decades to overcome the destruction of war. More recently cities such as Groznyi in Chechnya and Faluja in Iraq have been all but destroyed by war, and, so far, the prospects of reconstruction and achieving social development goals are poor. The widespread use of torture and other abuses associated with military occupation in these and other places is hardly conducive to realizing economic and social progress.

Political oppression and the denial of basic freedoms also impede social development efforts, and many examples can be given of how the activities of totalitarian governments have inhibited economic growth and social progress. On the other hand, it has been argued that political authoritarianism can promote development, and examples can also be given of the positive economic performance of countries such as Chile and South Korea under authoritarian, military governments. The economic successes of nonmilitary authoritarian governments such as China, Singapore and

Taiwan are also cited. However, as Freeman (2002) has shown, these are exceptions and do not negate the argument that civil and political freedoms are conducive to economic growth and the attainment of social development goals.

Entrenched inequalities, racism, and discrimination against women and minorities also obstruct social development programs. The problem of distorted development is exacerbated in situations where race and ethnicity are associated with patterns of economic participation. The exclusion of ethnic, religious, and other minority groups from participating fully in the political, social, and economic life of the community has resulted in violence and impeded development programs in many parts of the world, retarding improvements in living standards. The legalized racism of the apartheid regime in South Africa produced huge disparities in living standards between the white minority and the African majority, as well as glaring inequalities in educational, health, and nutritional status, all of which impeded the attainment of social development goals.

The active pursuit of human rights can address these problems and create a social and political climate conducive to realizing both economic and social development goals. Fortunately the importance of addressing factors that impede successful social development efforts are being increasingly recognized, and more emphasis is now being placed on the need to promote democratic institutions, ensure civil liberties, foster good governance, facilitate social integration, and encourage full participation in political and social affairs. Today these activities are seen as integral to social development. As the Copenhagen Declaration and Program of Action adopted at the 1995 World Summit on Social Development stated, "Social development and social justice cannot be an obtained in the absence of peace and security or in the absence of respect for human rights and fundamental freedoms" (para. 5).

Facilitating the Implementation of Social Development Policies and Programs

In addition to clarifying the goals of social development, a rights-based approach can facilitate the implementation of social development policies and programs. This is because formal international human rights instruments, as well as the institutional system of information dissemination, program implementation, and accountability that has been created to promote human rights, both nationally and internationally, can be mobilized to support social development efforts. Both public organizations and NGOs are involved in this task. Although the latter have been primarily concerned with civil and political rights, they have also become involved in the promotion of economic, social, and cultural rights.

Accession to an international human rights treaty through signature and ratification obligates States Parties to comply with the treaty and fulfill its requirements. Most governments that ratify human rights instruments do so with the intention of complying, but ratification does not always result in effective implementation. Some governments have ratified human rights instruments yet flagrantly violated their provisions. Others have ratified but cannot comply, primarily for budgetary reasons. Treaties such as the International Covenant on Economic, Social, and Cultural Rights have many provisions that require major budgetary allocations, and many developing countries simply do not have the resources to meet their obligations. This problem is recognized in the Covenant on Economic, Social, and Cultural Rights, which requires the progressive implementation of its provisions.

Formal mechanisms have been created at the international level to foster the implementation of human rights. In addition to the United Nations Commission on Human Rights and the Office of the High Commissioner for Human Rights, a number of specialized committees have been established to deal with compliance issues. In some cases these committees are authorized under optional protocols to hear complaints. Several UN agencies also offer administrative and logistical support. Some governments have also created mechanisms at the national level that promote the implementation of human rights. Participation in a treaty requires that national law be modified to comply with the treaty, and, for this reason, rights are justiciable through national courts. Of course, many governments have also enacted their own human rights statutes, and many national constitutions contain human rights provisions. In addition, some governments have created human rights commissions, ombudsman offices, and other bodies charged with advising on human rights, educating people about rights, and advocating for human rights. Human rights advocates hope that these efforts will foster the emergence of a culture, nationally and internationally, that institutionalizes human rights. Although this goal is far from being realized, they are optimistic that efforts to promote human rights through-

out the world will garner widespread support and that a "culture of compliance" (Overseas Development Institute, 1993) will evolve and eventually
reduce the necessity for formal legal recourse.

It is in the context of an emerging culture of rights that human rights
instruments can play a critical role in supporting the implementation of
social development policies and programs. By acceding to a human rights
treaty, and being genuine in their commitments, government programs
dealing with education, health, nutrition, maternal well-being, and shelter
are no longer discretionary but have the force of law. This gives programs a
legalistic claim to budgetary and administrative priority, infuses them with
the language and culture of human rights, and integrates programs into
wider human rights efforts. As noted earlier, some governments have used
international treaties such as the Convention on the Rights of the Child to
modify their child welfare programs, and to set specific targets based on the
provisions of this convention. These efforts have fostered the integration
of human rights into government social development programs in some
countries. Moser and Norton (2001) point to the family planning services
of Zimbabwe, which adopted a "charter of rights" based on international
declarations and treaties. This decision has enhanced the program's conventional social service delivery approach by giving women access to services as a right, significantly extending their control over their own fertility.
Although opposed by tribal leaders, the charter is prominently displayed in
all government health centers and family planning clinics, and its adoption
has empowered women to more effectively negotiate the expectations and
demands of their traditional culture.

Despite the claim that economic, social, and cultural rights are not justiciable, many documented examples can be found of the successful use of
legal means of redress. Known as public interest litigation, these cases are
often brought by human rights advocacy organizations working together
with NGOs engaged in social development. The United Nations Development Program (2000) documents the case of a low-income community
in South Africa that obtained redress through the legal system when the
local municipality arbitrarily cut its water supply. The court ruled that
the municipality's action infringed on the community's human rights as
guaranteed under the country's constitution. Another example is the Self-
Employed Women's Association (SEWA) in India, which embarked on a
long but successful litigation campaign that eventually required industries
contracting with home workers to comply with the country's wage and em-

ployment statutes. The result has significantly improved their incomes and living standards (Moser & Norton, 2001). As the Centre for Development and Human Rights (2004) has shown, public interest litigation has been frequently used to promote social development ideals in India in recent years. However, these efforts are not always successful. For example, Cook (2001) reveals that more than a million women die each year because of the complications of pregnancy and childbirth; although the courts in several countries require governments to provide emergency health care or HIV treatment, none has been legally required to offer maternal services that could prevent these unnecessary deaths.

Nevertheless, the use of public interest litigation has an empowering effect, and many low-income and oppressed communities have mobilized toward this end. A good example comes from the efforts of a Palestinian housing association to use the International Covenants on Economic, Social, and Cultural Rights to challenge the Israeli government's land confiscation and house demolition policies. Although the association has had only modest success, it mobilized resistance among local people and shamed the Israeli government into ratifying the convention, and it prides itself on its democratic achievements (Farha, 2001). Molyneux and Lazar's (2003) case studies of rights-based development activities in Latin America provide other examples of the campaigns of local NGOs to secure human rights that directly impact social development.

In addition to these community-based efforts, attempts to implement social development policies and programs have been supported through the advocacy of national and international human rights organizations. As noted earlier, much of this effort has been directed at violations of civil and political rights, but economic and social issues are increasingly being addressed. One example is the advocacy campaigns against multinational corporations that pay low wages and otherwise exploit workers, including child workers, in different parts of the world. These campaigns have also targeted multinationals, particularly in the oil and mineral extraction industries, which have supported brutal regimes that violate human rights. As a result of these activities, public opinion around the world has not only been educated but has mobilized to challenge these activities. Gradually a number of leading multinationals have succumbed to pressure and changed their policies. These efforts have also resulted in the adoption of the 1999 Global Compact, under the auspices of the United Nations and voluntary compliance codes in several countries (Freeman, 2002). Coupled with organized protest and growing popular disquiet with the negative impact of neo-liberal economic globalization policies, efforts to integrate human rights and social development through a rights-based approach may yet enhance the well-being of all the people in the world.

References

Arndt, H.W. (1978). *The rise and fall of economic growth: A study in contemporary thought*. Chicago, IL: University of Chicago Press.

Boeke, J.H. (1953). *Economics and economic policy of dual societies*. Haarlem, Netherlands: Willink.

Bromley, R., & Gerry, C., (Eds.). (1979). *Casual work and poverty in Third World cities*. Chichester: Wiley.

Centre for Development and Human Rights. (2004). *The right to development: A primer*. Thousand Oaks, CA: Sage.

Chenery, H., Ahluwalia, M., Bell, C., Duloy, J. H., and Jolly, R. (1974). Redistribution with Growth. Oxford: Oxford University Press.

Cook. R.J. (2001). Advancing safe motherhood through human rights. In I. Merali & V. Oosterveld (Eds.), *Giving meaning to economic, social and cultural rights* (pp. 109–123). Philadelphia: University of Pennsylvania Press.

Farha, L. (2001). Bringing economic, social and cultural rights home: Palestinians in occupied East Jerusalem and Israel. In I. Merali & V. Oosterveld (Eds.), *Giving meaning to economic, social and cultural rights* (pp. 160–179). Philadelphia: University of Pennsylvania Press.

Freeman, M. (2002). *Human rights*. Malden, MA: Polity.

Green, M. (2002). Social development: Issues and approaches. In U. Kothari & M. Minogue (Eds.), *Development theory and practice* (pp. 52–70). New York: Palgrave.

Higgins, B. (1956). The dualistic theory of underdeveloped areas. *Economic Development and Cultural Change, 4*, 22–115.

Independent Commission on International Development Issues (Brandt Commission). (1980). *North South: A programme for survival*. London: Pan Books.

International Labour Office. (1972). *Employment, incomes and equality: A strategy for increasing productive employment in Kenya*. Geneva: International Labour Office.

International Labour Office. (1976). *Employment, growth and basic needs: A one world problem*. Geneva: International Labour Office.

Ishay, M.R. (2004). *The history of human rights: From ancient times to the globalization era*. Berkeley: University of California Press.

Lewis, W.A. (1955). *The theory of economic growth.* London: Allen & Unwin.

Lloyd, G.A. (1982). Social development as a political philosophy. In D.S. Sanders (Ed.), *The development perspective in social work* (pp. 43–50). Manoa: University of Hawaii Press.

Merali, I., & Oosterveld, V. (Eds.). (2001). *Giving meaning to economic, social and cultural rights.* Philadelphia: University of Pennsylvania Press.

Midgley, J. (1995). *Social development: The developmental perspective in social welfare.* Thousand Oaks, CA, and London: Sage.

Midgley, J. (2003). Social development: The intellectual heritage. *Journal of International Development,* 15(7), 831–844.

Molyneux, M., & Lazar, S. (2003). *Doing the rights thing: Rights-based development and Latin American NGOs.* London: ITDC.

Moser, C., & Norton, A. (2001). *To claim our rights: Livelihood, security, human rights and sustainable development.* London: Overseas Development Institute.

Overseas Development Institute. (1999). *What can we do with a rights based approach to development?* ODI Briefing Paper. London: Overseas Development Institute.

Puta-Checkwe, C., & Flood, N. (2001). From division to integration: Economic, social and cultural rights as basic human rights. In I. Merali & V. Oosterveld (Eds.), *Giving meaning to economic, social and cultural rights* (pp. 39–51). Philadelphia: University of Pennsylvania Press.

Streeten, P., & Burki, S.J. (1978). Basic needs: Some issues, *World Development, 6,* 411–421.

United Nations. (1971). Social policy and planning in national development, *International Social Development Review, 3,* 4–15.

United Nations. (1975). *Popular participation in decision making for development.* New York: United Nations.

United Nations. (1996). *Report of the World Summit for Social Development: Copenhagen, March 6–12, 1995.* New York: United Nations.

United Nations. (2005). *Investing in development: A practical plan to achieve the millennium development goals.* New York: United Nations.

United Nations Development Program. (2000). *Human development report 2000: Human rights and human development.* New York: United Nations.

United Nations Development Program. (2003). *Human development report 2003: Millennium development goals—A contract among nations to end human poverty.* New York: United Nations.

World Commission on Environment and Development (Brundtland Commission). (1987). *Our common future: From one earth to one world.* Geneva.

6

Using Economic Human Rights in the Movement to End Poverty

The Kensington Welfare Rights Union and the Poor People's Economic Human Rights Campaign

MARY BRICKER-JENKINS, CARRIE YOUNG, AND CHERI HONKALA

This chapter argues that economic human rights should have the same legal and moral status as civil and political rights. No subset of human rights can be realized without promoting and protecting the entire set of human rights.

The Plight

When Robin and her three young children lost their apartment because Robin couldn't pay rent and utilities from her $8 per hour job, she and her children moved in with her sister while Robin looked for affordable housing. After three months the sister's landlady said she would have to evict the entire household because of overcrowding if Robin didn't leave, as the landlady had to comply with federal "Section 8" regulations. Wanting to be helpful, the landlady contacted the local child welfare agency. She had read of a new program that provided housing assistance on a priority basis to families who were at risk of having their children placed in foster care without housing assistance. The landlady was told that Robin could get into the program through the city's shelter system. Desperate, Robin agreed to go with the landlady to a family shelter. It was mid-morning. The landlady left for work, promising Robin to give her priority in one of her other subsidized apartments if Robin could "get on the program." Robin and her three children, who had not eaten since breakfast, waited four hours for the shelter intake worker to see them. A child welfare worker arrived just as Robin was about to lose her temper with her hungry, whining toddler. Joni, the child welfare worker, picked up the child to relieve the pressure on the overwhelmed mother. Robin's insides turned to ice; in poor communities, child welfare workers are often more feared than the police. "This was a trick! You came for my kids! You ain't taking my kids!" she screamed.

Joni handed the terrified toddler back to Robin, assuring her that she had come to help Robin get on the housing program. She asked if the family had eaten, and offered to go to the corner market for sandwiches. On the way out she told the uniformed guard to be sure the family did not leave. Upon her return with sandwiches and drinks, Joni explained the program: Robin and the children would stay at the shelter for a while. Joni would "open a case" so Robin could obtain preventative services, and that would make her eligible for the special housing program. There was a waiting list for apartments, so she couldn't say how long the family would be at the shelter.

The family and the child welfare worker waited another hour while Joni went to fill out paperwork to open the case. Finally, five hours after Robin's arrival, the shelter intake worker appeared and asked to speak with Joni. There was no room in the shelter for a woman with three children, she explained. Two might have to be placed in foster care, at least for a few days, but she and the child welfare worker would see what they could do to keep the family together. Frantically the two workers called every shelter in the city looking for space for the family. They tried unsuccessfully to reach Robin's sister's landlady to see if one or two of the children could return to the apartment for a few days. They called the domestic violence shelter, but Robin had no history of domestic violence and was denied service. Meanwhile, Robin called her employer, who told her that he could give her only two days off. After that, he'd have to replace her.

Joni returned to Robin to explain the situation. The best they could do, she said, was to decide together which children would be placed, and she promised to try to place them nearby and together. It was now late in the day. Joni called to alert her supervisor about the need for placement. Robin closed her eyes, and then stared out the window.

The children sensed the tension. Terrified, two clung to their mother while the oldest crossed the room and forcefully pushed another child off the bench that faced the television. The guard approached the children. As he leaned over the child on the floor, Robin scooped up her toddler, and screamed, "Run!" With one child in her arms and two racing behind her, Robin ran into the now dark street, down an alley, and hid behind a dumpster. Later, much later, the family made its way to the one-room apartment of a friend, who said they could stay the night. Huddled together on their friend's couch, Robin tried to explain to the children what had happened.

The next morning Robin's friend went out to get food for Robin and her children. When she came back, she told Robin about a group she had heard about in the neighborhood called the Kensington Welfare Rights Union (KWRU). "It's a group of people who are struggling like us," she explained, "and they help people get places to live without going to the shelters." Robin's friend told of a neighbor who had gone to KWRU when she had been cut off from welfare. The KWRU helped her get her welfare back and her medical assistance, too. They also helped people with food, clothing, and utilities. Robin agreed to go with her friend to the KWRU office to see what they could do.

Later that day Robin and her children arrived at the KWRU office, located in the heart of Kensington—a poor, multiracial, formerly industrial community in North Philadelphia. They were greeted by Lisa, who said she was a member volunteering in the office. She asked Robin to tell her why she had come. When Robin explained the events of the previous day, Lisa shared her own story about being homeless with her children. "I came to this organization when I was homeless, too," she said, "and I learned that I wasn't alone. I also learned that I have rights, including a right to have housing, health care, and other things I need for me and my family to survive." Lisa asked Robin to wait for Mark, one of the leaders of the organization, who was on his way and could help her. Meanwhile she told Robin that the organization had some clothes and food, and if Robin needed anything she was free to help herself. She also showed Robin's children a room with toys where they could play while they waited. They hesitated for a moment to leave their mother, but soon they were happily playing with a few other children in the next room. For the first time in days, Robin started to relax.

Mark arrived a few minutes later and introduced himself to Robin. After Robin told him her story, he explained that he also had come to KWRU a few years before when he was homeless with his family, and that he had won housing through the organization. He explained to Robin that KWRU had a number of houses in Kensington that were called "human rights houses." Sometimes people actually donated houses to the organization, but many of these houses were so-called abandoned houses that were owned by a federal agency called Housing and Urban Development, or HUD. He explained the KWRU position—that the United Nations' Universal Declaration of Human Rights, which the United States signed in 1948, guaranteed that housing was a human right, and that if the government was not providing housing for its people, then groups like the KWRU were prepared to organize and take what they needed.

Robin was apprehensive about living in a house that seemed "illegal," but Mark assured her that she and her children would be safe. They would be sharing the house with a longtime member of the organization who had access to a phone and knew exactly what to do in case there were any problems. He also described the organization's "Underground Railroad," a network of other poor people, students, social workers, doctors, and lawyers, who were part of the organization and would do whatever was necessary to support families living in the human rights houses. In short, Robin and her children would not be alone.

The Fight

Mark began to explain to Robin the way KWRU operated. Robin would not have to pay rent to the organization or meet a long list of criteria in order to obtain housing as was the case in a shelter, but she would be expected to join the organization. In addition to fighting for permanent housing for her family, Robin would fight for other people to obtain housing, health care, and other human rights. Membership meetings were held every Monday night, where she would learn more about the organization and human rights. All the meetings provided child care so that she could bring her children with her to the meetings. Later she could join one of the organization's committees, such as the Education Committee, Local Organizing Committee, Media Committee, or others, where members planned the work of the organization. The KWRU, he explained, was not a social service agency but an organization run and led by poor and homeless people. "No one here earns a salary," he said, "but we work with this organization every day because we are fighting for our rights, for our lives."

Robin told Mark that she needed housing for herself and her children, but that she did not want to go into a shelter and, most important, she

Mary Bricker-Jenkins, Carrie Young, and Cheri Honkala

did not want anyone to take her children away. Robin had never thought of housing as a right, and she wanted to join the organization and learn more while she was fighting for her own right to housing. Mark welcomed her to the organization and made a few calls to arrange for someone with a truck to take Robin, her children, and their belongings to their human rights house. He invited her to attend a movie night that evening at another human rights house, where she could learn more about economic human rights and meet other members of the organization.

During the year that followed, Robin developed her leadership skills:

- She attended many movie nights and other "educationals."
- She participated in food distributions and direct actions at city hall.
- She went to jail for civil disobedience with other KWRU members.
- She testified before a House Select Committee on Economic Human Rights about her plight.
- At the end of the year she joined nineteen other women from Canada and the United States to tell her story to a United Nations official investigating the effects of violations of women's economic human rights around the world.

After two years in the organization, having taken on increased responsibility in several of the committees, Robin was elected to the "War Council," KWRU's policy-making body. Having secured her right to housing, she was helping others do the same; having pursued KWRU's curriculum, Robin had become a leader in the movement to end poverty.

A Brief History of KWRU and the PPEHRC

The Kensington Welfare Rights Union (KWRU) began in the Kensington neighborhood of Philadelphia, the poorest district in Pennsylvania, when a group of mothers on welfare began meeting in a church basement to talk about how recent cuts in welfare and medical assistance would affect their ability to feed themselves and their children. Early members of KWRU distributed flyers and food in front of welfare offices, held educational meetings in the community, organized protests and demonstrations, and set up Tent Cities for homeless families in North Philadelphia.

In 1996 families living in a Tent City called "Ridgeville" (named after

Tom Ridge, then governor of Pennsylvania) decided to march to Harrisburg to meet with the governor to find out what he was going to do to help the thousands of homeless families in Pennsylvania. Arriving in Harrisburg, the families set up "Ridgeville" at the Capitol—first inside its Rotunda and later, after building rules were changed in order to keep the building locked at night, on the Capitol steps and lawn. Families lived there quietly for weeks, explaining to tourists, elected officials, and other passersby why they were there. One day they marched a few miles to the governor's mansion, where families observed that the governor's dogs were better housed and fed than they. Then the governor, still refusing to meet with the families during their nearly two-month wait, ordered the Capitol Police to remove the blankets from those sleeping on the grounds. It was the coldest night of October. Through this experience of being treated as less than human, members of KWRU began to understand and use the language of economic human rights.

This was a critical development in the history of KWRU, for it had become clear that the plight of folks like Robin could not be addressed solely through patchwork reforms in the welfare system. Nor could even the most kind-hearted and skillful social workers like Joni provide resources that simply were not being made available by legislators and those who financed their campaigns. Poverty could not be ameliorated; it had to be ended. The concepts and language of economic human rights provided key elements of the conceptual and strategic apparatus needed to move to the next phase—building a mass social *movement* to end poverty.

KWRU leaders and members began to study the Universal Declaration of Human Rights (UDHR), adopted unanimously and proclaimed by the UN General Assembly on December 10, 1948. They then set out to teach others about it. It became a primary organizing tool of KWRU and, later, of the Poor People's Economic Human Rights Campaign (PPEHRC), the national organization spearheaded by KWRU. While affirming that human rights are indivisible, primary emphasis in organizing is on the articles that encompass economic human rights—Articles 23, 25, and 26 (United Nations, 1948):

ARTICLE 23

(1) Everyone has the right to work, to free choice of employment, to just and favourable conditions of work and to protection against unemployment.

(2) Everyone, without any discrimination, has the right to equal pay for equal work.

(3) Everyone who works has the right to just and favourable remuneration ensuring for himself and his family an existence worthy of human dignity, and supplemented, if necessary, by other means of social protection.

(4) Everyone has the right to form and to join trade unions for the protection of his interests.

ARTICLE 25

(1) Everyone has the right to a standard of living adequate for the health and well-being of himself and of his family, including food, clothing, housing and medical care and necessary social services, and the right to security in the event of unemployment, sickness, disability, widowhood, old age or other lack of livelihood in circumstances beyond his control.

(2) Motherhood and childhood are entitled to special care and assistance. All children, whether born in or out of wedlock, shall enjoy the same social protection.

ARTICLE 26

(1) Everyone has the right to education. Education shall be free, at least in the elementary and fundamental stages. Elementary education shall be compulsory. Technical and professional education shall be made generally available and higher education shall be equally accessible to all on the basis of merit.

(2) Education shall be directed to the full development of the human personality and to the strengthening of respect for human rights and fundamental freedoms. It shall promote understanding, tolerance and friendship among all nations, racial or religious groups, and shall further the activities of the United Nations for the maintenance of peace.

(3) Parents have a prior right to choose the kind of education that shall be given to their children.

Leaders of the emerging movement were drawn to the *concept* of economic human rights, as their absence reflects the daily conditions of increasing numbers of people in the United States, and their fulfillment offers the perceived promise of the United States to its people since the nation's inception. Further, they were drawn to the *instruments* of the UDHR, and especially to its derivative treaty, the Covenant on Economic, Social, and Cultural Rights (United Nations, 1966). Such instruments have, at the very least, legitimacy and moral force in world opinion, and they speak starkly and simply to people, creating a potential basis for unity around a common vision.

Members of KWRU began to train people as human rights monitors and undertook a massive campaign to document economic human rights violations. They then organized a month-long bus tour in June 1998, called "The New Freedom Bus—Freedom from Unemployment, Hunger, and Homelessness." In addition to providing a means of collecting documentation from people living in poverty in urban and rural communities throughout the United States, the bus tour would serve to link the KWRU with other grass-roots organizations interested in working to ensure that economic human rights were guaranteed in America. The final tour stop was New York City, where thousands, led by the New Freedom Riders and representatives from organizations around the country, marched across the George Washington Bridge and down the streets of Manhattan to the United Nations to present the documentation. At a tribunal organized by KWRU, experts on international and constitutional law, social welfare, and labor listened to marchers' testimony. These experts then declared that the United States government was in fact guilty of violating the economic human rights of its citizens.

Following the New Freedom Bus Tour, people from more than forty states and Puerto Rico met at Temple University in Philadelphia for a "Poor People's Summit." Out of the Bus Tour and Summit was born the Poor People's Economic Human Rights Campaign. Over the next few years, as the structure of the PPEHRC and the growth of the membership continued, KWRU and PPEHRC continued to organize locally, nationally, and, increasingly, internationally. Member organizations pursued their own agendas consistent with their local analyses and missions but came together around joint events that spoke to their common cause: claiming economic human rights.

In October 1999 KWRU and other PPEHRC organizations were joined by representatives from Canada and Central and South America on a March of the Americas. Beginning in Washington, DC, the march culminated a month later in New York City with a conference focused on organization and education for building the movement. During the conference PPEHRC leaders formally established its Steering Committee. The loose coalition spearheaded by KWRU was becoming a formal national organization.

The next major PPEHRC event was a massive march down Broad Street in Philadelphia on the opening day of the 2000 Republican National Convention. The Democrat mayor, eager to please his Republican guests, ordered official opposition to the march. City child welfare authorities warned KWRU and PPEHRC leaders that their social workers would be present if the march took place; they would take children into custody if they were perceived to be "at imminent risk of serious harm"—that is, if riot police moved to break up the "illegal" march and make arrests. Nevertheless, thousands of people marched down Broad Street, crowds swelling behind the poor— the only group that had been denied a permit to march. Leading up to the march, a week-long Tent City, dubbed "Bushville," housed and educated leaders of the march in movement strategy and tactics. Thus the University of the Poor (UP), launched at the culmination of the 1999 March of the Americas, fully implemented as the national education arm of PPEHRC. Although not a university with credentials or one able to offer degrees, the UP is nevertheless at the core of a movement that views education and organizing as essential, interrelated elements in the progression of the movement.

Over the next few years the many schools of the University of the Poor were established, using the web for communication, exchanging "educationals" among PPEHRC member organizations and helping them develop political education for their members. Many PPEHRC organizations undertook statewide marches and national campaigns. For example, the Oakland-based Women's Economic Agenda Project (WEAP) organized a statewide New Freedom Bus Tour, helping to establish Economic Human Rights Committees throughout California. In Pennsylvania KWRU joined with the Pennsylvania Chapter of the National Association of Social Workers and a visionary state legislator to undertake statewide organizing around economic human rights; the coalition used legislative hearings and a resolution as a tool—the first state resolution to legitimate economic human rights as standards for evaluating social programs (Bricker-Jenkins, 2004). The Florida-based Coalition of Immokalee Workers (CIW) organized the "Taco Bell Truth Tour" and a successful national Taco Bell Boy-

Using Economic Human Rights in the Movement to End Poverty

cott. PPEHRC groups from around the country also joined two Utah-based organizations, Mormons for Economic and Social Justice (MESJ) and JEDI Women, in protests and demonstrations during the 2002 Winter Olympics, held in Salt Lake City.

Eight years after its inception, PPEHRC has grown to include more than a hundred organizations, community groups, and nonprofit organizations concerned with economic human rights in urban, suburban, and rural communities throughout the United States. Most member organizations are community-based and led by people living in poverty. Annual joint events, national in scope and representation, provide opportunities for the formal structure and leadership of PPEHRC to evolve while underscoring the commonality of social, political, and economic challenges faced by member organizations. They galvanize attention of the participants—and the press—to the systematic denial of economic human rights in the United States and to those who benefit from this denial of rights. Events have included the following:

- a second national Freedom Bus Tour that crossed the country between November 10 and December 10, 2002 (the anniversary of the UDHR);
- a Poor People's March for Economic Human Rights through the South, in August 2003, commemorating the Thirty-fifth Anniversary of the 1998 Poor People's March which Martin Luther King was organizing when he was assassinated
- a second successful march, in August 2004, on opening day of the 2004 Republican National Convention in New York City
- a week-long University of the Poor Leadership School, in July 2005, which brought together at Bryn Mawr College more than a hundred leaders of PPEHRC member organizations from across America for classes, workshops, and other activities
- a National Truth Commission, in July 2006, in Cleveland, Ohio, where a panel of international and domestic commissioners heard and evaluated testimony on violations on the rights to housing, health, education, water, and other basic needs, and on the removal of children from their homes, or the failure to return children to their homes, as a result of the government's failure to meet families' economic human rights

Mary Bricker-Jenkins, Carrie Young, and Cheri Honkala

Analysis and Strategy in the Movement to End Poverty

In 1967 Martin Luther King asserted that it was "necessary for us to realize that we have moved from the era of civil rights to human rights" (King Jr. 1967, May). Proposing mass action by people of all colors, Reverend King stated:

> There are millions of poor people in this country who have very little, or even nothing, to lose. If they can be helped to take action together, they will do so with a freedom and a power that will be a new and unsettling force in our complacent national life. (King Jr., 1967, p. 60)

In the spring of 1968, before he could lead his envisioned Poor People's March to Washington to demand that the government ensure all human rights, Dr. King was murdered.

The Poor People's Economic Human Rights Campaign has taken up the program Reverend King proposed, as seen in its mission statement:

> The Poor People's Economic Human Right's Campaign is committed to the unity of the poor across color lines as the leadership base for a broad movement to abolish poverty. We work to accomplish this through advancing economic human rights as named in the Universal Declaration of Human Rights—such as the rights to food, housing, health, education, communication and a living wage job.

Both Dr. King and PPEHRC emphasize the strategic imperative of the *unity of the poor*, but changes in the objective conditions in the United States (and the world) have, in the decades since Reverend King was organizing, given new meaning to this mandate. We have moved from an industrial age to a global, electronically based economic system that has resulted in an ever widening gap between rich and poor, increases in the percentage of "officially" poor, as defined by federal guidelines, and the production of what we refer to as a "new class of poor." This "new class" is comprised of people who have followed all the rules to achieve "middle-class" status and yet now find themselves overwhelmed with debt, working longer hours for lesser wages, and either permanently displaced or threatened with possible displacement. In the new economy, the dictum that, with economic growth, "a rising tide lifts all boats," is no longer true. Even as vast fortunes are amassed by a global "elite," the boats of the "backbone worker" in the United States are sinking.

In working for the *unity of the poor*, PPEHRC embraces both those currently living in "official" poverty and the "new class of poor"—the employed and unemployed struggling to meet their basic needs. Strategically this leads to working with unions, displaced workers, and "welfare populations"; emphasizing the task of organizing in small towns and cities where plant closings devastate entire communities, and thus conditions lend themselves to fashioning unity across "class lines" and between "poor" and "worker"; and stressing the high cost of health care, which threatens the financial stability of millions, and the inadequacy of health care insurance that reveals the inability of government and corporations to deliver on the American Dream—the goal they promote to buy loyalty from labor. Through this work we foster the development of a subjective consciousness that is in line with today's objective conditions, a consciousness that enables effective political struggle.

Organizing and uniting the poor *across color lines* is, as Dr. King understood, strategically imperative. Despite some instances of remarkable unity, the use of racism and ethnic-based "pride," has, throughout U.S. history, vitiated efforts to organize across color and obscured common class interests. As the new economy produces both abundance for some and abandonment for many, however, it is increasingly clear that the abandoned share a new equality, an equality of poverty. Our educational program focuses on the history of the use of race-based stereotypes, myths, and fears in the effort to disrupt movements, and we strongly emphasize organizing among poor white populations. To prepare the nation for the shredding of the welfare state, and the fabric of rights and entitlements from which it was woven, President Ronald Reagan created the myth of the "welfare queen," implicitly fat, hyper-fertile, and black. In contrast, we hold up the true picture of poverty: a group of people of many colors struggling to care for themselves, their families of diverse composition, and their depleted communities.

We believe that the *leadership base* for the movement must be comprised of people with no stake in the status quo, namely, the poor as a united and organized force. Professional advocates, particularly those who make their living in the social welfare system, have a stake only in "reducing, managing, or moderating" poverty, not ending it. For those who do well from their investments (including labor) in the economy, poverty is raw material in the productive enterprise. If we are to *end* poverty, we must pursue a vision and program fashioned from the experience of the poor—experience examined collectively to develop a political consciousness and commitment to meeting everyone's basic needs. This leadership base—those with no stake in the status quo—are the core of Reverend King's "unsettling force."

This does not mean that all leaders in the movement must live in poverty. It does mean, however, that the leaders of PPEHRC *identify* with the *program* of the poor, that is, the effort to protect and promote everyone's economic human rights. A basic assumption in PPEHRC strategy is that we are at a very early stage of building the movement and must therefore focus on "panning for gold," looking for and developing people from all sectors of the population who will study and advance the program of the poor. Robin's story, related at the beginning of this chapter, illustrates this process of leadership development.

Advancing economic human rights, as previously stated, is both a conceptual framework and a primary organizing tool in PPEHRC's work. Again, Robin's story illustrates this. Redefining social conditions from "individual deficits" to "collective denial of human rights" challenges the "blame and shame" dynamic that justifies institutional repudiation of rights and shuts down action to claim them. Encouraging people to reframe their stories, relating them in terms of human rights, conveys the message that "you are important and are not to blame for all that has happened to you. Come join others who share the same story—and the same dreams."

The language of "poverty" is so tainted and toxic that it is difficult for people who are using it—particularly with reference to themselves—to conceive of the poor as worthy and, when united, able to participate in the decisions that profoundly shape their lives. The language of "rights," on the other hand, expresses a universal longing, a legitimate collective claim of humanity on the prerequisites for a life of dignity. The language of rights has particular potency in the United States, of course, where rights denied have historically moved people to action. Thus PPEHRC's educational work and materials use the language of economic human rights to underscore the indivisibility of economic human rights from other human rights stipulated in UN instruments.

Another strategic implication of the use of a human rights framework is that action to claim any economic right—safe and affordable housing, health, livable wages, water, and so forth—can reveal both the structural nature of the denial of human rights by government and corporations and the inherent unity of interest between so-called poor, working-class, and middle-class people. Nowhere is this clearer today than in the struggle for health care (mental as well as physical); thus, for example, PPEHRC strategically focuses intensively on the right to health.

Not all the approximately one hundred-member organizations of PPEHRC have the same structure or type of program, nor do they all focus exclusively or even primarily on economic human rights, but they all agree to endorse and, as resources allow, participate in the collective work of the campaign. Gradually and strategically, the language and concepts of human rights are being infused at the grass-roots level into the discourse of conditions in the country today.

Roles for Social Workers in the Movement for Economic Human Rights

Since its inception, social workers have been active in this wave of the movement to abolish poverty. They have worked as allies, coalition partners, interns, members, and leaders, many moving along this spectrum from "supporter" to immersion in the work of KWRU and other PPEHRC organizations.

As allies, social workers have made referrals to PPEHRC organizations, contributed money and supplies, carried out fund raising, conducted research, exposed their colleagues and students to the organizations and PPEHRC literature, organized and attended trainings and lectures on economic human rights and social work, and spoken out in their agencies and communities when PPEHRC organizations and members were trivialized, marginalized, or under attack.

As coalition partners, social workers and their organizations have joined PPEHRC in legislative actions, marches and demonstrations, and other efforts to secure resources and rights. In New Jersey, for example, labor unions, social workers, and a PPEHRC organization (Poor Voices United, which was co-founded by a social worker) came together to work for health care, producing a documentary film with the assistance of the Media College of the University of the Poor. Coalition partners and allies have created opportunities in their organizations, schools, newsletters, and conferences for their members to learn about the movement.

Scores of social work students have done internships and field placements in PPEHRC organizations, involving themselves in all aspects of the work from case advocacy to major event organizing. Two such students learned to document economic human rights violations and, from that base, wrote the legislative resolution that passed in Pennsylvania. Students that followed them organized hearings and, ultimately, the PPEHRC-PA statewide organization. Many students began their involvement in such organizations as the Underground Railroad, established in 1995 at Temple University School of Social Administration as a KWRU ally, members declaring that they were "partners in crime" in a system that was rapidly criminalizing the poor.

Many former students and interns became members of KWRU and other PPEHRC organizations around the country, joining with faculty and agency-based social workers to take on increasing responsibility in the organizations. Staffing committees, offering workshops, lectures, and "reality tours," working with families in crisis, doing administrative and research tasks, chairing study groups, sometimes going to jail—all these responsibilities, among others, are carried out within PPEHRC organizations by social workers committed to advancing the program of the organized poor. Nationally, the Social Welfare Action Alliance (SWAA) has been accepted as a member organization of PPEHRC and is represented on its Coordinating Council.

Some social workers have become leaders in the movement, committing themselves to carrying out major responsibilities. Several organizations were co-founded by social workers. One such group, Women in Transition in Kentucky, has taken leadership in the Claiming our Rights/Reclaiming our Children (CORROC) initiative, working to prevent unjust removal of children from poor families, ensuring effective representation in Family Courts, and promoting timely and adequate reunification services. They are assisted by members of the University of the Poor School of Social Work and Social Transformation (SSW&ST), which has also developed and delivered workshops and lectures on economic human rights and the movement to abolish poverty across the nation. SSW&ST members have also conducted research in support of the movement, publishing in professional literature and newsletters. Finally, members of the SSW&ST are working to articulate an organically emerging approach to social work practice based in an economic human rights framework, one that is being used in clinical settings, child welfare agencies, youth settings, and elsewhere.

Clearly, an economic human rights framework for social work has the potential that few other approaches have had for enabling us to fulfill our ethical mandate to work for social and economic justice.

References

Bricker-Jenkins, M. (2004). Legislative tactics in a movement strategy: The Economic Human Rights–Pennsylvania Campaign. *Meridians, 4*(1), 108–113.

Bricker-Jenkins, M., & Baptist, W. (2006). The movement to end poverty in the United States. In Howard-Hassman, R.E., & Welch, C.E., Jr. (Eds.). *Economic rights in Canada and the United States* (pp. 103–117). Philadelphia: University of Pennsylvania Press.

King Jr., M.L. (1967). Speech at the staff retreat [of the Southern Christian Leadership Conference (SCLC)] at Penn Center, Frogmore, SC. Mimeographed transcript (p. 2). Available at the Rev. Martin Luther King Jr. Archives, Atlanta, GA.

King Jr., M.L. (1967, May). *The trumpet of conscience.* New York: Harper & Row.

United Nations. (1948). *Universal declaration of human rights.* Adopted December 10, 1948, GA Res. 217 AIII (Un Doc. a/810).

United Nations. (1966). *International covenant on economic, social, and cultural rights.* Adopted December 16, 1966. GA Res 2200A XXI. Retrieved January 14, 2004, from www.unhchr.ch/html/menu3/b/a_cescr.htm.

Economic and Social Rights

The Neglected Human Rights

SILVIA STAUB-BERNASCONI

A primary conception of human rights is that they are indivisible and inter-dependent, meaning that no single human right is more or less important than another. In practice, however, individual human rights have been any-thing but equal: economic and social human rights continually occupy a second level of rights, especially below political and civil human rights. In the words of Steiner and Alston (2000, p. 238):

> [There is a] shocking reality . . . that States and the international commu-nity as a whole continue to tolerate all too often breaches of economic, social and cultural rights which if they occurred in relation to civil and political rights, would provoke expressions of horror and outrage and would lead to concerted calls for immediate remedial action. In effect, despite the rhetoric, violations of civil and political rights continue to be treated as though they were far more serious, and more patently intoler-able, than massive and direct denials of economic, social and cultural rights. . . . Statistical indicators of the extent of deprivation, or breaches, of economic, social and cultural rights have been cited so often that they have tended to lose their impact. The magnitude, severity and constan-cy of that deprivation have provoked attitudes of resignation, feelings of

helplessness and compassion fatigue. Such muted responses are facilitated by a reluctance to characterize the problems that exist as gross and massive denials of economic, social and cultural rights. Yet it is difficult to understand how the situation can realistically be portrayed in any other way. (UN Doc, E/199/22, Annex III, paras. 5 and 7)

Most international nongovernmental organizations (NGOs), as well as national governments, have neglected economic and social human rights, and concentrated mainly on torture, arbitrary detention, and capital punishment. Without belittling the importance of civil and political rights, perhaps the following question highlights the fallacy of relegating economic and social rights to the background: What permanent achievement is there in saving people from torture, only to find that they are killed by famine or disease that could have been prevented had the will and appropriate controls been in place? Thus grave cases of corruption may also imply violations of economic, social, and cultural rights (Eide & Rosas, 2001, p. 7).

Taking economic, social and cultural rights seriously requires a commitment to social integration and a response to the complex question of income distribution and the national gross product. Economic, social, and cultural human rights apply to all persons but especially economically vulnerable groups and individuals, such as the unemployed, the working poor, children, the disabled, cultural minorities, and indigenous peoples. Unfortunately vulnerable persons often serve as scapegoats, made possible by existing prejudices: "The individuals in question must appear to be too weak to fight back successfully when attacked. And . . . the society must sanction the scapegoating through its own institutional structures" (Saenger, 1953, quoted in Adams, Blumenfeld, Castaneda, Hackmanh, Peters, & Zuniga, 2000, p. 24). As long as economic, social, and cultural rights are insufficiently institutionalized, satisfaction of basic needs rests not on a mandate but on the mercy of governmental policies and programs.

Considering the current decline of the nation-state and welfare state in Western, economically advanced countries, as well as ongoing economic struggles in Third World countries, the importance of mandated economic, social, and cultural human rights can only increase. New actors, like international financial and development institutions, the private sector, and local government will be responsible for the integration of social rights into policies and programs. Thus economic, social, and cultural rights will and should play an important role in "keeping the notion of universal solidarity" on the world agenda and in "working for the betterment of the lives of vulnerable and excluded individuals and groups" (Eide & Rosas, 2001, p. 6).

This chapter traces the historical origins of the inferior status now occupied by economic, social, and cultural rights within the overall human rights structure. In taking the position that these neglected rights are as important as political and civil rights, the chapter provides criteria for a just society and guidelines for social workers to promote neglected rights.

Historical Dissent Over the Proper Status of Economic and Social Rights

After completing its work on the Universal Declaration of Human Rights in 1947, the United Nations Commission on Human Rights started to draft conventions on human rights that would be legally binding, as opposed to the nonbinding, inspirational role of the Declaration. The Commission could not decide whether to establish only one covenant that would reflect all articles in the Declaration or two covenants that would separate civil and political from economic, social, and cultural rights.

In 1950 the UN General Assembly passed a resolution to emphasize the interdependence of all human rights and called on the Commission to adopt a single convention. However, the United States and Western European states then pressured the Commission to draft two separate covenants, one on civil and political rights and the other on economic, social, and cultural rights (Eide & Rosas, 2001, p. 3). Yet the official position on human rights doctrine is that human rights are "universal, indivisible, interdependent and interrelated" and that the international community must treat them in a fair and equal manner, "on the same footing, and with the same emphasis" (Vienna Declaration, 1993, para. 5).

This formal consensus masks a deep and enduring disagreement over the proper status of economic, social, and cultural rights. At one extreme, promoted by the former Soviet Union and many developing countries, economic rights have greater social value than civil and political rights. At the other extreme, the United States is in the forefront of claiming that economic and social rights do not even constitute rights. Treating them as rights undermines the enjoyment of individual freedom, distorts the functioning of free markets by justifying large-scale state intervention in the economy, and provides an excuse to downgrade the importance of civil and political rights (Steiner & Alston, 2000, p. 237).

> Those who were in favor of drafting a single covenant maintained that human rights could not be clearly divided into different categories, nor could they be so classified as to represent a hierarchy of values. All rights should be promoted and protected at the same time. . . . Those in favor of drafting two separate covenants argued that civil and political rights were enforceable, or justiciable, or of an "absolute" character, while economic, social and cultural rights were not or might not be; that the former were immediately applicable, while the latter were to be progressively implemented; and that, generally speaking, the former were rights of the individual "against" the State, that is, against unlawful and unjust action of the State, while the latter were rights which the State would have to take positive action to promote. (Steiner & Alston, 2000, p. 244)

Listed below are some of the arguments that initially framed the discussion centering on whether to fully recognize economic and social human rights:

AGAINST LEGAL STATUS OF ECONOMIC AND SOCIAL RIGHTS
- Freedom must be freedom from something; economic and social rights require the state to take positive action, not refrain from acting.
- Economic and social rights require the state to define what the happiness of its people must be and so are apt to result in a coercive benefactor (e.g., the former Soviet Union).

FOR LEGAL STATUS OF ECONOMIC AND SOCIAL RIGHTS
- The right to life is illusory without a right to the protection of means by which life can be lived; democracy without socioeconomic development has often led to fascism, racism, and generally to the negation of freedom.
- Certainly if the state dictated people's lifestyles, thinking, social mores, and speech, enforcement of economic and social rights could be coercive; however, a more reasonable view is that by promoting

these rights the state would do what it already does, which is to facilitate infrastructure, partially regulate economic investments, and provide education, health care, and other necessary services without discrimination.

Yet, after much discussion within the Commission, the question of drafting one or two covenants became more pragmatic than anything else, and centered on implementation. Civil and political rights were generally thought to be "legal" rights best be implemented by the creation of a good offices committee, whereas economic, social, and cultural rights were thought to be "program" rights best implemented by establishing a system of periodic reports. Because the rights could be divided into two broad categories, each subject to different procedures of implementation, it would be both logical and convenient to formulate two separate covenants (Annotations on the Text of the Draft International Covenants on Human Rights, UN Doc.A/2929 [1955], at 7) (Steiner & Alston, 2000, pp. 244–245). The result of creating two covenants with one emphasizing legal enforcement (political and civil rights) is now obvious: civil and political human rights generally have more importance than economic, social, and cultural human rights.

Current Status of Economic, Social, and Cultural Rights

On a regional level, various charters or mission statements include economic, social, and cultural rights as guiding principles. For example, the European Social Charter, the Additional Protocol of the American Convention on Human Rights, and the African Charter on Human and People's Rights all include economic and social rights (Ishay, 1997). Yet in Europe and elsewhere enforcement of those rights appears weak. Applicants for membership in the Council of Europe must ratify the European Convention on Human Rights, but they are not required to give assurances regarding the European Social Charter. The Organization of American States adopted an additional protocol in 1988 (the "Protocol of San Salvador") that included economic and social rights, but not all countries supported it, with only eleven out of a possible twenty-five having approved it (Steiner & Alston, 2000, p. 249).

Although recognizing the importance of economic and social rights at least superficially, most countries did not openly criticize the inclusion of those rights in charters and other guiding documents. The only blatant hostility to this group of rights has come from the United States, whose attitudes have varied considerably from one administration to another. Certainly the current status of those rights in the United States is one of outright neglect (Steiner & Alston, 2000).

Perhaps the most curious aspect of economic and social rights has occurred in the East European countries that were formerly part of the Soviet bloc, which held economic and social human rights on the same plane as civil and political ones. After the fall of communism in 1989, East Europe had the opportunity to integrate a more liberal version of social rights with Western civil and political rights, but this has not occurred. The following is a convoluted rationale used by former proponents of economic and social rights to now diminish those rights:

> If we look at the actual and proposed constitutions for Eastern Europe, we will find a truly dazzling array of social and economic rights. . . . I think that this is a large mistake, possibly a disaster. It seems clear that Eastern European countries should use their constitutions to produce two things: (a) firm liberal rights . . . and (b) the preconditions for some kind of market economy. The endless catalogue of what I will be calling "positive rights," many of them absurd, threatens to undermine both of these important tasks. Three qualifications are necessary at the outset. First, the argument against these rights applies with distinctive force to countries in the unique position of transition from Communism to a market economy. . . . Second, there is a big difference between what a decent society should provide and what a good constitution should guarantee. A decent society ensures that its citizens have food and shelter; it *tries* to guarantee medical care; it is concerned to offer good education, good jobs, and a clean environment . . . Third, not all positive rights are the same. The right to education, for example, is more readily subject to judicial enforcement than the right to a clean environment. Some of the relevant rights pose especially severe risks; others are relatively harmless. But I believe that few of them belong in Eastern European constitutions. Here's why: Governments should not be compelled to interfere with free markets . . . For countries that are trying to create market economies,

this is perverse. ... Many positive rights are unenforceable by courts. Courts lack the tools of a bureaucracy. They cannot create government programs ... The inclusion of many positive rights could work against general current efforts to diminish sense of entitlement to state protection and to encourage individual initiative.

... In these circumstances ... I suggest three routes for the future. First, people now drafting constitutions for Eastern Europe should delete or minimize provisions that call for positive rights. ... Second, (they) might put the positive rights in a separate section ... making clear that such rights are not for judicial enforcement ... Third, judges and lawyers in Eastern Europe ... might adopt the notion that rights are "nonjusticiable"—not subject to judicial enforcement—when they call for large-scale interference with the operation of free markets, or when they call for managerial tasks not within judicial competence. Any such notion must, however, make it clear that courts will vigorously enforce the basic political and civil rights whose violation was a daily affair under Communist rule—rights such as free speech, religious liberty, freedom from police abuse, due process, and nondiscrimination on grounds of ethnicity, race, religion, and sex. (Steiner & Alston, 2000, pp. 280–282)

Considering the above dominant thought in East Europe, no former Soviet bloc country has incorporated economic and social rights into its constitution. Nor have Western European countries done so. In some European countries those rights have the status of programs. In most countries, however, they are part of the welfare state that guarantees differing levels of social security. All European countries now have to cope with "globalization" and economies that are internationally oriented. Government, business, and many individuals view as undesirable the high taxes that could guarantee a decent level of social insurance, medical aid, and social welfare. This anti-tax view has created an ever increasing theme that extensive social benefits have simply become unaffordable.

Why Have Economic and Social Rights Become "Leftovers" of Civil and Political Rights: A Hidden Gender Bias?

Virtually all major religions manifest concern for the poor and oppressed (Ishay, 1997, pp. 1–72). Religious teachings highlight the need of those who are well off to give to the less fortunate. Political and philosophical writings from authors as diverse as Kant, Rousseau, Paine, Marx, and John Rawls are other secular sources promoting similar ideas (ibid., pp. 73–232). Considering the clear precedent of economic and social rights within religious, political, and philosophical teachings, why have those rights not received the same stature as political and civil rights? Thomas Marshall, a sociologist-economist at the London School of Economics, rarely cited in American literature, provides a historical analysis that answers this question (Marshall, 1992/1982).

In feudal societies men defined justice and participation in society. Rights granted were strictly local and bound to the societal status and norms of the work or profession to which they belonged. This basis for participation within society favored men, who occupied all significant labor positions. Individuals (serfs) bound to property owners had no rights, as was usually also the case with women. As nations and states began to develop, laws began to become national in scope. The French Revolution in the late eighteenth century was instrumental in abolishing slavery, involuntary servitude, and hereditary bondage, which led to the concept of free labor and the freedom to make contracts in a free market. Serfs fled to the cities and were declared free and equal, but still not all men enjoyed political and civil rights. These were reserved only for those who owned land or a business, were economically successful, or were allowed to wear a weapon. The societal structure kept women under tutelage. Women had no rights at all; they had the obligation to obey their husband who was the one to decide where they would and whether a wife should work:

> The husband is the guardian of the wife by law. He is entitled to spend and enjoy the fortune of his wife. The interests and the additional gains of her fortune and what his wife earns by her labor are property of the husband. (Zürcher Privatgesetzbuch Paragraph 138; in Joris, 1997, p. 85)

Thus men essentially controlled women's lives and had the right to determine the use of the woman's income and property.

Although women, as well as men, initiated the French Revolution, after the revolution men quickly sent women back home. As before the revolution, women had no right to education, property, or access to participation in public affairs. The justification was that family harmony would be destroyed if men and women had equal rights; moreover, because women and children are considered weak and vulnerable, men must protect them, thus eliminating their "right to have rights." Similar views about the authority of men over women existed within major religious documents and teachings (e.g., the Qur'an states that men are entitled to exercise authority over women and not the reverse) (Abdullah Ahmed An-Na'im; in Steiner & Alston, 2000, p. 394). This may be well intentioned by some men, but the power to protect can be associated with the power to discriminate and exploit, with no possibility for the powerless to claim (social) justice.

The historical status of male dominance in many societies shaped the development and emphasis of today's human rights. In contrast to the establishment of men's political and civil rights, which became nationally and constitutionally protected, a different history transpired in relation to economic and social rights. The source of social rights in Europe was membership in local communities, where community members assisted one another in time of need, and the concept of reciprocal help was partially institutionalized in cooperatives. As the numbers of poor persons increased as a result of famines, local wars, and other societal breakdowns, so-called poor laws replaced reciprocity and self-help. Poor laws provided minimal assistance to needy individuals outside the family but were not seen as social entitlements. Those laws remained local in scope. Had national governments incorporated poor laws into their constitutions as guaranteed rights, property owners and other wealthy individuals would have viewed those rights as infringing upon the liberal market economy from which governments were not to interfere. Also, poor laws were the antithesis of political and civil rights. Poor laws belonged to the hated feudal society, reminiscent of local feudal instead of universal principles. Political and civil rights belonged to the enlightened society and its great promises of freedom, national and international progress, and wealth. Except for the right to primary education, especially for boys, no other economic or social right obtained legal status.

In the second half of the nineteenth century, the growing misery and distress of the labor class led to the notion that political and civil rights did not guarantee a free life. This notion challenged the superiority status of political and civil rights. If an individual does not have the economic means to pursue happiness or go to court and receive justice, any political right is, in effect, a mockery. Slowly this budding challenge to the primacy of political rights gave rise to the idea that everyone had the right to a living standard based not on economic market value but on an individual's inherent human value and dignity.

Behind this still present asymmetry between political and social rights lies a well-hidden historical gender bias. The concealed, hegemonic logic of gender relations—free autonomous man versus woman under guardianship—continues to exist as a subtext in social welfare policies and in many religious texts.

Gender-Based Rights in Different Social Welfare Systems

As the concept of social welfare developed, the gender bias in policies of social insurance and assistance became clear. Two distinct models have evolved: (1) the masculine interpretation or pattern of social rights, and (2) the feminine interpretation or pattern of social rights (Fraser, 1994).

Masculine Interpretation of Social Rights

The masculine interpretation or pattern of social rights defines individuals as free and autonomous citizens who bear rights. Individuals maintain their status as autonomous consumers who decide for themselves how to manage their income. Social insurance with a masculine orientation has the following characteristics:

- Rules apply nationally
- Payments are the same nationwide
- Access to insurance requires only a small amount of bureaucracy, without a means-and-needs-test
- Payments are sent to individuals
- Weak or nonexistent control over what the recipient of insurance does with the payments
- Little control over social relationships, such as new female acquaintances of divorced men

Individuals who receive social insurance under the masculine pattern are defined as "possessing individuals." They are subjects making rational market choices, and have the freedom and competence to make the best bargains. On the whole they have more rights than duties.

Feminine Interpretation of Social Rights

Under the feminine interpretation or pattern of social rights, the hidden gender bias previously discussed plays a large role in defining economic and social benefits. This pattern has the following characteristics:

- Welfare programs are mostly the result of political bargaining on the local level
- Welfare programs greatly differ in financial assistance
- Many programs are voluntarily if eligible persons earn less than the poverty level
- Access to a program requires extensive paperwork, imposes a long waiting time, and is means-tested
- Control over expenditures and lifestyle often exists; the state assumes the controlling function of the husband and wants to know if there is a new man in the family and may even inspect the applicant's home, possibly violating the woman's right to privacy
- Assistance often occurs as an in-kind benefit, not as financial aid

Individuals—mostly women with children—who receive economic and social assistance are defined as the alternative to "possessing, autonomous individuals." Government and society do not view these individuals as citizens able to make rational choices. They are not persons with individual needs, but members of an incomplete or failed/destroyed family, mothers with duties who lost control and protection of their husband or partner and thus have to be controlled by the state. If the former husband/father cannot pay support for the children, he is not required to go to the public aid office and be subjected to the myriad of control mechanisms. Instead, it is the woman/mother who is left to pursue relief. When public assistance ends, the mother is forced to work without the support of a social day care structure for her children; this would require the implementation of some social rights especially for women. The mother, not the delinquent father or partner, loses the entitlement for welfare after a couple of months or years.

Welfare programs constructed under the feminine pattern are not inspired by human rights but harbor a deep mistrust of women's competencies and derive their policies from the principle notions of begging, humiliation, dependency, and control. Yet, even in contrast to the beggar, who is free to do what he or she wants with the received money, welfare recipients depend on the prevailing political constellation and mood.

The underlying message of the masculine versus feminine pattern of social rights is that one segment of individuals can benefit from autonomy and ego-centered care, whereas the other receives little empathy and care, an inequality often supported by law. The thinking is that those unable to care for themselves who must depend on the state should be punished. The problem is not unwanted pregnancy, poverty, or unemployment but rather dependency. And this justifies the guardianship, not only for women but also for men with little income. Instead of developing the idea that all human beings have a social right to live decently, independent of their societal contribution, modern thought about social rights centers on how to hinder the legalization and implementation of social rights. Even where economic benefits exist, reducing those benefits and routing out "cheaters" occupies the powers that be (see the summary of national studies on food stamp practices reported in the New York Times, August 12, 2000).

Economic and social human rights have yet to reshape power relations for a better world as occurred with political and civil rights. Governments and the well off perceive these positive rights as obstacles to the exercise of real power, especially over the resources of the world. They perceive such rights as threats coming from insatiable, deceptive individuals who simply want to cheat the system and possibly overturn the government. Yet precisely these rights—education, food, employment, decent housing, and medical care—would make at least the same contribution as political and civil rights to a safer and more secure world.

What Is a Just Society?

The historical origins of the determination of governments and leading policy makers to elevate political and civil human rights over economic, social, and cultural human rights are important to understand from both policy and practical viewpoints. Social workers can hardly begin to implement economic, social, and cultural rights without appreciating why current policies fail to adequately reflect key human rights principles. However, knowing the historical origins of human rights establishes only a foundation for social work policy and practice. The next step requires an examination of what we mean by a just society, and by social justice, which is a key component of social work values.

Characteristics of a Just Society

The departing point in defining a just society is in Article 29 of the UN Universal Declaration of Human Rights: "Everyone is entitled to a social and international order in which the rights and freedoms set forth in this Declaration can be fully realized" (UN Declaration, 1948, Art. 29).

·A just society has extensive interconnections between the enjoyment of civil and political rights and the appreciation of basic economic and social rights. Individuals can only realize freedom and political participation if they are freed of always balancing precariously on the edge of financial disaster. On the other hand, enjoying economic and social rights without political and civil rights clearly is paternalistic in its mildest form but autocratic and authoritarian in the logical extreme. The extreme situation leads to the unacceptable condition in which society must first provide economic rights while suppressing political rights. The former Soviet Union, with its suppression of political and civil freedoms, is an example of this extreme position. A just society must also avoid the temptation to provide social justice only for its members; this is an ethnocentric view. Each society is part of a world society and needs to view social justice as both an external and internal factor.

To be internally just, a society recognizes the following characteristics (Bunge, 1987, p. 372f):

- Every member of the society receives what she requires to meet her basic needs;
- Every member can earn, by doing socially useful work, what she requires to satisfy legitimate aspirations;
- Every member fulfills the obligations assigned her by family, workplace, and social circle(s)—assignments which, in the case of adults, are made by mutual agreement;

- Every member is free to satisfy her or his legitimate aspirations and to pursue inclinations that are not antisocial.

To promote the above characteristics, an internally just society allows every member to work toward those characteristics, whether alone or in association with others.

To be externally just, a society must not hinder the development of other societies and must actively contribute to the development of those societies.

A just society must be both internally and externally just. Internal (or social) and external (or international) justice is desirable not only for moral reasons, but it is also a prudent, rational, and lasting means of preventing civil strife and international conflict (Bunge, 1987, p. 373). A just society institutionalizes the noted characteristics within its constitution to "prevent discrimination on the grounds of race, color, sex, language, age, religion, opinion, national origin, property, birth, or other status from impairing equal enjoyment or exercise of economic, social, and cultural rights" (Eide, 2001, p. 27). Thus liberal and social rights are complementary. A society must be criticized when it denies basic resources to human beings in order to protect the resources of the rich. And one has to speak of a scandal when individual and corporate property is protected by law, constitution, and liberal rights while the satisfaction of survival or basic needs cannot be guaranteed, with the result that social assistance can be questioned and shortened at any time by political parties.

Leaders, when promoting a just society, often perpetuate a common misunderstanding that the state must provide economic, social, and cultural rights. Such action is costly and creates an overgrown government apparatus. Political and civil rights require only that the state renounces certain activities, which costs little and does not establish unwieldy bureaucratic structures. Yet the opposite may be true, as implementation and protection of freedom and political rights results in enormous expenditures to protect these rights, such as for police, courts, lawyers, education, experts, prisons, and detention centers. Without substantial resources, liberal and political rights have little significance.

In reality, the funds that a state must provide to ensure economic and social human rights often pale next to those required to effect liberal rights. With respect to economic and social rights, individuals are expected to find ways to ensure the satisfaction of their own needs through their own resources or initiative, both individually and in association with others (Declaration on the Right to Development, Art. 2). But this expectation requires that individuals have resources, typically land, labor, or other productive assets and capital that can be used to meet their needs. Without these resources social rights impose three types of state obligations (Eide, 2001).

Three Types of State Obligations

- Respect the resources owned by individuals; ensure a job and take necessary individual or collective action to meet economic and social needs
- Protection of individual resources and the freedom to act unimpeded by assertive or aggressive entities—powerful lobby groups; fraudulent officials, groups, or individuals; discriminatory actors; and unethical actors in trade and contractual relations
- Fulfillment of rights through the concept of (1) facilitation or improvement of means to produce, conserve, and distribute food and other necessities by utilizing scientific and technical knowledge and reforming agrarian or tax systems, or (2) direct provision to make available requirements for basic needs, including food, medical assistance, shelter, or social security, when no possibility of self-sufficiency exists (e.g., unemployment, recession, elderly, children, natural disasters).

Only *direct provision* requires the State to allocate resources directly to individuals or groups to meet economic and social human rights, although other obligations require expenditures to develop infrastructure. In view of these different types of obligations, of which all but one require direct expenditures, it becomes clear that the provision of economic and social rights becomes practicable, even essential.

A Just Society and the Priority Principle

Within the realm of economic and social human rights, a transfer of some resources inevitably must occur. This raises the crucial question: How much sacrifice can reasonably be expected from one person, an organization, or a country for the sake of another? To answer this question, a priority principle based on different levels of need and desires can assist in determining whether a transfer of resources should occur (Shue, 1996). The priority principle distinguishes between various rights and desires:

- Basic rights—refers to biological, psychic, and social needs that must be fulfilled unless the psychic structure and organism collapses
- Non-basic rights—refers to legitimate subjective wishes, that is, wishes that do not harm other individuals or groups or whole populations
- Cultural enrichment—refers to wishes of cultural enrichment, the promotion of creativity, and innovation
- Preference satisfaction—refers to wishes of luxury and greed (Shue, 1996, p. 114)

The priority principle establishes a structure by which "(1) fulfillment of basic rights takes priority over all other activity, including the fulfillment of one's own non-basic rights; (2) the fulfillment of non-basic rights takes priority over all other activity except the fulfillment of basic rights, including the enrichment of culture and the satisfaction of one's own preferences; and (3) the enrichment of culture takes priority over the satisfaction of preferences in ways that do not enrich culture" (Shue, 1996, p. 118).

Within the structure of the priority principle, fulfillment of basic needs has primary importance. Therefore taking resources away from those who can barely meet basic needs is prohibited. Not adhering to this principle increases the probability of fascist, fundamentalist, or extreme leftist movements and racism. After the fulfillment of basic needs, a society can negotiate and bargain as to the allotment of resources to the other categories, but always by the order of priority listed above (p. 123).

Needs Versus Wishes

Certainly a common objection to defining a just society through terms such as basic needs rests on the belief, if not reality, that human beings have insatiable needs. Also, needs are subjective and not clearly definable. Thus no consensus can ever exist on the level of need that must be fulfilled and protected as part of economic and social human rights. A further argument is that needs are determined by history, social context, and culture, meaning they are relative to any given society. However, although these may appear to be valid objections, research indicates otherwise, though this is not the place to extend this argument (see Doyal & Gough, 1991; Nussbaum, 1993; Sen, 1999; Ross & Miller, 2002; Grawe, 2004; Obrecht, 2005). Needs are part of objective human survival and development condition, and they are identifiable. They are also finite and have a definite saturation limit. In contrast to needs, wants or wishes do not have this limit; they are subjective and insatiable. Social and cultural factors determine, furthermore, an individual's wishes and the means and forms with which that individual satisfies needs and wishes. Those factors also determine the amount of resources produced and available for distribution within and between societies. Confusion about needs and wishes often occurs by reference to the means by which needs are met. For instance, in meeting the basic need of housing, a person does not need an expensive tablecloth or designer furniture; these would be wishes. But a need does exist for secure housing, including adequate furnishings to cope with climate and health concerns. The economic structure in most societies today focuses not on needs but on wishes.

Economic and social rights provide a reference and tool with which to fulfill universal physical, psychic, and social needs. How a society satisfies those human rights often becomes confused with wishes or preferences for resources that go far beyond the satisfaction of needs. It is the notion of universal needs common to all human beings that is one of the legitimate bases of the claim for their protection and fulfillment through a human rights structure (Galtung, 1994; Marshall, 1992; Staub-Bernasconi, 2003).

Economic and Social Rights Within Social Work Education and Practice

Social work defines itself as a profession dedicated to social justice and, more recently, human rights. Yet if social work is to contribute to the future development and implementation of human rights, especially economic, social, and cultural rights, social work education and practice must change, especially internationally. "Internationalization is more than the addition of a course on international issues or human rights to a curriculum or the insertion of a unit of comparative policy into a course on welfare" (Healy, 2002, p. 181). The new accreditation norms of the Council of Social

Work Education (CSWE) go in this direction when they say that students should be prepared to "recognize the global context of social work practice" (CSWE, 2001, p. 6). In addition, programs must now provide content in knowledge and skills to analyze "international issues in social welfare policy and social service delivery"; they must further "integrate social and economic justice content grounded in an understanding of distributive justice, human and civil rights, and the global interconnections of oppression" (pp. 6, 10). Globalization "has impacted on social welfare as much as on the aspects of daily life, and now requires all social workers to place their local activities in a wider frame, or, in some cases, to operate outside or across political boundaries. . . . [S]ocial work is a local and global profession" (Lyons, 2000, p. 1).

In addition to making social work education more international in focus, which should encourage the study of human rights, the human rights cause should be helped by transforming commonly perceived private social ills, such as poverty, unemployment, and domestic abuse of women and children, into public issues. Social work has increasingly restricted itself to the private, intimate domain supported by therapeutic methods. Yet human rights issues are viewed more as public than private issues, one factor that has led to social work not being closely identified as a human rights profession. But it is in this private sphere where many human rights violations occur. Social work education should emphasize a strong connection between individual problems and public issues to help illustrate economic and social human rights issues prevalent within social work (Ife, 2001).

Knowledge alone, however, will not provide a sufficient tool for applying human rights. In addition to acquiring specific knowledge of the terms and definitions used in human rights, social workers need to understand how to translate human rights into the social work profession. This ability requires an understanding of government agencies, clients, and social work concepts (Reichert, 2003, p. 224). Beginning in the late 1980s the International Federation of Social Workers (IFSW) adopted a strong program of human rights. Because of the interdependence between human rights and social work practice, the IFSW has focused its work in the area of human rights, especially economic and social rights. Human rights are inseparable from social work theory, values, ethics, and practice. It is therefore difficult to perform social work in a society where basic human rights are not met (Healy, 2001, p. 58).

Of course, the above statements resemble a foundation, not an actual course of action. How, then, does social work actually contribute to the further development of human rights, especially economic and social rights?

Action for Human Rights and Social Justice

Social workers should directly assist *individuals* in obtaining access to education, work, and social, cultural, and medical services by mobilizing necessary resources if the individuals themselves are unable to do so. The social work profession has an obligation to contest cuts to social assistance that would place recipients under the poverty level as a violation of human rights. The profession should promote consciousness-raising and lobbying for economic, social and cultural rights that require a sound knowledge of those rights.

Social workers should identify prejudices and scapegoating in relation to individuals, families, and *vulnerable, oppressed groups*, whether or not these occur as structural norms of deprivation, privilege, and discrimination. Practitioners must consider whether these prejudices violate economic and social human rights. Social workers will need to gather facts and analyze specific situations to determine the degree to which prejudices or biases impact human rights violations. The profession can also join the worldwide movement of "local economy" in order to establish social enterprises to provide jobs for people excluded from the labor market (Elsen, 1998). It should consider methods of community organizing, focusing on mediation on the premise of social justice (Montada & Kals, 2001; Staub-Bernasconi, 2004a). Community organizing that empowers individuals to actually obtain economic or social rights from those who are reluctant to relinquish entrenched benefits can also be a valuable tool for social work action (Alinsky, 1971; Simon Levy, 1994; Staub-Bernasconi, 2004b).

On the organizational, especially *social agency level*, the profession could develop a human rights culture in everyday life (Wronka, 1995a, 1995b). Social workers could become involved at the workplaces of social agencies or in social settings, such as schools, leisure centers, homes, hospitals, and prisons, with the goal of evaluating and furthering human rights within the organization. People who have lost faith in the political system are often more accepting of organizations as a kind of functional equivalent in promoting human rights and social justice (Sheppard, Lewicki, & Minton, 1992; Sing, 1997; Gilliand, Steiner, & Garlicki, 2001). The skeptic can directly observe how structural norms, activities, and decisions hurt or enhance the fulfillment of needs and the interests of individuals on different organizational levels as victims and violators. Here they are able to take remedial, organizational, or political action. The main questions to be answered in the organizational context are the same as in politics: Who is entitled to what, and who owes what to whom, and why, and according to what human rights standards? The result could be a monitoring and reporting system as a base for organizational improvements and formulations of social policy as a form of organizational advocacy (Taylor, 1987).

On an *international level,* the profession should refer to documents specifically issued by the UN through its human rights branches, like periodic nation reports on economic, social, and cultural rights and compliance with these rights. Entities of the profession specifically targeted for human rights issues include the IFSW and the International Association of Schools of Social Work (IASSW) commissions on human rights. Everyday activities of the profession bring it into close contact with victims and violators of human rights. This proximity to human rights issues allows social workers to gather relevant information about circumstances of the most vulnerable individuals and groups.

The profession should acknowledge that enough money and resources exist to abolish extreme poverty and hunger, and implement the priority principle at both national and international levels. Scarcity of resources and fiscal crises are generally artificial creations of government that often promote wars, tax benefits for the wealthy and for corporations, and other preferential policies that do little to satisfy economic and social human rights.

Conclusion

Social work as a discipline and profession needs a voice in affairs relating to human rights at all social and governmental levels. The profession will have to find ways to further develop economic and social rights than those currently available. It will have to find ways to inform and educate clients, students, and colleagues about their rights, and collect data to support the promotion of human rights.

Human rights give the profession the opportunity to clarify the moorings and long-term objectives of social work. Human rights will disturb the complacence of the individual social worker who may be tempted to acquiesce in the values of the local community even when those values conflict with the broader principles of the profession. Human rights will compel the organized profession to take clear positions on economic and social issues. In the midst of a plurality of cultures and values there will be a need for the affirmation of one acceptable common denominator. The Universal Declaration of Human Rights provides this necessary standard and direction to all constructive action (Gore, 1996, pp. 67–68). That declaration makes no distinction between political and economic human rights. The profession should follow the lead of the Universal Declaration and make every effort to promote all human rights with the same vigor.

References

Adams, M., Blumenfeld, W. J., Castaneda, R., Hackmanh, H. W., Peters, M. L., & Zuniga, X. (Eds.). (2000). *Readings for diversity and social justice: An anthology on racism, antisemitism, sexism, heterosexism, ableism, and classism.* New York and London: Routledge.

Addams, J. (1902): *Democracy and social ethics.* New York: Macmillan.

Alinsky, S. D. (1971). *Rules for radicals.* New York: Random House.

Bielefeldt, H. (1998). *Philosophie der Menschenrechte. Grundlagen eines weltweiten Freiheitsethzos.* Darmstadt: Primus.

Blumenfeld, W. J., & Raymond, D. (2001). Prejudice and discrimination. In M. Adams et al., *Readings for diversity and social justice: An anthology on racism, antisemitism, sexism, heterosexism, ableism, and classism* (pp. 3–30). New York and London: Routledge.

Bunge, M. (1989). *Ethics: The good and the right.* Vol. 8, *Treatise in basic philosophy.* Dordrecht: Reidel.

Chesnais, F. (2001/1998). *Tobin or not Tobin.* Konstanz: Universitätsverlag Konstanz.

Coote, A. (Ed.) (1992). *The welfare of citizens: Developing new social rights.* London: IPPR/Rivers Oram Press.

Copranzano, R., Kacmar, S., & Michele, K. (Eds.). (1995). *Organizational politics, justice, and support: Managing the social climate of the workplace.* Westport, CT: Quorum Books.

Doyal, L., & Gough, I. (1991). *A theory of human need.* London: Macmillan.

Eide, A. (2001). Economic, social and cultural rights as human rights. In A. Eide, C. Krause, & A. Rosas (Eds.), *Economic, social and cultural rights: A textbook* (2nd ed., pp. 9–28). Dordrecht, Boston, and London: Martinus Nijhoff.

Eide, A., Krause, C., & Rosas, A. (Eds.). (2001). *Economic, social and cultural rights: A textbook* (2nd ed.). Dordrecht, Boston, and London: Martinus Nijhoff.

Eide, A., & Rosas, A. (2001). Economic, social and cultural rights: A universal challenge. In A. Eide, C. Krause, & A. Rosas (Eds.), *Economic, social and cultural rights: A textbook* (2nd ed., pp. 3–7). Dordrecht, Boston, and London: Martinus Nijhoff.

Elsen, S. (1998). *Gemeinwesenökonomie—eine Antwort auf Arbeitslosigkeit, Armut und soziale Ausgrtenzung?* Neuwied: Luchterhand.

Fox-Genovese, E. (1989). Freiheitskämpfe: Frauen, Sklaverei und Gleichheit in den Vereinigten Staaten, In H. Olwen (Ed.), *Menschenrechte in der Geschichte* (pp. 194–235). Frankfurt am Main: Fischer. (Originalausgabe, *Historical change and human rights*. Oxford Amnesty Lectures. New York: Basic Books.)

Fraser, N. (1994/1989). *Widerspenstige Praktiken. Macht, Diskurs, Geschlecht.* Frankfurt am Main: Suhrkamp.

Frei, B. S., & Stutzer, A. (2002). *Happiness and economics. How economy and institutions affect human well-being.* Princeton, NJ, and Oxford: Princeton University Press.

Galtung, J. (1994). *Human rights in another key.* Oxford: Blackwell.

Gilliland, S., Steiner, D., & Skarlicki, D. (2001). *Theoretical and cultural perspectives on organizational justice.* Greenwich, CN: Information Age.

Gore, M. S. (1969). Social work and its human rights aspects. In International Council on Social Welfare (Ed.), *Social welfare and human rights* (pp. 56–68). Proceedings of the Fourteenth International Conference on Social Welfare, Helsinki, Finland, August 1968.

Grawe, K. (2004). *Neuropsychiatrie.* Göttingen/Bern/Oxford/Toronto: Hogrefe.

Healy, L. M. (2001). *International social work: Professional action in an interdependent world.* New York: Oxford University Press.

Healy, L. M. (2002). Internationalizing social work curriculum in the 21st century. In N-T. Tan & I. Dodds (Eds.), *Social work around the world* (2nd ed., pp. 179–194). Berne: IFSW.

Hufton, O. (Ed.) (1998). *Menschenrechte in der Geschichte.* Frankfurt am Main: Fischer. (Originalausgabe, *Historical change and human rights.* Oxford Amnesty Lectures. New York: Basic Books.

Hussbaum, M. C. (1993). *Menschliches tun und soziale Gerechtigkeit.* In M. Brumlik & H. Brunkhorst (Eds.), *Gemeinschaft und Gerechtigkeit* (pp. 323–361). Frankfurt am Main: Fischer.

Ife, J. (2001). *Human rights and social work: Towards rights-based practice.* Cambridge: Cambridge University Press.

Ishay, M. R. (Ed.). (1997). *The human rights reader: Major political essays, speeches, and documents from the Bible to the present.* London: Routledge.

Kälin, W. (2000). Soziale Menschenrechte ernst genommen. In *Sozialalmanach. Sozialrechte und Chancengleichheit in der Schweiz* (pp. 69–82). Luzern: Caritas.

Laqueur, W., & Rubin, B. (Eds.) (1989). *Human rights reader.* New York: Penguin.

Lyons, K. (2000/1999). *International social work: Themes and perspectives.* Ashgate, Aldershot: Ashgate.

Marshall, T. H. (1992/1982). *Bürgerrechte und soziale Klassen* [Civil rights and the welfare state]. Frankfurt am Main: Campus.

Montada, L., & Kals, E. (2001). *Mediation.* Weinheim: Beltz.

Mullaly, B. (1997). *Structural social work: Ideology, theory, and practice* (2nd ed.). Oxford and New York: Oxford University Press.

Obrecht, W. (2005). Umrisse einer biopsychosozialen Theorie menschlicher Bedürfnisse. Interdisziplinärer Universitätslehrgang für Sozialwirtschaft, Management und Organisation. Sozialer Dienste (ISMOS) der Wirtschaftsuniversität, typescript, Vienna.

Rawls, J. (1999/1971). *A theory of justice.* Cambridge, MA: Harvard University Press.

Reichert, E. (2003). Social work and human rights: A foundation for policy and practice. New York: Columbia University Press.

Rosenfeld, J. M., & Tardieu, B. (Eds.) (2000). *Artisans of democracy: How ordinary people, families in extreme poverty, and social institutions become allies to overcome social exclusion.* New York and Oxford: University Press of America

Ross, M., & Miller, D. T. (Eds.) (2002). *The justice motive in everyday life.* Cambridge: Cambridge University Press.

Satka, M. (1995). *Making social citizenship: Conceptual practices from the Finnish Poor Law to professional social work.* Jyväskyla, Finland: University of Jyväskyla.

Sen, A. (1999). *Development as freedom.* New York: Knopf.

Sheppard, B. H., Lewicki, R. J., & Minton, J. W. (1992). *Organizatonal justice: The search for fairness in the workplace.* New York: Macmillan.

Shue, H. (1996). *Basic rights: Subsistence, affluence, and U.S. foreign policy* (2nd ed.). Princeton, NJ: Princeton University Press.

Simon Levy, B. (1994). *The empowerment tradition in American social work: A history.* New York: Columbia University Press.

Singer, M. S. (1997). *Ethics and justice in organisations: A normative-empirical dialogue.* Aldershot: Ashgate.

Staub-Bernasconi, S. (2000). Sozialrechte—Restgrösse der Menschenrechte? In U. Wilken (Ed.), *Soziale Arbeit zwischen Ethik und Ökonomie* (pp. 151–174). Freiburg and Berlin: Lambertus.

Staub-Bernasconi, S. (2003). Soziale Arbeit als (eine) Menschenrechtsprofession. In R. Sorg (Ed.), *Soziale Arbeit zwischen Poliltik und Wissenschaft* (pp. 17–54). Münster: LIT-Verlag.

Staub-Bernasconi, S. (2004a). Mediation and empowerment: Two complementary approaches to social justice and to a human rights practice. Presentation at the 2004 Congress of IASSW/IFSW, typescript, Adelaide.

Staub-Bernasconi, S. (2004b). Menschenrechtsbildung in der Sozialen Arbeit—Ein Master of Social Work als Beitrag zur Thematisierung von Sozialrechten. In C. Mahler & A. Mihr (Eds.), *Menschenrechtsbildung. Bilanz und Perspektiven* (pp. 233–244). Wiesbaden: VS Verlag für Sozialwissenschaften.

Staub-Bernasconi, S. (2005). Die würdigen und unwürdigen Armen von heute. Menschenwürdige Existenz und Sozialarbeitswissenschaft. In W. Schmid & U. Tecklenburg (Eds.), *Menschenwürdig leben? Fragen an die Schweizer Sozialhilfe* (pp. 113–132). Luzern: Caritas.

Staub-Bernasconi, S. (2006). Soziale Arbeit als Dienstleistung oder Menschenrechtsprofession? Zum Selbstverständnis Sozialer Arbeit in Deutschland mit einem Seitenblick auf die internationale Diskussionslandschaft. In Lesch, W. & Lob-Hüdepohl, A. (Eds.), *Einführung in die Ethik der Sozialen Arbeit.* Schöningh-Verlag: UTB.

Steiner, H. J., & Alston, P. (2000). *International human rights in context: law, politics, morals* (2nd ed.). New York: Oxford University Press.

Taylor, E. D. (1987). *From issue to action: An advocacy program model.* Lancaster, PA: Family and Children's Services.

United Nations/IASSW/IFSW. (1994/1992). *Social work and human rights: A manual for schools of social work and the social work profession.* Professional Training Series no. 4. New York and Geneva: Centre of Human Rights.

Wahl, P., & Waldow, P. (2001). *Devisenumsatzsteuer—Ein Konzept für die Zukunft. Möglichkeiten und Grenzen der Stabilisierung der Finanzmärkte durch die Tobin-Steuer.* Bonn.

Wronka, J. (1995a). Creating a human rights culture. *Brandeis Review,* 28–31.

Wronka, J. (1995b). Human rights. In R. Edwards (Ed.), *Encyclopedia of social work* (19th ed., pp. 1405–1418). Washington, DC: NASW Press.

8

Human Rights and Women

A Work in Progress

JANICE WOOD WETZEL

History of Social Justice and Human Rights

Concern for social justice has been documented ever since Hammurabi's *Code of Laws*, in Babylon, and later espoused in certain quarters of ancient Chinese, Greek, and Roman cultures. The religious tomes of ancient Jews, early Christians, and Moslems all honored the dignity and worth of human beings. Great Britain's *Magna Carta* in the Western world followed suit in 1215 (Falk, 1998; Laquer & Rubin, 1979; McKinney & Park-Cunningham, 1997; National Association of Social Work (NASW, 2000); Wronka, 1994, 1998).

The French Declaration of the Rights of Man and the Citizen, and the U.S. Declaration of Independence and Bill of Rights advanced the cause of political rights. But not until the nineteenth century were beginning efforts made to win rights for women and ethnic minorities (Falk, 1998; Laquer & Rubin, 1979). Unfortunately, although women in many parts of the world have made great progress in achieving human rights, much still has to be done to fully realize these rights.

The Universal Declaration of Human Rights

Under the leadership of Eleanor Roosevelt in 1948, the Universal Declaration of Human Rights gave the world a landmark document that recognizes the inherent dignity and worth of all members of the human family, and the equal and inalienable rights of both men and women. Her attention to women remains an unheralded legacy, for the very mention of human rights at that time was alien to the culture. The common reference to man or mankind implied, but the terms symbolically rendered women invisible and powerless. Men decided when the word *man* was generic and when it was exclusively male. Mrs. Roosevelt made a case against the use of the male pronouns, but they remained in the Declaration. On the occasion of the fiftieth anniversary of the drafting of the Declaration, a history of the process was written to commemorate the day.

The efforts of the Commission on Human Rights would prove unrivaled in world history. Although attempts to describe the rights of men and women had been previously undertaken, the outcome had only applied to members of a particular society. Never before had the community of nations successfully identified the rights and freedoms to be enjoyed by people the world over, for all time (Universal Declaration of Human Rights [UDHR], 1998).

The Universal Declaration of Human Rights is unique in that it gave the United Nations the right to ask sovereign nations questions that were previously considered to be internal affairs. It is customary now for international law even to scrutinize non-member nations. Even so, the human rights of women all too often are ignored, largely interpreted as local civil rights shaped by political, religious, and cultural customs in relation to the place of women in a given society. To this day, those who deny the principles of the Universal Declaration of Human Rights argue that intruding on such conditions violates societal self-determination. Such interpretations are direct contradictions of the intent of the Declaration, as well as of the agreements that follow. The international agreements underscore the requirement that human rights are to be expressed concretely in the real lives of people, both women and men (Evans 1998).

The International Human Rights Covenants

More than the Declaration was needed, whether or not gender issues were in question, if the UN was to have legal force to implement the collective ideals of its member nations. Two international Covenants were presented for ratification in 1966 to meet the challenge. The first was the International Covenant on Civil and Political Rights, a defensive stand against oppression referring to "rights devised to ensure freedom from any curtailment of individual liberty." The second was the International Covenant on Economic, Social, and Cultural Rights, an affirmation of the right to the fulfillment of material and nonmaterial needs, "aimed at ensuring social justice, freedom from want, and participation in the social, economic and cultural aspects of life" (International Association of Schools of Social Work [IASSW] & International Federation of Social Workers [IFSW], 1994, p. 4; Tessitore & Woolfson, 1997, 1998). The ramifications of these agreements are particularly salient to the domestic and international policies and practices of the United States (Wetzel, 2001).

Human Rights and the U.S. Government

The United States has never signed the International Covenant on Economic, Social, and Cultural Rights which affects, inter alia, the right to education, housing, health care, and income maintenance. The U.S. government does not consider these to be human rights, and hence the difficulty of passing social legislation and the associated lack of support for social work issues. Historically, when under conservative leadership, the U.S. government has had an aversion to the concept of human rights as compared to social and cultural rights. Unlike civil and political rights that can be modified based on internal, cultural, and religious values, human rights are universally applied and transcend discriminatory customs. There has been a consistent attitude that signing on to international treaties is an impingement on U.S. sovereignty. The rejection of the International World Court, the Convention on the Elimination of All Forms of Discrimination against Women, and the Convention on the Rights of the Child are cases in point. The world has seen the unfortunate effects of these anti-human rights mind-sets.

Human Rights as an International Social Work Principle

The International Association of Schools of Social Work (IASSW) and the International Federation of Social Workers (IFSW) are two professional international organizations committed to educational and practice excellence. They collaborated, in 1994, in writing the first human rights and social work manual for the profession. Noting that a purely social justice orientation is based on needs fulfillment which in turn is based on choice, they called for human rights to be considered an organizing principle for professional practice. The fundamental nature of human needs, they maintain, requires these rights to be met not as a matter of choice but as an imperative of basic justice. A shift was needed in the way human rights principles were viewed (IASSW & IFSW, 1994, p.5). Plans for the revision of *The Human Rights and Social Work* manual are currently in progress.

In 1996 the IFSW summarized their stance in their updated policy statement: "Human Rights condense into two words the struggle for dignity and fundamental freedoms which allow the full development of human potential. Civil and political rights have to be accompanied by economic, social and cultural rights."

These core values also have been integral to the Council on Social Work Education's (CSWE) Educational Policy Statement since its inception as an accrediting body in the United States (Council on Social Work Education [CSWE], 2005). Although this interpretation of human rights as a basic social work principle is straightforward, its application is fraught with hidden issues that demand transparency. A simple examination of the meaning of the word *dignity* is a logical place to begin our exploration. *Dignity*, a hallmark of social work values, is defined as "the quality or state of being worthy, honored, or esteemed." *Self-worth* and *self-esteem*, in turn, are defined as "a confidence and satisfaction in oneself." Such confidence and satisfaction require *self-respect*, "a proper respect for oneself as a human being, a regard for one's own standing and position" (*Merriam-Webster Online Dictionary*, 2005). In the absence of attainment of these qualities, much less the social conditions required to make them possible, fundamental freedoms are found wanting. The reality is particularly salient when we apply it to the lives of the world's women whose economic and social conditions are not likely to foster a sense of self-worth anywhere, much less fundamental freedoms in many cultures. This reality challenges social workers every day.

Janice Wood Wetzel

Women's Right to Development

The UN High Commissioner for Human Rights, Mary Robinson, has stated that development must be based on human rights (Robinson, 2002). She was referring to social development, but I suggest that the principles hold true for personal development as well. To grant women human rights is simply attesting to the fact that women are human and therefore have human needs. But to advocate for human rights is more controversial than one might think. It means that the human rights of women are sacrosanct; they are not just civil rights that can be bent to the will of the powerful, whether that power resides in the home, the community, the courts, or the pulpit.

Human rights transcend cultural, religious, and ethnic customs. That means that it is wrong to physically or psychologically restrain and control women, regardless of religious insistence on their subservience. It is not all right to demand dowries when women marry, regardless of ritual beliefs. Nor is it acceptable to genitally mutilate girls and women, regardless of ancient mores. To pay women at lesser rates than men for the same work is not all right, regardless of common practices. To expect women to work all day outside the home for inequitable wages, in addition to having responsibility for unpaid home maintenance and child care, is wrong, even if "everyone does it." And to blame women for being poor or not having a home when their wages are less than life-sustaining, and when affordable housing is unavailable, is not all right. Women's human rights are being violated.

The Human Rights of Women Mandate

The "human rights of women" mandate was first passed in Vienna, at the 1993 World Conference on Human Rights, and again in Beijing at the 1995 Fourth World Conference on Women, and yet again at the 1999 National Association of Social Workers' Delegate Assembly in Washington, DC. The mandate is now an official policy of the National Association of Social Workers (NASW) (NASW, 2000). Although NASW delegates were persuaded to adopt the policy without a penalty, Mary Robinson paid a price for her human rights advocacy; The U.S. government pressured her to leave her UN post as a result of airing U.S. human rights abuses. Upon stepping down from her position, she wrote, "If you believe in human rights, then they must be applied without fear or favour" (2002, p. 22). Her courage is a touchstone for those who stand up for human rights around the world, across all cultures. It is my hope that social work educators will equip their graduates "to stand up and be counted."

Attention to the human rights of women empowers them to change their communities, their lives, and the lives of their children. The reframing of social problems as human rights, so many of which concern women, creates an international context in which to understand them more fully (Reichert, 2001; Wetzel, 1993). The global issues can no longer be viewed as simply an individual woman's personal problem or even her culture's unique issue (Beneria, 2003).

Clinically the understanding of human rights as basic to all humanity frees us of our societal and institutional myopia that encourages us to wrestle with less intrinsic values and ethics. Further, our clinical understanding of the internalization of social norms, regardless of their destructive nature, frees us of the option to view women's denigration of themselves as self-determination. We must rethink our own values on behalf of oppressed people everywhere (Wetzel, 2005). Multicultural policies designed to protect "culture," whatever the culture or religion, usually contribute to the repression of women. Tradition and the servitude of women are virtually synonymous (Cohen & Howard, 1999; Okin, 1999). Powerful forces do not dissipate easily.

Women's Economic Rights

The UN has concluded that there is no country in the world where women have equal status with men. The nuances vary, but the story line remains the same. International research documents that women are more likely to be economically deprived the world over. Much of their work contributes to their oppression, rather than to their independence and sense of self-worth. It is likely to be unpaid, low-paid and labor-intensive. Their benefits are almost nonexistent, and often their working conditions are dangerous. In addition to maintaining the home and caring for children, men, and relatives, they contribute to the economic support of the household. In Africa they provide all the family's food by personally farming the land. And, contrary to the common perception, women are responsible for 80 percent of productivity in the Muslin world (Keshavarz, 2003; Wetzel, 2004).

Over the past decades women have clearly been the ultimate victims of the economic "structural adjustment" policies of wealthy nations. Their demand for repayment of debts required poor nations to scale back and even eliminate social programs for their people. It is women who have had to take on the burden of unmet societal needs, on top of their already back-breaking workload (Tsikata, 2002). It will be important to follow the outcome of the debt relief agreed to in June 2005 by the world's wealthiest nations on behalf of sixty of its poorest. It remains to be seen whether governmental social services will be reinstituted (Becker, 2005).

The notion of equal sharing of family responsibilities between women and men was first formally proposed in 1975 by women in nonaligned countries at the first United Nations Decade of Women conference in Mexico City (Wetzel, 1996, 2003). The concept was incorporated as a transformative strategy for poverty eradication in the New Delhi *Report on Empowerment of Women throughout the Life Cycle* (United Nations, 2001). They further contend that child care support services must be provided "to allow both women and men, especially in poverty, to utilize their employment opportunities and build their capacities" (p. 36).

Women's Right to Health

The Harvard World Study reports that women's work burden is incapacitating. More likely to live in poverty, they are subject to physical and mental health risks, including chronic fatigue, malnutrition, depression, and anxiety, usually a result of unconscionable social conditions. Women and girls are particularly vulnerable to poverty-related physical and emotional suffering because of their inferior social status. Even in wealthy nations like the United States, 78 percent of all people living in poverty are single women and hungry children who are swelling the ranks of soup kitchens throughout the country (Wasserman, 2002). There is a continued lack of physical and mental health services for women, or research concerning their needs, even in the United States. Understanding the sources of ill health for women means understanding how cultural and economic forces interact to undermine their social status (Desjarlais, Eisenberg, Good, & Kleinman, 1995). Violence against women is one such force.

Violence, Health, and Women's Rights

Violence affects women disproportionately and comes in many guises the world over. Among them are psychological threats, isolation, and denigration; beatings, disfigurement, even murder; sexual coercion and slavery; genital mutilation, forced veiling, and harsh social constraints; and lack of personal control and identity. Depression, anxiety, post-traumatic stress disorder (PTSD), eating disorders, and chemical dependency in women are all thought to be directly or indirectly related to psychological, physical, and sexual abuse. Violence, whether imposed within the family or as a result of war and terrorism, corrodes the very essence of self-worth (Morrow, 1999). Awareness of these facts was incorporated in the work of Van Soest (1999) under the rubric of the NASW's Violence and Development Project in the United States. Violence at the institutional, systemic, and international levels that wreak untold havoc on human beings can be as devastating as individual acts of violence perpetrated against them. The toll of domestic violence against women is universal from all perspectives.

Among women in the United States, battering is the greatest single cause of injury. Four million American women a year are physically assaulted by their male partners. Over 60 percent of them are beaten while pregnant (Katz, 2005). Internationally the picture is shockingly similar. It has been reported that the rates of domestic violence against married women range from 20 percent in some countries to over 80 percent in others (Kansas Coalition against Domestic Violence [KCSDV], 2005). When associated with male alcohol abuse, these numbers skyrocket (Office of the Prevention of Domestic Violence [OPVD], 1995).

One woman, on average, is raped every two minutes in the United States (Katz, 2005). The culture of rape exposed in recent years in our military establishments indicates the significant prevalence of institutional rape in the U.S. (Janofsky & Schemo, 2003; Quindlen, 2003). In the past human rights were relevant only in the private realm, traditionally that of men, and abuses such as rape and other acts of mental or physical violence were relegated to the public sector, the civil and political arenas. Religious and cultural customs held sway in those domains, ensuring male power and the perpetuation of women's subjugation. Until the late 1970s rape by a husband was considered legally impossible, as a married couple is as one and that one is the man. "A man can't rape himself," so went the logic (Brownmiller, 1993).

Although rape in wartime has been common since time immemorial, it was not until the war in the Balkans in 1998 that it was considered to be a criminal act of war and recognized as a form of torture (Neil, 2005). "Amnesty International has concluded that women suffer more violations of human rights than any other group in the world, both in times of war and through traditional practices excused by culture" (Behar, 1996, p. 107; Wetzel, 2001).

Seventy-nine percent of those who are maimed, tortured, or killed in wartime are civilian women and their children. Acknowledging this phenomenon, one theologian commented, "at least from the middle of the twentieth century, it is safer to be in the military than to be a civilian (Keating, 2002, p. 4).

When women are immigrants or refugees, the violence is endemic. Eighty percent of the world's refugees are women and their children (Pittaway, 1999). A high percentage of these women are sexually abused by their husbands, gangs on the high seas, or in refugee camps by the men in their families, other sexual predators, or the very guards meant to protect them. The women have no recourse, and their rapes stigmatize them for life; their reputations are beyond repair. They are thought to be "spoiled goods" and may be killed by a male family member "to cleanse the family honor" (Desjarlais et al., 1995, p. 189). The wonder is that refugee women, like so many others, exhibit superior coping abilities, resilience, and capacity to thrive in the face of heavy burdens, responsibilities, and trauma (Ferguson, 1999; Ferguson & Pittaway, 1999). One refugee expert calls them the "unsung heroes" (Pittaway, 1999, p. 1).

Mental Health Consequences

Despite women's reported endurance, one should not be surprised that anxiety and PTSD among girls and women are sharply increasing. Depression is out of control the world over, showing up earlier and earlier in the lives of girls and women. By the year 2020, according to the World Health Organization, unipolar major depression is projected to be the second largest cause of disability-adjusted life years overall, and the leading cause in females and in developing countries (Saraceno, 2006). When coupled with other high risk factors, such as alcohol-related violence, the figures rise markedly. More and more girls and women at younger and younger ages are consuming alcohol and other drugs. Girls in the United States with histories of sexual abuse have similar eating disorders with girls in such unlikely places as Africa, Southeast Asia, and even Fiji (World Health Organization [WHO], 2002b; United Nations (2003 a); United Nations (2003 b).

Harvard world mental health researchers have concluded that the problems they found in developing countries cannot be separated from those in the developed world. They are shared by nations rich and poor. Women in abusive relationships, for example, face physical and emotional hardship, even death, wherever they live. The researchers call this shared reality "the global distribution of psychosocial disorders" (Desjarlais et al., 1995, p. 261). The goal to achieve dignity and fundamental freedoms is elusive for such women.

According to the Beijing Platform for Action (United Nations 1995), health and well-being elude the majority of the world's women. Whether speaking of physical, emotional, or social well-being, the absence of equality is at the root of their suffering. As recognized from the first Women's World Conference in Mexico City, in 1975, equality (including shared family responsibilities), development, and peace are essential to optimal well-being. Public health spending everywhere has decreased as social contracts have been abridged in both the developed and developing world. Recall that it is women who pay the dearest price, for they must take on the burden of caretaking, usually unpaid or at best low paid, in addition to their already overwhelming work obligations.

Women's Reproductive Health

Women's reproductive health is particularly vulnerable to social control, rendering them powerless in their personal relationships with men who are not educated to respect them, allow them self-determination, or take equal responsibility for sexuality and reproduction. Religious institutions often collude with governments in their restrictive fiats concerning women (United Nations 1995). The United States has gone so far as to create a "gag rule" for any women's health service that so much as mentions abortion as a possibility. Funds are withdrawn even though the health service is not performing abortions and is using its own monies to educate women. International policies that are against the law in the United States are thus mandated in the developing world. Women are losing their lives as a result of forced pregnancies, illegal abortions, and absence of prenatal and post-partum health care (Darvich-Kodjouri & Bonk, 2001). In the UN General Assembly, the U.S. stands against all nations that support family planning, thus voting with Syria, Iran, North Korea, and the Sudan to disallow it. The United States colludes with adversaries, and women pay the price.

HIV/AIDS and Women

The vulnerability of women to human rights abuses is also increased by the HIV/AIDS epidemic that today disproportionately affects women worldwide as a result of biology and second-class status. Social and cultural patterns lead to discrimination and stereotyped sex roles, ranging from sexual division of labor and sexual exploitation that favors men at home and at work, to multinational sexual trafficking, second only to the global drug trade. Women are infected with HIV/AIDS because they do not have the power to insist that their partners wear condoms, and because they are forced to have sex with their husbands who bring the virus home.

Evidence indicates that women who are especially at risk are in a hetero-sexual marriage or a long-term union in a society where men commonly engage in sex outside the union, and women suffer abuse if they demand condom use (Human Rights Watch, 2005a, p. 1).

Although one tends to think of women's vulnerability in the developing world, it is no less true in the United States. Violations of women's human rights begin in the home everywhere. Human Rights Watch observes that "the deadly link between women's rights abuses and the spread of HIV/AIDS is slowly gaining recognition, but not before millions of women lost their lives to the disease" (2005a, p. 1). The Beijing Platform for Action (United Nations 1995) asserts that the health, social, and developmental consequences of HIV/AIDS and other sexually transmitted diseases must be viewed from a gender perspective. Not to do so is to ensure its proliferation. And so it is with other social problems that challenge social workers every day.

A Psychological Analysis of Women's Universal Oppression

Just as it is erroneous to think that social and economic oppression does not take a toll on the psyches of women, so, too, is it a mistake not to explore why their oppression has been so ubiquitous since time immemorial. On the occasion of the fiftieth anniversary of the UN's Universal Declaration of Human Rights, Evan's (1998) noted the disjuncture between the theory and practice of human rights. He cites an abundance of "literature about utopian visions and legal solutions, but [with] little to say about the social and political context in which violations take place" (p. 1). Examples from the historical documents referred to at the start of this chapter support Evan's view.

Peterson and Parisi (1998) go even further in providing a conceptual framework and analysis of the time-worn oppression of women. Their analysis begins with the ancient Greeks and their efforts to normalize heterosexuality by "engraving in stone the rejection of all but heterosexual forms of identity and subjectivity" (Wetzel, 2001, p. 22). Peterson and Parisi report, too, that family forms with centralized authority and hierarchical divisions of labor were made manifest at that time. These policies led to the government-sanctioned denial of women's self-determination, decision making, and subordination to male-defined interests. Repudiation of bonding among women in their own interest was normalized, along with heterosexual masculine privilege.

Gender hierarchies sanction asymmetries that are replicated within and between families and other groups. When females are denigrated, so, too, is anyone or anything associated with femininity. Women, in effect, are not considered "fully human" and, by extension, are not worthy of human rights (Peterson & Parisi, 1998). And so it is that the most common male insult, the ultimate derision, is to call a man by a female name. "Sissy" in childhood is just the beginning of a long line of sexually explicit, generally vulgar female epithets targeted at boys and men as they get older. Any attitude or behavior that may be attributed to the feminine is thus kept in check (Wetzel, 2001).

Lesbian, Gay, Bisexual and Transgendered Movement

The Lesbian, Gay, Bisexual and Transgendered (LGBT) movement, according to Amnesty International, "owes a major debt to the women's movement which opened up issues of sexuality and sexual identity as legitimate areas of collective struggle" (1999, p.15). The LGBT movement has become international in scope. The global studies of human rights conducted by

Amnesty International—United Kingdom (1997) brought that organization to the conclusion that gay men and lesbians worldwide remain at risk.
Human rights violations on the grounds of sexual identity are not yet expressly forbidden by any international law (p. 8.)

The Psychosocial Dynamics of Homophobic Hatred

Women's subordination to males, normalized in ancient Greece, has continued to this day, according to Peterson and Parisi's historical research.
From that time on, anything other than heterosexual male and masculine
privilege have been denied and repressed. Male-defined interests over females and femininity rule. Indeed, any person or object considered to be
feminine are objectified as an appropriate target of domination and deemed
unacceptable. Gay males and women who are lesbians fit this profile (Peterson & Parisi, 1998; Wetzel, 2001).

It is perhaps understandable, then, that many heterosexual men are
threatened by lesbians. They may feel rejected as males, or they may feel
that it is unacceptable for a woman not to depend on a man. But why are
traditional heterosexual women also threatened? It is likely because, con-
sciously or unconsciously, they are male-defined as a result of their socialization. The same things that trouble men trouble women who have inter-
nalized the rules of society and their own oppression (Wetzel, 2001). In
any case, the oppression and abuse of women is compounded when they
identify as lesbian and bisexual women, and their human rights are violated in the process.

Aging Women

The explosive growth of older populations worldwide in recent decades
has, historically, never been seen before. One out of every ten people in
2003 was sixty and older; by 2050 the ratio will be 1 to 5; and by 2150 it
will be 1 to 3 (United Nations, 2003 c) Population Division, Department of
Economic and Social Affairs [DESA], UN). The UN has called the world's
exploding aging population an "agequake." The rapidly increasing aging
population with all its serious ramifications of disability and poverty has

become an international phenomenon affecting both the developing and developed world. In the U.S., as in other countries, women represent the majority of that burgeoning population. They also represent the majority of the elderly poor. In this regard, their economic status is directly linked to their second-class status throughout their lives. It should come as no surprise that they are more likely to live in poverty at all ages. The "feminization of poverty" is old news. The vulnerable situation of women in old age does not descend on them out of the blue. In the words of Julia Tavares Alvarez, a UN Ambassador and tireless global advocate for older adults, "Simply put, no country on the planet treats women as well as it does men. The best we can say is that some countries are not as bad as others" (Alvarez, 1999, p. 10).

Suffice it to say that role loss has been a dominant perspective for obvious reasons. But contrary to popular opinion, in some cases the loss of roles that are not valued or even desired can free an older person in the final years of their lives. This has been found to be particularly true in the case of women who are more likely to have constraining social roles thrust upon them earlier in life (Wetzel, 1993, 2003). In such cases, role loss is not a negative at all, although it is important that new, positive social roles be developed to substitute for the void.

The social roles assigned from birth often are associated with gender, ethnicity, race, and class, and their attendant constraints, expectations, and responsibilities. Such roles are usually power-based, rewarding one group over another. Despite their strengths, the damage to those relegated to second-class status takes its toll over a lifetime, often leaving them vulnerable to poverty. By the second half of their life span, however, there are some surprising results. This is particularly true in relation to gender roles throughout the world. There has been research over the past quarter of a century revealing that older women are more resilient than men, more emotionally secure and able to take care of themselves. This is true even though they are more likely to live alone and to be poor as a result of previous, lifelong discrimination carried into old age, as well as discrimination against the elderly per se. Perhaps the necessity for women to be resourceful and resilient throughout their lives, coupled with their more relational attributes, position them to be stronger in old age. Then again, having been told of their lesser worth overtly and indirectly over the years, in later years they appear to realize they have been given misinformation. As they mature, they learn to appreciate themselves, sometimes for the first time. It is a tragedy that it takes so long, or that their reality needs to be revisited. Such are the fruits of oppression.

A study of twenty-eight thousand nurses between the ages of sixty and seventy-two concluded that women living on their own are not socially isolated or at increased risk for declining health as generally believed. In fact, they appear to fare better psychologically than women living with spouses (Mitchell, 2001). Contacts with friends and family and social activities seemed to bolster the mental health of older women who live alone or with people other than a spouse. The study does not conjecture why this is so, but we might consider that the absence of traditional marital roles and the relative freedom of other relationships might make the difference. In any case, the phenomenon may be universal.

Feminist Life Span Perspective on Aging

Feminist theories provide another lens through which to view the interaction between people and their environments. Nowhere is the influence of the social environment clearer than in its impact on the well-being of women throughout their lives. A feminist life span perspective on aging recognizes the oppression of girls and women over the course of their lives and the heavy price women and society pay (Browne, 1995). The biological, psychological, social, and economic realities of their lives are all brought to bear. The feminist perspective also is philosophical, in that it provides a way to view the oppression of women and to ponder it in an attempt to explain it. But it is not just an intellectual exercise, and it is not just about females. Rather, feminism is a practical worldview that challenges oppression in all populations and seeks to honor the uniqueness and strengths of all human beings, as well as unity in diversity. The feminist gender lens recognizes that economic, political, and social forces collude to create the situation of women that culminates in old age.

The International Women's Movement

The international women's movement was ushered in by the United Nations' International Women's Year, in 1975, to acknowledge the plight of women throughout the world. It soon became clear that a year was grossly inadequate, so a Decade of Women was proclaimed. Women worldwide met initially in Mexico City in 1975, in Copenhagen in 1980, and in Nairobi in 1985. Ever escalating numbers of women, totaling twelve thousand by the end of the decade, forged a Magna Carta for women's human rights, the Convention on the Elimination of All Forms of Discrimination against Women (CEDAW) (1980), and the Nairobi Forward-Looking Strategies: a Platform for Action (1985). The end of the Decade of Women marked the beginning of an international women's movement the world was yet to recognize. Ten years later, in Beijing (United Nations 1995), fifty thousand women came together and forged a Program of Action based on the outcome documents of the Decade. In the year 2000 a follow-up meeting was held at the UN in New York to assess the progress of all member states.

As the years passed, governments were threatened by the enormous success of the world's women. No longer considered a benign movement, efforts were made to reign in the progressive momentum. Although this had occurred in previous conferences to a degree, by 2000 ultra-conservative delegates crowded the UN meetings. Seldom had these newcomers had previous involvement or background on the subject of women's rights. Barriers were created not only to stem progress but also to turn back the clock. The U.S. administration and other conservative governments tried every means possible to deny decisions that had already been agreed on by consensus at previous conferences. They generally were unsuccessful, but deterring them fragmented the energies of the participants, minimizing new gains.

Global reports in 2005 consistently revealed that despite the efforts of the women of the world, the outcome to date has been a disappointment. The report of the Women's Environment and Development Organization (WEDO) (2005, p. 1), *Beijing Betrayed*, concluded: "Governments worldwide have adopted a piecemeal and incremental approach to implementation that cannot achieve the economic, social and political transformation underlying the premises and vision of Beijing."

And the advance report of Social Watch, *Unkept Promises*, another telling title, measured the progress of sixty member states against their commitments about poverty and gender. This Uruguay-based global research organization finds that the promises have been largely unmet. What is clear is that gender and inequality are entwined (Bissio, 2005). To get a clearer picture of the issues, it is important to be aware of the context.

CEDAW

Understanding CEDAW, the Convention on the Elimination of All Forms of Discrimination against Women, is fundamental. As of May 2006, 183 countries had ratified this treaty. The United States continues to be the only industrialized nation and the only Western nation not to do so (Human Rights Watch, 2005c; Division for the Advancement of Women, 2006). CEDAW is essentially a Bill of Rights for women that sets forth internationally accepted standards for achieving their equal rights. The document specifies policies that must be implemented to challenge women's universal oppression, addressing, inter alia, patriarchal systems that ensure continued subservience as well as vulnerability to poverty, sexual exploitation, lack of health care or access to education, and their role as peacemakers with little or no voice in arbitration.

Social and cultural patterns lead to discrimination and stereotyped sex roles including the sexual division of labor that forces women into unpaid work, sexual exploitation at home and at work, and global sex trafficking. From grade school to graduate school, the substance of what women are learning tends to ignore or trivialize knowledge specifically relevant to females. Women are less likely to have access to education in many cultures, leading to the greater likelihood that they will be illiterate, even in the United States where women today often outnumber men in colleges. Despite their educational status, however, women's socialization, opportunity, and aspirations culminate in a lack of awareness about their situation. They continue to see themselves, and to be seen, as less deserving and less knowledgeable than men, despite information to the contrary. The UN concept of "gender-mainstreaming" would go a long way toward remedying that vacuum.

Gender-Mainstreaming Human Rights

The social work profession has long committed itself to the idea of social justice, and today there are a growing number of educators throughout the world who are committed to human rights principles (Reichert, 2001; Reichert, 2006)). Still, to bring life to a human rights commitment, social work must grapple with the hard work of applying the concept to their values, theories, therapies, practice, programs, policies, research, and work in the community, rethinking and fine-tuning them when necessary.

The concept of "gender-mainstreaming" provides a template for the task at hand. Endorsed by the UN Economic and Social Council, in 1997, the idea is to mainstream a gender perspective in all policies and programs. Before decisions are taken, the effects of a policy on women and men must be analyzed (United Nations, 1997). The detailed recommendations for implementing this concept drew directly on the 1995 Beijing Platform for Action, the concluding document of the Fourth World Conference on Women (Wetzel, 2005). By endorsing and implementing gender mainstreaming, social workers will gain clarity of purpose, while ensuring research, policy, program, and practice relevance.

Women and the Law

Throughout the world, women lack equality in terms of laws and experience in the courts. So, in the absence of oversight, even when laws are instituted, they do not necessarily translate into rights. This has been obvious in recent years in the U.S., where women's rights have been steadily eroding (Milani & Albert, 2003). Organized advocacy and educated awareness are essential to their implementation. But that does not mean that legislation is not important. Without it, there is little chance of realizing personal, social, and economic development. Equality with men under the law is fundamental to women's human rights. According to Human Rights Watch (2005b): "Laws and practices governing women's personal status—their legal capacity and role in the family—deny women human rights in many countries. While the type of discrimination varies from region to region, women throughout the world find that their relationship to a male relative or husband determines their rights." Given that the Equal Rights Amendment was defeated by conservative forces in the U.S. in the 1970s at the height of the women's movement, it is not surprising that support for CEDAW today is proving to be a particularly difficult challenge. In fact, some of the same players are behind the resistance.

Women's Human Rights Capacity Development

The term "capacity development" refers to the desired outcome of the capacity-building process and is an essential approach to ensuring the human rights of girls and women of any age. As social workers know, development is not just a geographic, economic, or societal concept. It is also about human development involving emotional well-being and personal growth. It is, in effect, about human rights. Without attention to the inner self, there can be no real social or economic development.

Over time, the evolution and implementation of capacity building and development have gained breadth and depth. A definition from the field of lifelong learning is particularly pertinent to social work. In their experience, "capacity-building includes developing the critical understanding to effectively challenge the vested interests of the powerful, identifying the spaces within which to promote social change" (Mayo, 2000, p. 24).

Challenging "the vested interests of the powerful," then, is fundamental to women's advancement. If ignored, women do not "own" the policy or program; it fails as their morale fails. Further, policy direction is unclear and implementation difficult. Dobie (2000), the chief author of the United Nations' Century 21 capacity building program, also advises that without the full participation of women, development is not sustainable.

Speaking in the context of health promotion, Labonte and Laverack (2001a, 2001b) make it clear that capacity building is at once an individual and community enterprise—a means and an end. While improved economics may be an honorable goal, the very process of getting there is in itself capacity building.

Micro-Credit and Capacity Building

Micro-credit to develop the capacities of the poor, and particularly poor women, has become a mantra throughout the world, and for good reason. Such human rights programs, providing poverty relief by granting small loans to small businesses, have been touted as unusually successful since their introduction in the early 1970s by the renowned economics professor and recent Nobel Prize recipient Muhammed Yunus in rural Bangladesh (Yunus, 1987; Yunus & Jolie, 1989). Yunus, like his program heirs, found, early on, that attention had to be paid to women's low self-esteem and personal development before economic programs could be established. Once women were given the opportunity to bond in groups, and their sense of self-worth in the context of their families and the community was attended to, the women flourished. What is more, they pay back their loans over 98 percent of the time, a higher rate than men. The trend continues to this day all over the world.

Despite the rave reviews for Yunus's work, there is one critique that should be considered. Yunus himself testified to a U.S. Congressional Forum about why a high percentage of his loans go to women: "Women have plans for themselves, their children, about their homes, the meals. They have a Vision. A man wants to enjoy himself" (quoted in Goetz & Gupta, 1996, p. 55). This reality has been mirrored in micro-credit programs around the world. But instead of calling into question self-serving male behavior, the behavior is accepted as "boys will be boys." It is an excellent example of lost opportunity. Although it is true that women's capacity is expanded thanks to micro-credit programs, the men's capacities are not. Their limitations do not bode well for gender relations and families, much less for communities. That does not mean that any of these critics would want women to be rejected for loans as they have been in the past. Their very strengths, their excellent credit risk, and unselfish use of profits are deserving of reward. Rather, the psychological development of boys and men must be addressed as well if capacity development is to be realized by societies.

Conclusion

Social deprivation and gender inequality go hand in hand, for women are among the most socially deprived people worldwide, as this inequality incorporates economic, social and political ramifications Bassuk et al. (2004). Women's subjugation and inequity compromises not just their lives but also the lives of everyone in the community. Not only is their capacity to thrive diminished, they are less able to support and care for their families and participate equally in community life. Clearly the human rights of woman go far beyond their own well-being to the well-being of the family, the community, and, by extension, the world. Women's human rights are indeed a work in progress. I believe that social workers, given their values, education, and skills, can—indeed, must—move that work forward.

References

Alston, P. (1990). U.S. ratification of the covenant on economic, social and cultural rights: The need for an entirely new strategy. *American Journal of International Law, 84,* 365–393.

Alvarez, J. T. (1999). *Reflections on an agequake.* New York: NGO Committee on Aging, United Nations.

Amnesty International--United Kingdom. (1997). *Breaking the silence: Human rights violations based on sexual orientation.* London: Amnesty International—United Kingdom.

Amnesty International United Kingdom. (1999). *The louder we will sing: Campaigning for lesbian and gay human rights,* handbook. London: Amnesty International—United Kingdom.

Bassuk, E,; Salomon, A.; Browne A.; Bassuk S.; Dawson R.; Huntington N. (2004). Secondary Data Analysis on the Etiology , Course , and Consequences of Intimate Prtner Violence Against Extremely Poor Women.. NCJ 199714 , http://www .ccmc.org/global.htm, retrieved Jan. 13, 07)

Becker, E. (2005, June 11). Odd alliance brings about debt relief: Leading rich to help poor. *New York Times,* p. C1.

Belser, J. W. (2003, February). Fostering women's health around the world. *Response: The Voice of Women in Mission,* 33–35.

Beneria, L. (2003). *Gender, development and globalization: Economics as if all people mattered.* New York: Routledge.

Bissio, R. (Ed.). (2005). Gender and poverty: A case of entwined inequalities. Unkept promises: What the numbers say about poverty and gender. In *Advance Social Watch Report 2005* (pp. 19–21). Montevideo, Uruguay: Instituto del Tercer Mundo.

Brownmiller, S. (1993). Against our will: Men, women and rape. New York: Ballantine Books.

Cohen, J., & Howard, M. (Eds.). (1999). *Is multiculturalism bad for women.* Princeton, NJ: Princeton University Press.

Council on Social Work Education (CSWE). (2005). Educational policy statement. Alexandria, VA: Council on Social Work Education. Retrieved June 27, 2005, from http://www.cswe.org.

Darvich-Kodjouri, K., & Bonk, K. (2001). Global population media analysis. Communication Consortium Media Center. Washington, DC. http://www.ccmc.org/global.htm.

Desjarlais, R., Eisenberg, L., Good, B., & Kleinman, A. (Eds.). (1995). *World mental health.* New York: Oxford: Oxford University Press.

Division for the Advancement of Women. (2006). Convention on the elimination of all forms of discrimination against women. Department of Economic and Social Affairs, United Nations. CEDAW. Retrieved June 6, 2006. http://www.un.org/womenwatch/daw/cedaw/.

Dobie, P. (2000, June). Approaches to sustainability: Models for national strategies: Building capacity for sustainable development. In J. McCullough (Ed.), *Building capacity for a sustainable future* (pp. 25–35). Geneva: United Nations Development Program.

Elden, M., & Chisholm, R. F. (1993). Emerging varieties of action research. *Human Relations, 46*(2), 121–141.

Evans, T. (1998). Introduction: Power, hegemony and the universalization of human rights. In T. Evans (Ed.), *Human rights fifty years on: A reappraisal* (pp. 1–23). Manchester and New York: Manchester University Press.

Falk, D. (1998). Human rights in global perspective. Unpublished monograph, Pomona, NJ: Richard Stockton College of New Jersey.

Ferguson, B. (1999). The shadow hanging over you: Refugee trauma and Vietnamese women in Australia. In B. Ferguson & E. Pittaway (Eds.), *Nobody wants to talk about it: Refugee women's mental health* (pp. 21–30). Transcultural Mental Health Centre. Parramuta, BC: Australia.

Ferguson, B., & Pittaway, E. (Eds.). (1999). *Nobody wants to talk about it: Refugee women's mental health*. Transcultural Mental Health Centre. Parramuta, BC: Australia.

Goetz, A. M., & Gupta, R. S. (1998). Who takes the credit? Gender, power and control over loan use in rural credit programs in Bangladesh. *World Development, 24*(1), 45–63.

Hannum, H., & Fischer, D. (1993). *Guide to international human rights practice.* Philadelphia: University of Pennsylvania Press.

Human Rights Watch. (2005a). Women and HIV/AIDS. Retrieved June 15, 2005, from http://www.hrw.org/women/aids.html.

Human Rights Watch. (2005b). Women's rights under attack. Retrieved June 15, 2005, from http://www.hrw.org/english/docs/06/06/global602.htm.

Human Rights Watch. (2005c). CEDAW: The women's treaty. Retrieved June 21, 2005, from http://hrw.org/women/legal.html.

International Association of Schools of Social Work (IASSW) & International Federation of Social Workers (IFSW). (2004, October). *Global qualifying standards for social work education and training. Global social work congress: Reclaiming civil society.* Adelaide, South Australia: IASSW & IFSW.

International Association of Schools of Social Work & International Federation of Social Workers. (1994). Human Rights & Social Work: A Manual for Schools of Social Work and the Social Work Profession, Geneva: Centre for Human Rights.

International Federation of Social Workers (IFSW). (1996). *Policy paper on human rights* (rev. ed.). Hong Kong: IFSW.

Janofsky, M., & Schemo, D. J. (2003, March 16). Women recount life as cadets: Forced sex, fear and silent rage. *New York Times*, p. A1.

Katz, N. (2005). Women's issues: Rape statistics. *About: News & Issues.* Retrieved June 27, 2005, from http://www.womensissues.about.com/od/rapecrisis/a/rapestats.htm.

Kansas Coalition against Domestic Violence (KCSDV) (2005). Statistics. Retrieved June 27, 2005, from www.kcsdv.org/stats.html.

Keshavarz, F. (2003, April 2). Arriving at the 21st century: Muslim women at home and at work. Presentation to Washington University at St. Louis alumnae conference, New York City.

Labonte, R., & Laverack, G. (2001a). Capacity building in health promotion, Part 1: For whom? And for what purpose? *Critical Public Health, 11*(2), 111–127.

Labonte, R., & Laverack, G. (2001b). Capacity building in health promotion, Part 2: Whose use? And with what measurement? *Critical Public Health, 11*(2), 129–138.

Laquer, W., & Rubin, B. (Eds.). (1979). *The human rights reader.* Philadelphia: Temple University Press.

Mayo, M. (2000, April). Learning for active citizenship: Training for learning from participation to regeneration. *Studies in the Education of Adults,* 22–35.

McGrew, A. G. (1998). Human rights: Coming to terms with globalization. In T. Evans (Ed.), Human rights fifty years on: A reappraisal (pp. 189–210). Manchester and New York: Manchester University Press.

McKinney, C. M., & Park-Cunningham, R. (1997). Evolution of the social work profession: An historical review of the U.S. and selected countries, 1995. In *Proceedings of the Twentieth-eighth Annual Conference* (pp. 3–9). New York State Social Work Education Association. Syracuse, NY: New York State Social Work Education Association.

Merriam-Webster Online Dictionary. (2005). Retrieved June 20, 2005, from http://www.m-w.com/cgi-bin/dictionary.

Milani, L. R., & Albert, S. C. (2003, May 11). Open letter to President George W. Bush from the Working Group on Ratificaton of the UN Convention on the Elimination of All Forms of Discrimination against Women. Washington, DC.

Morrow, M.H. (1999). Feminist anti-violence activism. In A. Brodribb (Ed.). *Reclaiming the future: Women's strategies for the 21st century* (pp. 237–257). Charlottetown, Canada: Ragweed Press.

National Association of Social Work (NASW). (2000). International policy on human rights. In *Social work speaks, 2000–2003* (5th ed., pp. 178–186). Washington, DC: NASW Press.

Neil, K. G. (2005). Duty, honor, rape: Sexual assault against women during war. *Journal of International Women's Studies*. Retrieved June 21, 2005, from. http://www.bridgew.edu/SoAS/jiws/.

Okin, S. M. (1999). Is multiculturalism bad for women? *Boston Review: A Political and Literary Forum*. Retrieved June 15, 2005, from http://www.bostonreview.net/BR22.5/okin.html.

Office of the Prevention of Domestic Violence (OPVD). (1995). *Domestic violence: The alcohol and other drug connection*. New York: OPVD.

Orr, R. (2002, fall). Governing when chaos rules: Enhancing governance and participation. *Washington Quarterly, 25*(4), 139–152.

Peterson, V. S., & Parisi, L. (1998). Are women human? It's not an academic question. In T. Evans (Ed.), *Human rights fifty years on: A reappraisal* (pp. 132–160). Manchester and New York: Manchester University Press.

Pittaway, E. (1999). Refugee women: The unsung heroes. In B. Ferguson & E. Pittaway (Eds.), *Nobody wants to talk about it: Refugee women's mental health* (pp. 1–20). Transcultural Mental Health Centre. Parramuta, BC: Australia.

Prigoff, A. (2000). Economics for social workers: Social outcomes of economic globalization with strategies for community action. Belmont, CA: Brooks/Cole.

Quindlen, A. (2003, April 7). Not so safe back home. *Newsweek*, p. 72.

Reichert, E. (2001, spring). Placing human rights at the center of the social work profession. *The Journal of Intergroup Relations*, 43–50.

Reichert, E. (2006). Understanding Human Rights: An Exercise Book. Sage, Thousand Oaks,

Robinson, M. (2002, December). Quoted in I. Williams, Reflections: Mary Robinson on rights-based development. *Choices*.

Saraceno, B. (2006, January 31). Presentation on the integration of mental health and social development, World Health Organization and NGO Committee on Mental Health. New York: United Nations.

Tessitore, J., & Woolfson, S. (Eds.) (1997). *A global agenda: Issues before the Fifty-second UN General Assembly*. New York: Rowman & Littlefield.

Tropman, J. E., Erlich, J. L., & Rothman, J. (Eds.) (1995). *Tactics and techniques of community intervention* (3rd ed.). Itasca, IL: Peacock.

Tsikata, D. (2002) Effects of structural adjustment on women and the poor. Position Paper. Commission on Social Development Women's Caucus. Retrieved June 21, 2005, from http://www.earthsummit2002.org/wcaucus/Caucus%20Position%20Papers/finance%20&%20trade/sap.htm.

United Nations. (1948). Universal Declaration of Human Rights. New York: United Nations.

United Nations. (1985). Convention on the Elimination of All Forms of Discrimination against Women (CEDAW). New York: United Nations.

United Nations. (1989). Convention on the Rights of the Child. New York: United Nations.

United Nations. (1993). Vienna Declaration and Programme of Action. World Conference on Human Rights. Vienna, Austria.

United Nations. (1995). Programme of Action. Fourth World Conference on Women. Beijing, China.

United Nations. (1997). The 1997 Report of the Economic and Social Council (ECOSOC). New York: United Nations.

United Nations. (2001, November 26–29). Empowerment of women throughout the life cycle as a transformative strategy for poverty eradication. Report of the Expert Group Meeting, Division for the Advancement of Women. New Delhi, India.

United Nations. (2003a). Commission on the Status of Women. , March 3–14). Forty-seventh Session of the Commission on the Status of Women. New York: United Nations.

United Nations. (2003b). Committee on Mental Health , (March 13). A mental health perspective: Violence against women and human rights, and the role of the media. Forty-seventh Session of the Commission on the Status of Women. New York: United Nations.

United Nations. (2003c). Development Fund for Women (UNIFEM). ,(March13). Voices of HIV women of Africa. MaryKnoll presentation at the Forty-seventh Session on the Commission on the Status of Women. New York: United Nations.

United Nations Development Programme. (2000). *Human Development Report.* New York: Oxford University Press.

Universal Declaration of Human Rights. (UDHR). (1998). Fiftieth anniversary. History of the Universal Declaration of Human Rights. Retrieved: June 20, 2005, from http://www.udhr.org/history/default.htm.

Van Soest, D. (1997, May). The Violence and Development Project, Washington, DC: NASW Press.

Wasserman, J. (2002, October 28). Hunger has a younger face. *Daily News,* p.A1.

Women's Environment and Development Organization (WEDO). (2005). *Beijing betrayed: Women's worldwide report.* New York: WEDO.

Weil, M. (Ed.). (1997). *Community practice: Models in action.* New York: Haworth.

Wetzel, J. W. (1993). *World of women: In pursuit of human rights.* New York and London: New York University Press.

Wetzel, J. W. (1995). Global feminist zeitgeist practice. In N. Van den Bergh (Ed.), *Feminist practice in the 21st century* (pp. 175–192). Washington, DC: NASW Press.

Wetzel, J. W. (1996, summer). On the road to Beijing: The evolution of the international women's movement. *Affilia: Journal of Women and Social Work*, *11*(2), 221–232.

Wetzel, J. W. (2001). Human rights in the 20th century: Weren't gays and lesbians human? In M. E. Swigonski & R. Mama (Eds.), *Hate crimes to human rights: Resources for lesbian, gay & bisexual empowerment & social action: A tribute to Matthew Shepard*. Special Edition, *Journal of Gay and Lesbian Social Services*. Copublished as monograph by Harrington Park Press.

Wetzel, J. W. (2002). The evolution of theories of aging in the United States." In V. Fokine (Ed.), *Social work with the elderly in the USA*. Ministry of Education of Russia. Tula, Russia: National Association of Social Work [Russian translation].

Wetzel, J. W. (2004). Mental health lessons from abroad. In J. Midgely & M. C. Hokenstad Jr (Eds.), *Lessons from abroad: Adapting international social welfare innovations*. Washington, DC: NASW Press.

Wetzel, J. W. (2005). Mental health consequences of the globalization of violence against women. *Proceedings of the Fourteenth Annual Conference*, Global Awareness Society International, Begni di Tivoli, Italy.

World Health Organization (WHO). (1975). *Report on World Mental Health*. Geneva: United Nations.

World Health Organization. (1992). *Women's Health across Age and Frontier*. Geneva: United Nations.

World Health Organization. (2002a). Mhgap (Mental Health Global Action Programme). Geneva, Switzerland: United Nations.

World Health Organization. (2002b). *Report on World Mental Health*. Geneva: United Nations.

World Health Organization. (2002c). *WHO Atlas*. Geneva: United Nations.

Williams, I. (2002, December). Reflections: Mary Robinson on rights-based development. *Choices*.

Wronka, J. (1994). *Human rights. Encyclopedia of social work* (18th ed.). Washington, DC: NASW Press.

Wronka, J. (1998). *Human Rights and Social Policy in the 21st Century* (rev. ed.). New York: University Press of America.

Yunus, M. (1987). *Credit for self-employment: A fundamental human right*. Grameen Bank. Dhaka, Bangladesh: Al-Falah Printing Press.

Yunus, M., & Jolie, A. (1989). *Banker to the poor: Micro-lending and the battle against world poverty*. New York: Public Affairs.

9

Human Rights Violations Against Female Offenders and Inmates

KATHERINE VAN WORMER

Anyone familiar with the scene inside the U.S. prison system would not be surprised by the shocking revelations of inmate abuse at Abu Ghraib and Guantánamo. Several prison guards in Iraq who were photographed psychologically torturing the detainees received their work experience as correctional officers in American prisons.

According to *The Fire Inside*, the newsletter of the California Coalition of Women Prisoners (2004, p. 3), the women striving to survive (emotionally and physically) inside the Chowchilla, California, prison walls were not stunned at the Abu Ghraib photographs. As one inmate sarcastically reported, "So what is new? They do this to us every day. I am strip-searched in a very humiliating way just coming to the visiting room and going back to my cell."

Readers will come to see just why the Chowchilla inmates were not surprised at the publicized atrocities against male prisoners, and why they were even less surprised by the less well-known sexual abuse of female prisoners at Abu Ghraib who were detained as a means of pressuring their husbands for information.

Readers will glimpse of the horrible events taking place closer to home, events that will be presented in a human rights framework. Of most relevance to women in prison are the following articles contained in the Universal Declaration of Human Rights (United Nations, 1948): Article 5, protection against inhumane and cruel treatment; Article 23, labor rights; and Article 25, health care and motherhood). Principle 9 of The Basic Principles for the Treatment of Prisoners, set forth by the United Nations in 1990, which states that prisoners have ready access to health services, can also be applied to the situation of female inmates.

Framing prisoner abuse as a human rights issue rather than a criminal justice issue, this chapter argues that whatever forms of government nations have, whatever the assumptions or policies of their criminal justice systems, they should not be allowed to violate the human dignity of persons in confinement. Thinking of the treatment of offenders in this way moves the issue from the realm of specific criminal justice systems into that of international human rights standards.

It is important at the outset to present the social and political context of the upsurge in female imprisonment, namely the anti-feminist backlash and the war on drugs. Within that context we consider the profile of the typical female inmate on her path to prison, a path characterized by chronic victimization. We then examine the considerable costs of female imprisonment to society, in terms not only of tax dollars but of broken families.

The impact of the criminal justice system on the human rights of women in confinement is introduced in the second portion of the chapter. Three major human rights issues highlighted are health care, prison labor, and personal safety. That the problem of sexual abuse of female inmates is exacerbated under the dictates of "modern correctional management" is a major argument of this chapter. The same economic incentives that encourage departments of correction to cut back on costs in staffing and treatment resources are also responsible for placing women at risk of violation by male predators who take advantage of their positions of power. The chapter concludes with a discussion of particular issues concerning specialized care of immigrant women in detention. The emphasis throughout the chapter is on the need for female inmates to receive particular care in order to meet their unique needs.

Correctional Trends

Each year the U.S. Department of Justice issues a statistical report titled "Prison and Jail Inmates at Midyear." From the most recent report (*Bureau of Justice Statistics*, 2005) we learn the following:

- More than two million people are confined in U.S. jails and prisons
- An estimated 12.6 percent of black males, 3.6 percent of Hispanic males, and 1.7 percent of white males in their late twenties were in jail or prison at some time in their lives
- Private facilities held 6.6 percent of all state and federal inmates, and the federal system continues to privatize
- Since 1995, the rate of growth in the number of female inmates has averaged 5 percent compared to an average increase of 3.3 percent for male inmates
- Women account for 6.9 percent of all inmates
- Black females were 2.5 times more likely than Hispanic females and nearly 4.5 times more likely than white females to be incarcerated

The crime rate has actually dropped, and for women the murder rate has declined markedly in recent years. According to the FBI (2005) *Uniform Crime Reports*, from 1995 to 2003 the murder rate for female offenders dropped from 1,400 known murders in 1995 to 1,123 in 2003, a 19.8 percent reduction in just eight years. Justice Department statistics show that violent crime in the United States fell by over 33 percent from 1994 to 2003, and property crime fell by 23 percent (Elsner, 2005).

The profiles of women in prison, in contradiction to the myth of the new, violent female offender, confirm the detrimental impact of mandatory sentencing guidelines. Singling out crack cocaine—the one drug used most frequently in the inner city—for harsh penalties leads to desperate consequences for black and Latina women. When their spouses and partners are arrested for drug dealing, these women are often brought down with them. Equality under the law may thus not adequately take into account the inequalities in most of these male/female relationships. In any case, the new sentencing guidelines weigh heavily upon the young women of color—most of them mothers—who are serving time in the nation's prisons. The backlash against affirmative action and women's "creeping equality" that has played out in U.S. courtrooms—termed "equality with a vengeance" by Chesney-Lind and Pollock (1995, pp. 155–177; Chesney-Lind, 2005)—is clearly also evident within the prisons, where women are held to an entirely inappropriate male standard.

A backlash against women at the higher echelons (by judges, prosecutors, etc.) who have reaped the benefits of affirmative action is played out against vulnerable women at the lower echelons (van Wormer, 2001). Consider, for example, the attempts to stymie women's reproductive freedom; the new coercive and highly punitive social welfare policies; the use of anti-conspiracy laws to punish the wives and partners of drug dealers for their role in perpetrating or covering up crime; extensive press coverage of domestic violence statistics that purport to show that women initiate violence against their partners as often as men do; and, most telling, a resurgence in the previously discounted myth of the "new female criminal."

Sadly, but predictably, the myth of the new female criminal has resurfaced in recent years to coincide with and justify women's harsh treatment by the courts, both civil (i.e., child custody) and criminal. Books, such as *Abused Men (Cook 1997)* and *When She Was Bad: How and Why Women Get Away with Murder* (Pearson, 1998) unabashedly present the case that the female offender has special exculpation privileges. Even *Psychology Today*, in an article titled "Bad Girls," attempts to link "women's liberation" with violent crime (Yeoman, 1999). Interestingly, The Canadian media, in fact, are promoting similar claims about the supposed new wave of female violence. However, writing in the *Toronto Star*, Michele Landsberg (1999) sets the record straight through interviews with criminologists whose data on girls and violence had been distorted in other news reports. More recently the emphasis has shifted to a focus on "mean girls" and female bullying at school (see, for example, the best-selling books by Simmons [2003] and Wiseman [2003], the latter adapted for the popular movie *Mean Girls*). The recent publication of an article in *Newsweek*, "Bad Girls Go Wild" (Scelfo, 2005), is a prime example of media sensationalism rather than journalism. To understand the actual state of affairs for incarcerated women, let us turn to a profile of the typical female criminal.

Women in prison are drawn from the ranks of the poor and uneducated (Shaw, 1994; van Wormer, 2001). Only four in ten women in state prisons were employed full-time prior to their arrests, compared to 60 percent of male inmates. Moreover, 30 percent of female inmates were receiving welfare assistance prior to arrest (Bureau of Justice Statistics, 1999). The class factor is at least as significant in the criminal justice system as in any other social institution.

The racist aspect of crime and punishment is evident in that African Americans are eight times more likely than non-Hispanic whites, and twice as likely as Latina women, to be imprisoned (Amnesty International, 1999). With most of these women singled out for crack cocaine, the drug associated with inner city crime, the war on drugs has become a war on minorities and women.

Nationwide, over 65 percent of women in state prisons are mothers of small children (Bureau of Justice Statistics, 1999). As an unintended consequence of harsh sentencing practices, the children of incarcerated mothers are placed at high risk of entering the vicious cycle of crime and punishment themselves (van Wormer, 2001). With women's facilities often located in rural areas, the mothers are often completely out of touch with their children.

Drug use at the time of arrest was reported more often among female inmates (about 40 percent), whereas alcohol use was more commonly reported among males. A finding that may be indirectly related to substance abuse is that 57 percent of women in state prisons reported that they were physically or sexually assaulted at some time during their lives; most reported that the assault occurred before the age of eighteen (Bureau of Justice Statistics, 1999).

In her explanation of the disproportionately high rate of multiple victimizations for female compared to male offenders, Meda Chesney-Lind (1997) maps out the pathway that leads girls, desperate to escape sexual and physical abuse at home, to run away, seek solace in drugs and the company of drug users, gang members, and the like, and survive on the streets through prostitution. This pattern is exacerbated among inner-city females, where prostitution may provide a means of survival in the face of extreme economic hardship. Rolison (1993) stresses the sexual and physical role of women who, in their economic oppression, come to assist the men in the commission of crime: to the degree that cross-gender relationships are still relatively class and racially homogeneous, women then involved with these men, become objects of discipline by public patriarchy because of their involvement with bad men. At the same time they become objects of discipline by these bad men who see the women as bad or devalued, or otherwise take out their aggression on them. The women's involvement in this vicious cycle of abuse by the state and by their partners can be seen as primary in paving the way for a lifetime on the margins.

The Impact of Prison Privatization

The prison industry, especially in its privatization dimension, is a significant force blocking criminal justice reform. As more private prisons are built, more lobbying of politicians will occur to keep prison construction going and beds full. The incarceration industry generates $30 billion a year in the United States (Mundon, 2001). One major advantage for the government in having privately owned and operated prisons is that it may exempt the state from lawsuits in cases of maltreatment and wrongful death (see Coyle, Campbell, & Newfeld, 2003). From 1995 to 2000 the three major prison companies—Corrections Corporation of America (CCA), Wackenhut, and Cornell—made a combined total of more than $528,000 in federal election contributions, much of it directly to political parties. In light of the spate of scandals and lawsuits involving these for-profit enterprises and numerous cancellations of state contracts, this attempt to influence politicians is understandable. And it has paid off. The headline from a 2001 *Wall Street Journal* article, "Federal Government Saves Private Prisons as State Convict Population Levels Off," tells all. According to the article, the contract signed with the Federal Bureau of Prisons was a bonanza for CCA (Hallinan, 2001). Notably the deal was signed despite initial resistance by the prison bureaucracy itself, and, in an unprecedented arrangement, payment for 95 percent of the beds was guaranteed.

Meanwhile, the war on terrorism is likely to bring further revenues to CCA and other private corporations in the increased detention of immigrants. Even as new anti-terrorism legislation was passed in Congress, the value of stocks in some private prison corporations soared by as much as 300 percent (Moorehead, 2001). In light of these recent developments, the earlier rumors of the demise of the prison industrial complex may have been premature (see Cheung, 2004).

According to the 2000 Census of State and Federal Correctional Facilities, 120 privately operated facilities are authorized to house women (Bureau of Justice Statistics, 2001). Thirty-seven of these facilities are exclusively female. Entries on the 2000 Census listing range from the Des Moines Women's Residential Center, which has an excellent reputation in Iowa for gender-specific programming, to the notorious correctional center at Florence, Arizona. Operated by CCA, this facility has been the subject of several successful lawsuits on behalf of women who have been sexually violated.

The prison privatization movement has enormous implications for female offenders, first, with regard to the increase in the number of women being incarcerated, and, second, in light of the recent history in private prisons of sexual abuse by male guards. If commercial enterprises take over the hiring and supervision of correctional staff, standards will be lowered. At the same time as the state relinquishes responsibility for the running of the prisons, public accountability for the abuses inflicted on female inmates will be even further reduced.

International precedents for these concerns have already been set. In this age of globalization, corporations easily expand into foreign markets. Wackenhut and CCA, for example, both had some initial success in selling their prisons overseas; private prisons for women sprang up in Australia, New Zealand, and England. Women's prison activists had several major concerns, including the removal of women to a large centralized prison far away from family; exemption of private prisons from freedom of information because of commercial confidentiality; economic and political influence of the multinational corporations on Australian sentencing; and use of cheapened prison labor. In October 2000, complaining of serious breeches of contract, the government of the Australian state of Victoria seized control of the maximum-security women's correctional center at Deer Park (People's Justice Alliance, 1999).

The profit motive not only provides an incentive to hold down costs at the expense of quality and care, but when punishment is an instrument of private business, there is a clear conflict of interest caused by the direct relation between profits, the prison occupancy rate, and cost-cutting in the provision of services. As Kate Krepel (2000) describes the situation:

Private prisons are in the business of making money off of incarcerating people. The more people in the beds, the more money they make. Our government pays these corporations the amount it would cost to house these criminals within their own system and the corporations choose how they will spend this money. The less money they spend on prison rehabilitation programs, guard training, and various other areas, the greater the profit margin. Additionally, private prisons can make money by offering cheap labor to other private corporations by paying the prisoners less than a dollar per hour to do entry-level work. Sound morally repugnant? These prisons aren't in the business to make society safer for all by trying to reform criminals. Profit margin is always the bottom line in these private corporations.

Subsidized programs offering job training and higher education are off-limits in this time of fiscal conservatism; poor women and children are the losers (Danner, 2000). Any money saved through cutbacks in welfare and health care aid is being funneled into the criminal justice system for expanded buildings and tighter security measures.

The new prison industrial complex will only impoverish communities as it enriches politicians and corporations. "Although women have largely been left out of the debate," Danner (2000, p. 222) argues, "it us women who are the quiet losers—the big-time losers—in the crime bills. Criminal justice reforms such as these are politically motivated, unnecessary, ineffective, and far, far too costly."

When women, most of them mothers, are sent to prison, their children are punished as well. Because such women are often single mothers, the children typically are sent to relatives or to an overloaded foster care system. Consumed by anger and rage, these children are clear candidates for developing emotional and legal problems down the road. In a 1999 nationwide poll by *U.S. News and World Report,* all but one of the juvenile justice agencies surveyed reported that more girls than boys had mothers who had been previously arrested. The state of Iowa reported that 64 percent of girls in that state in trouble with the law said their mothers had criminal records (Locy, 1999, pp. 18–21). Several other states were not far behind. Most of these mothers in prison are sentenced for drug-related offenses. Mandatory drug treatment with close aftercare monitoring, therefore, could provide tremendous cost savings for the community, thereby sparing the succeeding generation from following in their mothers' footsteps into crime (van Wormer & Davis, 2003). One thing is certain: building more prisons will *not* reduce the rate of intergenerational crime.

Human Rights and Women Prisoners

The United States was largely instrumental in the development of the United Nations Universal Declaration of Human Rights, which was enacted in 1948. The U.S. has continued to be a powerful moral force in monitoring international human rights abuses. But what about human rights abuses in the U.S.? Article 5 of the Declaration states, "No one shall be subjected to torture or to cruel, inhuman or degrading treatment or punishment" (United Nations, 1948). This standard, which seems identical to that of the U.S. Bill of Rights, is, in fact, a higher standard because it includes the word *or*. The application of the Eighth Amendment's "cruel and unusual" punishment, according to an article in the *Harvard Environmental Law Review* (Geer, 2000), requires that both elements apply at once—cruel and unusual. According to a recent Supreme Court ruling, the majority determined that if the cruelty is usual, then it is constitutional. In 1994 the United States ratified the Convention against Torture and Other Cruel, Inhuman or Degrading Treatment or Punishment. The U.S. government only signed this treaty with the stipulation that individuals would be given no more rights than those provided by the U.S. Constitution (Amnesty International, 1999). This restriction has important implications for prisoners who are mistreated in the custody of the state.

Of particular relevance to incarcerated women is that the U.S. resistance to international human rights commitments was even more pronounced in the failure of the Senate to ratify the Convention on the Elimination of all Forms of Discrimination against Women. This treaty's provisions of the right to adequate health care services and protection against gender-based violence are especially relevant to women (Human Rights Watch, 1996).

Other relevant UN documents are standards that carry less legal weight than treaties but nevertheless have moral power. Pertinent to women who are imprisoned is the UN Standard Minimum Rules for the Treatment of Prisoners. Rule 53 (3) provides that women should be attended and supervised only by women officers (United Nations, 1948). In the United States, however, nondiscrimination guidelines have removed most restrictions on women working in men's prisons. Accordingly, more often than not, women incarcerated in U.S. prisons are guarded by men; uniquely in this country, men are sometimes placed in contact positions over female inmates (van Wormer, 2001). Violations in the form of sexual harassment have been reported in virtually every state (Amnesty International, 1999).

The worst violations have come from privatized prisons, which are staffed by poorly trained and poorly paid correctional officers.

Sexual Abuse of Female Inmates

The stories of rape, revenge deprivations, forced nudity lockup, pregnancies in a closed system where the only males were the guards, forced abortions, and solitary confinement of complainants and witnesses to the abuses barely received notice until seven or eight years ago. Thanks to the facts revealed in a string of lawsuits, organizations such as Amnesty International and Human Rights Watch were able, through access to proof from court records, to run investigations of their own.

In practice unique to North America, male guards are placed in contact positions over female inmates, and the inevitable scandals and lawsuits follow. The facts are daunting, as are the individual stories that have come to light in lawsuits described in Human Rights Watch and Amnesty International reports as well as on national television and in personal correspondence from prisoners (Human Rights Watch, 1996; Amnesty International, 1999).

If not for the idealism and determination of legal aid lawyers and feminist organizations such as the National Women's Law Center, the stories might never have emerged. Across the country, incidents were reported of prison or jail staff sexually molesting inmates with impunity (Siegal, 1998). Ineffective formal procedures, legislation, and reporting capacity within U.S. jails and prisons account for much of the ongoing sexual abuse of women, according to Amnesty International (2005). If a prison official is found guilty, he is often simply transferred ("walked off the yard") to another facility instead of being fired. The inmate may also be transferred. The situation in privately owned prisons, with their poorly paid and trained staff, and little accountability, is the most unconscionable. Consider what happened at the predominately male-staffed, CCA-operated facility in Florence, Arizona.

Barrilee Bannister has written to me personally and been interviewed publicly concerning events that took place at the Central Arizona Detention Center (Bannister, 1998). When several female Oregon inmates were transferred to the for-profit, private facility in Arizona because of severe overcrowding in Oregon, they were subjected to unprofessional conduct.

Bannister, one of the prisoners transferred to Arizona and then back to Oregon when she complained, reported that a guard captain gave a marijuana cigarette to six women and then had men search their cells. They could avoid charges of drug possession, they were told, if they would perform a strip tease for the men. When they complied, the officers became sexually aggressive with them. After Bannister filed an official complaint, she was beaten by three officers.

A settlement reached in a suit filed by the Justice Department was flawed and weak, according to a Human Rights Watch report (Human Rights Watch, 2000). The Department of Corrections is allowed to continue to place women in solitary confinement after they have filed complaints of sexual abuse. No mechanism has been set up through which women can safely file complaints without fear of retaliation. The fear of retaliation silences many inmates from ever coming forward about the abuse. As we learn from Amnesty International (2005), many states give their guards access to the inmates' personal history files, which includes any record of complaints against themselves or other prison authorities. The correctional officers are even encouraged to review the files in many instances. In addition, as the report states, officers threaten the prisoner's children and visitation rights as a means of silencing the women. Guards also issue "rules-infraction" tickets, which extend the woman's stay in prison if she speaks out, and prisoners who complain are frequently placed on administration segregation.

In Texas, allegations of poorly staffed prisons and rampant sex behind bars caused Wackenhut to lose one of its jails when the staff conducted an audit and transferred the women to another facility. Many of the women had been raped. Similar stories emerged from a Texas women's prison and the Juvenile Justice Center, both run by Wackenhut (McNair, 2000). Few such cases are officially reported, however. A major setback to the civil rights of inmates came in the form of the passage of the Prison Litigation Reform Act in 1995, which limits judicial supervision of prisons and thereby reduces the civil rights of inmates. The difficulty of litigation notwithstanding, a substantial settlement was awarded to five female prisoners who had been coerced into sex with a correctional officer at a privately owned halfway house in Anchorage (*Prison Legal News*, 2001).

To appreciate the human side of some of the daily humiliations that takes place in women's prisons, here are several anonymous quotes from *The Fire Inside* (California Coalition of Women Prisoners, 2004):

Torture here is commonplace and daily. I came from an abusive relationship into much worse abuse here. It is so much worse partly because here there is no escape. If you try to stand up for yourself and fill out a 602 form complaining about anything, there is almost immediate retaliation. Humiliation is all pervasive. Some of the guards were reassigned here from Corcoran in the wake of the infamous staging of human cockfights. Does anyone think that their assignment here is to our benefit? They can do even more damage here. (p. 3)

The unmistakably sexual content of the abuse at Abu Ghraib is present here, too. For example, when we go to the infirmary to see a doctor, there is no cell with a bathroom there. We have to use a toilet in full view of male guards. The male gynecologist makes derogatory comments about us to other male guards after a gyn exam. (p. 6)

A medicated prisoner was raped but managed to snatch a piece of the condom with some pubic hair. Only with evidence like this is anything done at all. However, now she doesn't go to get her treatment, because she is worried that, when she is vulnerable, a buddy of his might get her. (p. 6)

Another female inmate from another system states, "To walk into the prison system is to be humiliated. Male guards make you take your clothes off, spread your butt cheeks, and lift your breasts ... While some officers really care, others treat us as meat and see us as savages" (Awilda Gonzalez, cited by Heather Haddon, 2001, p. 1).

Human Rights and Prison Labor

In 1979, to ensure a cheap labor pool, Congress began a process of deregulation that allowed private corporations to exploit the captive labor market for profit. Modern-day prison labor, argues Levin (1999), bears a frightening resemblance to slavery, with wages as low as eleven cents an hour in some places with no benefits or vacations. The prisoners must choose between taking low-paying jobs or serving longer sentences, since "good time" policies subtract days from one's total sentence for good behavior and days worked. In California prisoners who refuse to work are moved to disciplinary housing and lose canteen privileges, as well as "good time" credit that slices time off their sentences (Overbeck, 1997). In fact, although involuntary servitude as punishment for crime is legal under the U.S. Constitution (Thirteenth Amendment), it is prohibited by the UN's Universal Declaration of Human Rights (1948) which outlaws slavery in all forms.

Consider the fact that prison-made goods were initially only manufactured for state agencies; now they flow into all sectors of the economy, competing with outside companies and jobs. The extent of this exploitation of involuntary labor is revealed in an article in the 1997 summer issue of *Iowa Commerce Magazine:* "Employers pay an hourly wage only. No workers' compensation. No unemployment. No health insurance. No benefits" (Basu, 1998). Corporations ranging from JC Penney and Victoria's Secret to IBM and TWA utilize prison labor to cut costs and increase profit margins, although some inmates are relatively well paid by the companies that employ them—well paid, that is, by prison standards (Levin, 1999). Cheap prison labor may cost corporations very little in overhead, but profits of corporations utilizing prison labor ranges in the billions of dollars nationwide (Overbeck, 1997). In contrast, prison workers in countries with better welfare systems such as Sweden and Norway are well paid, unionized, and receive paid vacation time; in Canada, prison workers are paid a living wage, even for schooling (van Wormer, 2001). For the smooth running of a women's institution, these kinds of incentives for work and education are immensely helpful to correctional authorities.

Private prison companies have been predictably enthusiastic about the booming market for cheap convict labor. Whether they sew clothes or engage, for example, in data entry or telemarketing, inmates in the private system are paid far less than workers in the state or federal systems (Silverstein, 1997). Women typically are paid fifteen to thirty cents an hour, and even female juveniles may be forced to work a forty-hour week if they have been tried and sentenced as adults (Jordan, 1996).

The influence from the fear of losing jobs to cheap foreign labor has even pushed the general public into allowing the slave labor of inmates. In 1995 a constitutional amendment putting 100 percent of state inmates to work was overwhelmingly passed by Oregon voters (Overbeck, 1997). In 2000 there were thirty-six states permitting the use of convict labor in commercial enterprise resulting in eighty thousand inmates being employed in commercial activity (Whyte & Baker, 2000). Several states, moreover, now require prisoners to pay for basic necessities from medical care to toilet paper to the use of the library. Many states are now charging "room and board." Some jails, for example, Berks County Jail in Pennsylvania, are charging inmates money just to be there, and other states have similar legislation pending (Goldberg & Evans, 1997). So, although the government cannot (yet) actually require inmates to work at private industry jobs for less than minimum wage, they are forced to by necessity.

Recent developments are calling for change. The impetus is coming from business groups and corporations that want to obtain the federal government contracts (Arnold, 2005). Legislators, under pressure from the companies, are starting to cut back a federal program that puts prisoners to work making products for sale to the government. Although one of the stated aims is to bring in more educational and job-training programs, the extent to which this is a positive development for inmates remains to be seen.

Health Care and Human Rights

"Third Death in Two Months at Tutwiler Raises More Questions" announces a recent headline describing the scandal concerning medical treatment inadequacies at the Julia Tutwiler correctional facility in Wetumpka, Alabama (Associated Press, 2005). Since the prison health services there were privatized, three inmates have died. Negligent care was suspected. The lack of physician treatment in such cases as these had resulted in a federal lawsuit against the prison. An appointed court motion cited the lack of a treatment plan and failure to watch vital signs in seriously ill inmates as responsible for unnecessary deaths at the prison.

Health care for both male and female prisoners is sub par, but women face exceptional hardships in a system based on a military design, with young and healthy men as the treatment model (Cooper, 2002). The failure of the state to provide adequate medical care to meet the special needs of female prisoners was highlighted in the report of the U.S. General Accounting Office (1999), *Women in Prison: Issues and Challenges Confronting U.S. Correctional Systems*. Focusing on the nation's three largest correctional systems—the Federal Bureau of Prisons, the California Department of Corrections, and the Texas Department of Criminal Justice, a system holding collectively more than one-third of the nation's female inmates—the report found serious deficiencies in the areas of treatment for substance abuse, mental health problems, and HIV infection. Compared to men, women in prison have higher rates of illness in all three areas. For mental illness, for example, 13 percent of female inmates in federal prisons and 24 percent in state prisons report having a mental disorder or having spent time in a mental hospital (compared to 7 and 16 percent of men). The 1999 government report revealed that the prisons surveyed provided ready access to female-specific health care services, and that initial physical and pelvic examinations, mammograms, and routine pregnancy screening were done. Many of the prisons were under close external scrutiny as a result of lawsuits over neglectful health care in the past.

Substance-abuse treatment is the area of most striking deficiency; despite the fact that 70 to 80 percent of female inmates today have substance abuse problems, only about one-fourth of them receive the treatment they need. We must keep in mind that attendance at self-help group meetings, such as Alcoholics Anonymous, is counted as "treatment" in most prison surveys.

Partly because of the explosion in the female prison population, insufficient numbers of staff members are available to meet these physical and mental health needs. Legal cases based on medical abuse and neglect, accordingly, abound. Whereas prison administrators insist they are doing their job, health-care related complaints from female inmates and their legal advocates indicate otherwise. The denial of adequate medicine for chronic diseases, lack of timely treatment for spreading cancers, and dangerous delays in care for pulmonary and cardiac problems are among the allegations made (Talvi, 1999). From the California Women's Facility at Chowchilla come reports, contained in a lawsuit, of a mentally ill woman confined naked in a dirty cell, where she ingested her own feces; another inmate who died of untreated pancreatitis, having been denied access to her medications; and a new prison policy requiring HIV-positive patients to stand in long lines three times a day to receive doses of their medications (Clarkson, 1998). The biggest complaints from inmates at this facility concern health care. Even prison staff acknowledges that inmates often have to wait three months to see one of the five doctors who serve four thousand inmates. Accountability at Chowchilla for medical care is practically nonexistent (Cooper, 2002).

The situation in Nevada reportedly is similar, where the medical services provided by CCA at the women's prison in Las Vegas have been completely

inadequate to meet the women's needs. Such contractors save money by
hiring LPNs rather than RNs and by reducing qualifications in other areas (Dornan, 1999). For some women in prison, their ten- and twenty-year
sentences become death sentences, as their chronic illnesses become ter-
minal (Talvi, 1999). Thayer (2005, p. 2) sums up the situation pertaining
to cost cutting at the expense of women's health needs:

> Introduce the profit motive, and these challenges are exacerbated. In-
> carcerated women "are among the least favored people in society," says
> Si Kahn, executive director of Grassroots Leadership, a community-
> organizing effort that resists prison privatization in the South. "Almost
> no one cares about a woman in prison," so women's health care is "not
> something to which the government gives large amounts of money to
> start with. It's not like there's a lot of fat to be cut." And yet for a private
> company to get a prison health contract, "you're going to have to offer
> to do it for less money" than the government would charge, while also
> keeping shareholders and top executives happy. The chief executive of
> CCA, the nation's largest owner and operator of privatized prisons, made
> more than $1 million in 2003, not counting stock awards, according to
> the company's annual report.

That many states are guilty of medical neglect is highlighted in the Amnesty International (1999) report on human rights violations of women in
custody. Florida, Virginia, and Washington, DC, were singled out for their
routine medical neglect of female inmates. Amnesty International calls attention to the following health care failings:

- Inadequate staff that cannot meet physical and mental health needs
- Long delays in obtaining medical attention; disrupted and poor
  treatment causing the physical deterioration of prisoners with
  chronic and degenerative diseases, like cancer; and overmedicating
  prisoners with psychotropic drugs
- Using nonmedical staff to screen requests for treatment
- The serious lack of mental health staffing
- Routinely providing medication to women attempting to access
  mental health services but not giving them the opportunity to undergo psychotherapeutic treatment

- Keeping women in Security Housing Units for twenty-two to twenty-four hours a day in small, concrete cells, many of whom are later diagnosed with mental health problems (one California psychiatrist told Amnesty International that such harsh conditions can induce psychosis or exacerbate existing mental illness)
- Shackling all prisoners, including those who are pregnant, which is the policy in federal prisons and in the U.S. Marshall Service, and exists in almost all state prisons; shackling during labor, which may cause possible complications during delivery such as hemorrhage or decrease in fetal heart rate; delaying caesarean sections, when a delay of even five minutes can result in permanent brain damage to the baby
- Providing little or no access to women inmates suffering from treatable diseases such as asthma, diabetes, sickle cell anemia, cancer, late-term miscarriages, and seizures, sometimes resulting in death or permanent injury
- Failing to deliver lifesaving drugs for inmates with HIV/AIDS
- Charging inmates for medical attention, in violation of international standards, arguing that the charge deters prisoners from avoiding work or seeking medical attention for minor matters

Amnesty International makes the following recommendations:

- Local, state, and federal authorities should provide resources to ensure identification of the physical and mental health care needs of all inmates upon admission and while in custody, and provide necessary services and treatment
- Health care should be provided without charge
- Health care should accord with professionally recognized community standards for services to women
- Authorities should establish standards of adequacy and appropriateness for prison and jail health services, and conduct periodic, independent external reviews of the services
- People who are mentally ill should not be in jails and prisons but in mental health institutions
- The federal government should establish an inquiry into mental health services for women in jails and prisons, including the overuse of psychotropic medication

Poor prison health standards in the United States are in violation of international law. As states in Article 25, Part I, of the Universal Declaration of Human Rights: "Everyone has the right to a standard of living adequate for the health and well-being of himself and his family, including food, clothing, housing and medical care and necessary social services, and the right to security in the event of unemployment, sickness, disability, widowhood, old age or other lack of livelihood in circumstances beyond his control."

Unfortunately the United States did not sign this part of the U.N. Covenant so it does not carry the weight of a treaty. An international treaty that does have treaty status is the International Covenant on Civil and Political Rights (ICCPR), enforced in 1976. According to Human Rights Watch (2003), the ICCPR is the most comprehensive international human rights treaty the United States has ratified, and it includes provisions explicitly intended to protect prisoners from torture and cruel, inhuman, or degrading treatment or punishment.

Maternity Care, HIV, and TB

Whether the prison is privately operated or state-owned and operated, medical services tend to be privatized through contractual arrangements. Firms receive a fixed rate to provide medical care to prisoners, so every dollar *not* spent benefits the company's profit margin.

Because of the focus on short-term cost saving, privatization of medical care can be expected to make things worse. In California, for example, an investigation of medical care offerings showed a lack of prenatal care for pregnant women. Systemic problems at the contracting hospital included lack of coordination of services and medical information, as well as an abnormally high rate of miscarriage and babies who died at birth (Marshall, 1999).

Approximately 6 percent of women admitted to jails and 5 percent of women admitted to prisons are pregnant at the time of admission, and only slightly more than half receive prenatal care while incarcerated (Greenfield & Snell, 1999). Dangerous methods of restraint such as the use of leg shackles while women are in labor increased the health risks to mother and child. Most jails and prisons require women to be separated from their infants after delivering in a local hospital (Miles, 2004). In any case, care of newborns of HIV-infected mothers is a complex and daunting task, particularly if complicated by drug dependence in the infant. And since the drug use rates for female prisoners are higher than male prisoners, and given that 70 percent of federal inmates and 80 percent of state and local inmates report drug use, the rate of drug-dependent infants of incarcerated women is growing (U.S. Department of Justice, 2000).

Compared to men, women in prison have strikingly higher rates of illness in the areas of substance abuse, mental health problems, and HIV infection. All three areas of illness are interrelated. At year's end in 2002, 3.0 percent of all female state prison inmates were HIV-positive compared to 1.9 percent of male inmates (Bureau of Justice Statistics, 2004). Because the women drug-offender group is at high risk for contracting and transmitting HIV, AIDS has become the leading cause of death among female inmates (Brewer & Derrickson, 1992). A high correlation exists between HIV cases and tuberculosis; tuberculosis rates are falling for men in prison but are rising among female inmates. In some prisons TB infects one in four people compared to less than one in ten thousand in the general population (Bureau of Justice Statistics, 2000).

HIV, like other health problems of female inmates, is often a part of the cultural baggage brought into prison with those incarcerated. Because of their dire poverty and the failure of the United States to offer universal health care, jails and prisons are in the paradoxical position of providing access to health care services unavailable in the women's home communities. Helpful interventions that can and should be offered to high-risk female inmates include education about HIV and the risk of venereal disease, cognitive-behavioral and technical skills, such as cleaning needles in a high-risk environment, education concerning condom use after release from prison, and community public health resources.

Mental Health Care

Studies indicate that between 48 and 88 percent of women inmates have experienced sexual or physical abuse before coming to prison and suffer post-traumatic stress disorder (Amnesty International, 2005). Female inmates have twice the rate of mental illness as male inmates and almost three-quarters have attempted suicide at some point in their lives (Brennan & Austin, 1997). Yet very few prison systems provide adequate counseling, and, as noted, women attempting to access mental health services

are routinely given medication without the opportunity to undergo psychotherapeutic treatment. According to one report from the Bureau of Justice
Statistics (2000), about one in five female inmates receive medication for
psychological or emotional problems after admission to prison.

The most definitive report on the state of treatment of offenders with
mental illness is by Human Rights Watch (2003), which found gross violations of medical standards in prisons that were never intended to serve as
facilities for persons with mental illness. The report draws on interviews
with correctional officials, mental health experts, and inmates and their
lawyers to document deep-rooted patterns of neglect and even disregard for
the fate of these vulnerable and sick individuals. Some extreme cases cited
by the report were suicidal prisoners left naked and unattended for days on
end in cold observation cells; officers accidentally killing inmates while trying to subdue them; solitary confinement for lengthy periods in filthy and
hot cells; and deliberate mistreatment by prison staff. Punishing mentally
ill inmates for symptoms of mental illness which are seen as insubordina-
tion is a problem in most prisons. With the dismantling of public mental hospitals in the 1960s and the incarceration boom of the past decade,
prisons have become home for alarming numbers of mentally ill people.
Jails today have become the poor person's mental hospitals, the dumping
grounds for those whose bizarre behavior, which goes unmedicated, lands
them behind bars. Writing in *Prison Legal News*, Herivel (1999) describes
the "mental mayhem" at the Washington Corrections Center for Women
and shoddy medical and dental treatment of women . At the time of Herivel's report, only eight mental health care professionals served a population
of 730 women. Rather than receiving the necessary mental health treatment for suicidal and self-harming behavior, these women often end up in
segregation cells.

Social workers have long complained of the inadequacies of mental
health services in correctional facilities (Alexander, 1999). A task force
formed by the American Psychiatric Association in response to the abys-
mal lack of mental health services in jails and prisons delineated four core
elements of adequate care: mental health screening and evaluation; crisis
intervention; treatment; and discharge planning and referral.

Because of their smaller numbers, mentally ill women in prisons are
even more apt than their male counterparts to be housed with the general population and therefore to get into trouble. Some, as a result, end up
serving incredibly long sentences. One such case with which I am person-

ally familiar, having interviewed several family members along with two reporters from the Louisville press, ended in the inmate's death. I have written about the circumstances in detail elsewhere (van Wormer, 2001). Sherry Sloan from Bowling Green, Kentucky, was both mentally retarded and mentally ill. She had entered a plea of guilty to an earlier charge involving a fight. Her inability to function in jail and follow the rules had led to her serving years in prison, most of them in solitary confinement. The antipsychotic medication caused her weight to expand at some point in her confinement to more than four hundred pounds. She was twenty-seven years old at her death.

When Sloan died of mysterious circumstances, the case was initially reported in the local newspaper. According to claims made by her relatives, Sloan was killed by prison officers who were restraining her. The prison officials first claimed she had fallen off the "bed" (which was actually a mattress on the floor), and then claimed she had had an epileptic seizure. The autopsy report, which I read, confirmed there were bruises all over her body. Sloan's family members fought to publicize the case, file a civil lawsuit, and have federal authorities conduct an investigation. Lawyers refused to take the case, saying there was no monetary incentive to do so. The facts apparently were suppressed by the press, however, and the only report apart from initial news accounts was mine.

A similar case highlighted in the *New York Times Magazine* described the suicide of a mentally ill woman who had been confined to her cell for 250 days, and another 160 days in a barren chamber with a concrete floor called "the box" (Pfeiffer, 2004). As discussed in the article, the problem nationwide is in confining people to units where, if they were not already mentally ill, they would be at risk of suffering a mental breakdown. Modern research on prisoners of war, immobilized spinal-injury patients, solo, long-flight pilots, Antarctic dwellers, and prison inmates have shown that all were vulnerable to psychosis during their long periods of isolation and sensory deprivation (Pfeiffer 2004).

Treatment of Immigrants in Detention

Female immigrants, including refugees in detention, are another group of women who have suffered serious human rights violations. Even before the war on terrorism was declared, brutal treatment of detained political refugees was the norm. Yet, because the detainees are not U.S. citizens, they are considered to be outside the jurisdiction of U.S. constitutional protections. They are not, however, outside the scope of international law.

Amnesty International (1999) expressed the following concern about immigrants in detention: "Women asylum seekers are often subjected to harsh treatment. While awaiting action on the INS [Immigration and Naturalization Service] claims, they often languish in penal institutions facing the same human rights violations all women prisoners face. Many times they are placed in cells with hardened criminals." Fauziya Kassindja's (1999) harrowing memoir *Do They Hear You When You Cry?* recounts, in graphic detail, the horrors of her oppression during her confinement by the INS. Kassindja, who arrived in the United States as a refugee from forced genital mutilation in Togo, Africa, was successful in gaining eventual release only because her story received rare national press coverage (van Wormer & Bartollas, 2000).

New harsh sentencing laws have created a special population of prisoners—immigrant prisoners—whom the federal government segregates from the rest of the prison population and turns over to the private companies (Greene, 2001). When U.S. national security became the nation's top priority after the attacks of 9/11, the numbers of immigrants in detention increased in conjunction with new antiterrorism laws. In a personal interview with a social worker from Elizabeth, New Jersey, where immigrants, including refugees who request political asylum, are kept in the privately run Elizabeth Detention Center, I learned that conditions that would qualify as "cruel and unusual" clearly apply. Women in the detention center are all in one cell; no recreation is offered; and telephone calls cost an inmate $1.00 per minute. One woman has been detained in this way for five years. To what extent the usual protections offered to Americans under the Bill of Rights applies to these non-citizens is still not completely settled (Levy, 2002, Physicians for Human Rights, 2005). An Internet search reveals numerous reports on human rights violations, some in connection with facts that have emerged in lawsuits (*Star-Ledger*, 2004). Many of the terrorist suspects are currently being held, and have been since 9/11, at the Elizabeth Detention Center.

Conclusion

Because the violation of human rights is a systemic problem, the solution must change the overall system and not simply deal with individual jails and prisons that are ill equipped to deal with massive societal problems such as drug addiction and mental illness. The failure to define this problem as a health care issue rather than a criminal justice problem has created the extreme overcrowding and understaffing (especially of professional staff) that we see today.

As compassion has low priority in America's punitive society, women connected to crime through family ties—mothers who protect their drug-dealing children, or wives and girlfriends of drug-using men, for example—are now subjected to harsh punishment. Often they were turned in to the prosecutors by their men. Drug conspiracy laws and gender-neutral sentencing policies have resulted in a growth rate in incarceration for female offenders that exceeds the rate of increase for men. Constructed architecturally according to the same designs used for medium-security men's prisons and run by male correctional staff, many of the new women's facilities are privately owned and operated. For female offenders, the effects of treating them like men have been devastating. To do so is a violation of their womanhood and, in most cases, their motherhood.

This chapter has shown the many ways in which the privatization of a nation's prisons is associated with the loss of human rights, particularly for female inmates. In health care, mental health and addiction treatment, vocational training, and work, standards decline drastically when corporate interests supersede humanitarian concerns.

There are now at least some positive developments relevant to women in the criminal justice system. Drug courts have been established that send women addicts to treatment instead of prison, and there are restorative justice programs that focus on restitution rather than retribution. According to an earlier survey of women's prison wardens (van Wormer, 2001), tighter restrictions are quietly being placed on male officers supervising female inmates.

But until the U.S. government takes the constitutional rights of citizens more seriously and recognizes the force of international law, the human rights and human dignity violations as described in this chapter will continue.

References

Alexander, R. (1999). Social work and mental health services in jail. *Arete, 23*(3), 68–75.

Amnesty International. (1999). *Not part of my sentence: Violations of the human rights of women in custody*. New York: Author.

Amnesty International. (2005). *Women's human rights: Women in prison*. Retrieved June 6, 2005, from http://www.amnestyusa.org/women/womeninprison.html.

Arnold, L. (2005, May 30). Prison labor has its critics. *Asbury Park Press*. Retrieved from www.app.com.

Associated Press. (2005, May 7). Third death in two months at Tutwiler raises more questions. *Tuscaloosa News*. Retrieved from http://www.tuscaloodannews.com.

Basu, R. (1998, March 15). What's at work in Iowa prisons? *Des Moines Register*, p. A6.

Brennan, T., & Austin J. (1997). *Women in jail: Classification issues*. Washington, DC: National Institute of Corrections.

Brewer, T., & Derrickson, J. (1992). AIDS in prison: A psychosocial approach supports women and their children. *Women in Therapy, 21*(1), 103–125.

Bureau of Justice Statistics. (1999). *DWI offenders under correctional supervision*. Washington, DC: U.S. Department of Justice.

Bureau of Justice Statistics. (2001). *2000 census of state and federal correctional facilities*. Washington, DC; U.S. Department of Justice.

Bureau of Justice Statistics. (2000). Cited in *Incarcerated women in the United States: Facts and figures*. Curry School of Education. Retrieved from http://curry.edschool.virginia.edu/prisonstudy.

Bureau of Justice Statistics. (2004). *HIV in prisons, 2001*. U.S. Department of Justice Report; December 2004, NCJ 205333. Washington, DC: U.S. Department of Justice. Retrieved from http://www.ojp.usdoj.gov/bjs/abstract/hivp01.htm.

Bureau of Justice Statistics. (2005, April). *Prison and jail inmates at midyear 2004*. Office of Justice Programs, U.S. Department of Justice. Retrieved from http://www.ojp.usdoj.gov/bjs.

Bannister, B. (1998). Correspondence with B. Bannister on June 21 and July 5, 1998.

California Coalition for Women Prisoners. (2004, summer). *The Fire Inside, 28*, 1–9.

Chesney-Lind, M. (2005, May 12). Gender and justice: What about girls? Keynote presentation at the Whispers and Screams Conference, Ames, Iowa.

Chesney-Lind, M. (1997). *The female offender: Girls, women, and crime*. Thousand Oaks, CA: Sage.

Chesney-Lind, M., & Pollock, J. (1995) Women's prisons: Equality with a vengeance. In A. Merlo & J. Pollock (Eds.), *Women, law and social control* (pp. 155–177). Boston: Allyn & Bacon.

Cheung, A. (2004, September). Prison privatization and the use of incarceration: The sentencing project. Retrieved from www.sentencingproject.org.

Clarkson, W. (1998). *Caged heat.* New York: St. Martin's.

Cook, P. W. (1997). *Abused men: The hidden side of domestice violence.* New York: Praeger.

Cooper, C. (2002, May 6). A cancer grows: Medical treatment in women's prisons ranges from brutal to nonexistent. *The Nation.* Retrieved from www.indybay.org.

Coyle, E. A., Campbell, A., & Newfeld, R. (Eds.). (2003). *Capitalist punishment: Prison privatization and human rights.* London: Zed Books.

Danner, M. (2000). Three strikes and it's women who are out. In S. Miller (Ed.), *Crime control and women* (pp. 215–224). Thousand Oaks, CA: Sage.

Dornan, G. (1999, January 29). Privatization of prison medical services challenged. Retrieved from www.taho.com/bonanza/stories.

Elsner, A. (2005, April 24). U.S. prison population, world's highest, up again. Reuter's. Retrieved from http://www.reuters.com.

Federal Bureau of Investigation. (2005). *Uniform crime reports.* Retrieved from http://www.fbi.gov/ucr/ucr.htm.

Geer, N. (2000). Human rights and wrongs in our own backyard: A case study of women in U.S. prisons. *Harvard Environmental Law Review,* 13. Retrieved from www.lexis-nexis.com/universe/doc.

Goldberg, E., & Evans, L. (1997). The Prison industrial complex and the global economy. Prison Activist Resource Center. Retrieved from http://www.prison activist.org/crisis/evans-goldberg.html.

Greene, J. (2001, September). Bailing out private jails. *The American Prospect,* 23–25.

Greenfield, L. A., & Snell, T. L. (1999). *Women offenders.* Bureau of Justice Statistics Report, NCJ 175688. Washington, DC: U.S. Department of Justice. Massachusetts Public Health Association. Retrieved from www/mphaweb.org.

Haddon, H. (2001, March 20). Women suffering "extreme" sex abuse in U.S. prisons. AlterNet.Org. Retrieved from www.alternet.org.

Hallinan, J. T. (2001, November 6). Federal government saves private prisons as state convict population levels off. *Wall Street Journal,* pp. A1, A16.

Harding, T. W. (1997). *Do prisons need special health policies and programs?* University Institute of Legal Medicine, Geneva, Switzerland. Retrieved from http://www.drugtext.org/library/articles/97813.htm.

Herivel, T. (1999, September). Wreaking medical mayhem in Washington prisons. *Prison Legal News*, 1–4.

Human Rights Watch. (1996). *All too familiar: Sexual abuse of women in U.S. prisons*. New York: Author.

Human Rights Watch. (2000). *Nowhere to hide: Retaliation against women in Michigan state prisons*. New York: Human Rights Watch.

Human Rights Watch. (2003). *Ill-equipped: U.S. prisons and offenders with mental illness*. New York: Author.

Jordan, L. (1996). Drugs, minority women, and the U.S. prison economy. *Saxakali Magazine, 2*(2). Retrieved from http://saxakali.com.

Kassindja, F. (1999). *Do they hear you when you cry?* Los Alamitos, CA: Delta.

Krepel, K. (2000, November). No more prisons. In *The protest: Ideas and activism*. Retrieved from http://groups.northwestern.edu/protest/nov2000/krepel.html.

Landsberg, M. (1999, November 13). Feminism and the link between girls and violence. *Toronto Star*, p. L1.

Levin, J. (1999, February). Uncle Tom's cell: Prison labor gives a market face to an old idea: Slavery. *Perspective Magazine*. Retrieved from http://www.digitas.harvard.edu/~perspv/issues/1999/feb/unclean.shtml.

Levy, P. (2002). Personal communication with Patricia Levy, Elizabeth, New Jersey.

Locy, T. (1999, October 4). Like mother, like daughter? *U.S. News and World Report*, pp. 18–21.

Marshall, M. (1999, March). *Health care for incarcerated pregnant women*. American Society for Bioethics and Humanities. Retrieved from www.asbh.org/exchange/1999/w99mar.htm.

McNair, J. (2000, April 16). Wackenhut prisons mired in abuse scandal. *Miami Herald*. Retrieved from www.oregonafscme.com/corrections.private/pri.1196.htm.

Miles, J. (2004). The Public health burden in correctional facilities. Massachusetts Public Health Association. Retrieved from www/mphaweb.org.

Moorehead, M. (2001, October 25). Ominous growth industry, mass detention push up prison stocks. *Workers World Newspaper*. Retrieved from www.resist@best.com.

Mundon, A. (2001, May 12). The business of prison. *New York Times*. Retrieved from http://www.greaterdiversity.com.

Overbeck, C. (1997). Prison factories: Slave labor for the new world order? Parascope. Retrieved from http://parascope.com/articles/0197/prison.htm.

Pearson, P. (1998). When she was bad: Violence, women, and the myth of innocence. New York: Viking.

People's Justice Alliance (1999, January). Overseas news. *Newsletter*, p. 16. Retrieved from http://home.vicnet.net.au.

Physicians for Human Rights (2005) Examining asylum seekers. Retrieved July 1, 2005, from http://physiciansforhumanrights.org/library.

Prison Legal News (2001, July). $1.4 million awarded to raped Alaska women prisoners, Prison Legal News, p. 21.

Pfeiffer, M. (2004). A death in the box. New York Times Magazine, sec. 6, p. 48.

Rolison, G. (1993). Toward an integrated theory of female criminality and incarceration. In B. Fletcher, L. D. Shaver, & D. G. Moon (Eds.), Women prisoners: A forgotten population (pp.137–146). Westport, CT: Praeger.

Scelfo, J. (2005, June 13). Bad girls go wild. Newsweek, pp. 66–67.

Shaw, M. (1994). Women in prison: A literature review. Forum in Corrections Research, 6(1), 1–7.

Siegal, N. (1998). Women in prison: The number of women serving time behind bars has increased dramatically. MS, 9(2), 64–73.

Silverstein, K. (1997). America's private gulag. Prison Legal News, 8(6), 1–4.

Simmons, R. (2003). Odd girl out: The hidden culture of aggression in girls. Fort Washington, PA.

Star-Ledger. (2004, November 18). Judge allows detainees' lawsuit. Star-Ledger. Retrieved from www.nj.com/news.

Talvi, S.J. (1999, September). Is health care too much to ask for? Prison Legal News, pp. 5–7.

Thayer, L. (2005). Hidden hell: Women in prison. Amnesty International. Retrieved from http://www.amnestyusa.org/magazine/hidden_hell.html.

United Nations. (1948). Universal Declaration of Human Rights. Resolution 217A(III). Passed by the General Assembly. New York: United Nations.

U.S. Department of Justice. (2000, January). Bureau of Justice Statistics Special Report. Washington, DC: U.S. Department of Justice.

US General Accounting Office. (1999, December 28). Women in prisons: Issues and challenges confronting the U.S. correctional system. Washington, DC: Author.

van Wormer, K. (2001). Counseling female offenders and victims: A strengths-restorative approach. New York: Springer.

van Wormer, K., & Bartollas, C. (2000). Women and the criminal justice system. Boston: Allyn & Bacon.

van Wormer, K., & Davis, D. (2003). Addictions treatment: A strengths perspective. Belmont, CA: Brooks/Cole.

Whyte, A., & Baker, J. (2000, May 8). Prison labor on the rise in U.S. World Socialist Web Site. Retrieved from www.wsws.org/articles/2000.

Wiseman, R. (2003). Queen bees and wannabes: Helping your daughter survive cliques, gossip, boyfriends, and other realities of adolescence. New York: Three Rivers.

Yeoman, B. (1999, November/December). Bad girls. Psychology Today, pp. 54–57, 71.

10

Children's Rights
as a Template for Social Work Practice

ROSEMARY J. LINK

The United Nations Convention on the Rights of the Child is closely connected to social work practice and is useful in addressing issues concerning the well-being of children. In his introduction to the 2003 State of the World's Children, UN Secretary-General Kofi Annan invited the voices of children into the UN General Assembly and expected adults to make room for the children's views and experiences. The record shows exuberant pictures of young people under the age of eighteen, some younger than ten, finding their feet and sharing the microphone to discuss the Convention on the Rights of the Child:

> We are not asking too much! You said this Summit is about taking action! We need more than your applause and comments of "well done." We need ACTION. Think about the children, what kind of world do you want for them? Please hear us, we need time to learn. (United Nations Children's fund [UNICEF], 2003, p. 1)

The children addressed all the components covered in the fifty-four articles of the Convention, including education, protection preservation of identity, health services, and protection from armed conflict and dangerous labor

(UNICEF, 2003). In the last twenty-five years the Convention has slowly been ratified by a number of countries that have come to realize the multiple ways this richly layered document may be used, particularly in the field of social development and social work.

A vignette and brief history introduce and alert readers to the ways we are utilizing the articles of this policy in social work. This is followed by a more detailed presentation and analysis of the Convention in the context of human service and future work. Through discussion of eight clusters of articles, a number of questions for dialogue are raised, including

- How committed are human services in the U.S. to the rights of children?
- Why is there a tension between children's rights and family rights?
- What are the implications for social work when minors continue to languish on death row, and when young adults may carry concealed weapons?

As an international policy instrument the Convention is relatively new. It was passed in 1989 and has now been ratified by most countries of the world, with some few exceptions that include the United States and Somalia. More recently the articles have been implemented and momentum is gathering, as many countries use the Convention as a template for family and child services. The articles of implementation (Articles 42—54) and the mechanisms for reporting to the UN ensure consistency of planning and practice. It is an unfolding story, as the Convention has provided various frameworks and types of support to maintain the human rights of children, a story often overlooked in human service literature. Although adults have claimed the rights of parents to know what is best in disciplining children, the Convention commands attention to the protection of children from abusive punishment and recognizes that,

In all countries of the world, there are children living in exceptionally difficult conditions, and (we recognize) that such children need special consideration . . . and have agreed as follows . . . Article 19: State Parties shall take all appropriate legislative, administrative, social and educational measures to protect the child from all forms of physical or mental violence, injury or abuse, neglect or negligent treatment, maltreatment or exploitation including sexual abuse, while in the care of parent(s), legal guardian(s) or any other person who has the care of the child. (Human Rights Resource Center, 2003)

Introductory Vignette and History

A student participating in a summer school field placement in Koper, Slovenia, spoke of the indelible impression made by an evening picnic organized for her group (Link & Cacinovic Vogrincic, 2002). A child played an accordion and others danced, while their parents shared food and stories with visiting students and senior citizens. All the families present were recovering from drug addiction, and all the children had experienced the consequent stresses in their lives at home and at school, and in the community. The families were assigned mentors from the community: older, retired, previously isolated citizens who listened to and encouraged them. That evening the U.S. visitors became aware of the mutual respect between children, parents, and seniors. Circumstances of social service in relation to addiction vary considerably in the context of different countries. Where the "medical model" dominates, service often becomes "treatment," with professionals in control of clients, and intervention is separated from the needs of the children. The primary departure from that model at this picnic was the respect and seemingly equal power of all present. In Slovenia both families and children participate in recovery along with their mentors and the agency; everyone is equal in status and value. The families are matched with seniors who receive family help with transport, friendship, and meals; in turn, the elders become "grandparents" to the families and encourage their progress. A number of the group members had organized to run in a marathon, and the whole community focused on supporting them in this goal (Link & Cacinovic Vogrincic, 2002). Although Slovenia is a young country (it gained independence from the former Yugoslavia in 1991), its commitment to social services that use the Convention on the Rights of the Child as a template is exemplary (Slovenian Committee for UNICEF, 1995).

Social workers need to be familiar with the circumstances of the Second World War that gave rise to the United Nations and the concern for greater cooperation between peoples of the earth. Unlike preceding wars, children became victims as bombing took the lives of more civilians than military personnel (fire storms in Dresden and Coventry; two thousand people dying overnight in the "London Blitz"; and hundreds of thousands dying in the devastation and aftermath of the nuclear bombings of Hiroshima and Nagasaki) (Stearns, 1998, p. 732). The appalling loss of life led directly to the deliberations and agreements of the Declaration of Human Rights in 1948 and later the articles devoted to the rights of children (including that children not be pressed into serving as soldiers).

The specific focus on children manifested in the UN Convention for the Rights of the Child was long overdue, however. It moved through many revisions during its ten-year passage through the UN in the 1970s, before its approval in 1989. The Convention is seen by some as a fabulous testimony to our renewed commitment to children as people who happen to be under eighteen but have their own identity, voice, and ability to express themselves.

Arguably the Convention on the Rights of the Child affects all our lives but is rarely cited in U.S. agency documents. This is not just a negligent oversight; it may be another reflection of the more deep-seated antipathy to international "interference" in the nation's affairs. But such an oversight is also a threat to ethical professional practice, as demonstrated by the recent plight of the Seattle International Adoption Agency, when it was closed by federal agents out of concerns for international protocols and exploitation (Shukovsky, 2003). Following a presentation of the basic elements of the Convention and the ways it can be used as a framework for social work to support ethical practice, practice in fields including international adoptions illustrates the application of these concepts.

Articles, Goals, and a Framework for Service and Research

The UN Convention on the Rights of the Child has fifty-four articles that can be used as a natural framework for social service and research. The articles may be grouped into eight categories, each with standards and guidelines, and used as a framework for social work practice. The United States, in ignoring the Convention, is in danger of being at a disadvantage with a narrow vision for child development. The Convention also draws attention to the reality that these rights apply to more than just child protection; they involve respect and the inclusion of children in decision making. Other nations, however, are increasingly recognizing the Convention's usefulness. The following are the eight categories into which the articles fall:

1. Definitions of the child
2. Guiding principles (including nondiscrimination, the best interests of the child, and survival, development, and participation)
3. Civil rights and freedoms
4. Family environment and alternative care
5. Basic health and welfare
6. Education, leisure, and culture
7. Special protection
8. General measures of implementation. (International Federation of Social Workers [IFSW], 2007)

These clusters cover a wide array of vital issues for children's healthy development, including the plight of children pressed into fighting and killing as soldiers, the exploitation of young mothers who give their children up for adoption under the pressure of poverty, and the exploitation of child labor. To cover all eight categories at every level of practice would need separate discussion, but, for our purposes, the focus is on the implications of the clusters of articles of the Convention for social work practice, with at least one level of social work practice identified for each cluster. The following list points out the systems theory levels of practice whereby social work recognizes that every individual is part of a family and community system which interacts with surrounding systems, nations, and the world.

micro-practice / person-to-person / punishment and discipline
mezzo-practice / person-to-group / immunization
mezzo-practice / community-to-community / international adoptions
macro-practice / institutions-nations-the world / trafficking, child labor

A key goal of the Convention is to speak a universal language. In reaching for this goal, the Convention highlights the fact that many terms are misleading, whether local terms for marketplace negotiations or more abstract ideas. For example, the concept of "childhood" varies in age and cultural expectations from country to country, especially in relation to betrothal and marriage. Similarly, issues of child labor are interpreted differently: in Jamaica, the term "higgling" is an exchange of fruit and vegetables from family gardens that often occurs in schools among students and is an accepted way for families to survive. In the Convention, "child" applies to an individual under the age of eighteen. Similarly, the term "welfare" has different meaning from country to country; in many European, Asian, African, and Pacific countries it refers to "well-being" in a wider context. In countries with national health services with access to affordable day care and emphasis on public transport and housing availability, "welfare" reform is less harsh than in the U.S. (Scott & Ward, 2005).

Applying the Framework of the Eight Clusters of Articles

That the U.S. has failed to ratify the Convention may have led some policy makers to the false assumption that the Convention is irrelevant or that the U.S. has its own satisfactory systems in place. This is a serious barrier to sharing knowledge and gaining the benefit of the experience of countries that have established processes of participation, self-study, and reporting mechanisms. It also means a lack of attention in human services to children's issues that know no borders such as the provision of clean water.

Thus, although the essential elements of the articles relate to the social and economic well-being of children who are born into and endure acute poverty, certain aspects of children's rights cross all socioeconomic groups and cultures, including questions of identity, health, adoption, and sexual exploitation. Perhaps most important is the theme of worldwide cooperation invoked by the Convention of which Nelson Mandela spoke, in May 2000, in Johannesburg, at the Conference for Children: "This global partnership will be guided in its work by the Convention on the Rights of the Child, that luminous living document that enshrines the rights of every child without exception to a life of dignity and self-fulfillment" (Mandela, 2000).

The following sections present the articles in ways that illustrate the response of the social work profession to this seminal document and the connection to fields of practice.

DEFINITION OF THE CHILD

The eight clusters of articles represent the framework to connect policy ideas to social work. For example, the opening statement relates to the definition of a "child" as eighteen years old or younger. This is crucial to discussions of culpability, military service, marriage, and employment protections. Many western countries simply take for granted that children have the luxury of childhood and adolescence without the adult pressure of economic survival. Children's testimonies gathered by the international development and relief organization, Oxfam, express concerns about access to clean water and responsibilities as siblings rather than adults: Surma Begum moved from Bangladesh to Britain, and she speaks of people not having money for water wells and not understanding public health: "Some people, when no one is looking, they just pee in the water . . . that is how people get ill" (Oxfam, 1996). The definition of the child is part of the expectation that, "State Parties shall respect and ensure the rights set forth in the present Convention to each child . . . irrespective of the child's parent's race, colour, sex, language, origin, disability, birth or other status" (Article 2, UN Convention on the Rights of the Child).

For social workers, the right of every child to have his or her status defined and have a name is crucial for practice. In this author's experience as a school social worker in London during the 1980s, it was normal practice for a child born with a disability and placed for adoption to be called by a capital letter, such as Baby M or Baby P. Lacking a name implies that children do not exist in their own right until they are named by an adoptive parent, and this reduces their independent status and influences attitudes relating to practice. In Minnesota and Wisconsin laws have recently been passed to shelter newborns, so that a desperate mother can now take her child to a hospital, rather than abandon the child, and know that she will not be prosecuted by the state. Immediately at birth the child has status. The law affects social work practice in that it demands that we support and ensure these protections and the child's right to a name as the first step in our encounter. No child should be identified as a number or a category.

GUIDING PRINCIPLES

The second cluster relates to "guiding principles and the best interests of the child, including the right to survival and healthy development" (IFSW, 2007). There is a town in northern Italy called Postoia, which has been deemed a "child friendly city." The town abides by the Convention on the Rights of the Child, and the mayor and administration of the city define "child friendly" as placing children's needs as top priorities for the adult community. The Department of Education has developed preschool "nests," and interdisciplinary teams discuss the most effective ways to serve children, where those with the least resources are placed "at the front of the line" (GPN media, 2002). In reviewing and becoming more conscious of the terms we apply to children's services, we begin to realize how long it has taken to given them center stage and truly understand that they represent our future. This Italian town demonstrates the multiple ways in which adults can work to create the ideals of the Convention on the Rights of the Child by promoting safe and nurturing urban environments.

The idea of Boston, Minneapolis, or Madison establishing a "child friendly" set of policies and practices (which includes banning physical punishment) seems outlandish and impossible until one sees and hears the mayor, teachers, social workers, police officers, parents, and children working together in this sanctuary of commitment. The report of the European Network of Ombudsmen for Children (ENOC) is clear in its commitment to end physical violence in the guise of discipline, stating that,

> The Assembly considers that any corporal punishment of children is in breach of their fundamental right to human dignity and physical integrity. The fact that such corporal punishment is still lawful in certain member states violates their equally fundamental right to the same legal protection as adults. Striking a human being is prohibited in European society and children are human beings . . . the Assembly therefore invites the Council of Europe's Committee of Ministers to launch a coordinated campaign in all the member states for the total abolition of corporal punishment of children . . . to make Europe, as soon as possible, a corporal punishment-free zone for children. (European Network of Ombudsmen for Children [ENOC], 2005)

Social work practice is involved in myriad ways to enhance child development. These articles of the Convention remind practitioners of the obligation to ensure that children are free to learn and develop separately from their parent's impeding actions or crises. The meal program put in place by social workers at a number of agencies in Minnesota, including the Southside Family Nurturing Center, addresses this very concern; when children are hungry, it is harder for them to play and to learn. Issues of safety and hunger are central to child development and a priority for social work everywhere (Scott & Ward, 2005).

CIVIL RIGHTS AND FREEDOMS

The third cluster of articles refers to civil rights and freedoms needing protection from adults inclined to exploit children. The setting up of Ombudsman authorities in several countries, first in Norway as mentioned above, then in Sweden, and in some states (including Michigan) in the U.S. has led to delineating the rights and protections that children can seek of their own volition. This includes the rights of children not to be incarcerated with adults and not to be held on death row.

The 1999 case of the boys who bludgeoned a toddler to death in the United Kingdom shocked citizens into increased dialogue about the rights of children to due process, rehabilitative treatment, and anonymity. Following dissent by the UK courts, the case appeared before the European Union and the boys, who have now been released, are sequestered under new identities with the full protections of the Convention (*Financial Times*, 2005; Waldmeir, 2005). Similarly the U.S. Supreme Court has been criticized for its recent action in which Justice Anthony Kennedy ruled that the death penalty for juveniles is unconstitutional. In writing his decision, Justice Kennedy referred to international approaches to the death penalty and the Convention on the Rights of the Child (Waldmeir, 2005, p. 2). Waldmeir, in reporting on this decision, writes:

> Bowing in part to world opinion, the U.S. Supreme Court abolished the juvenile death penalty in a ruling that immediately sparked controversy over whether the justices should listen to the views of foreign countries when interpreting the U.S. Constitution. . . . Amnesty International welcomed the ruling saying that the U.S. court has ruled to protect child offenders in the U.S. from the premeditated cruelty of the death penalty. (2005, p. 2)

Justice Anthony Kennedy argued that "Neither retribution nor deterrence provides adequate justification for imposing the death penalty on juvenile offenders" (Waldmeir, 2005, p. 2). However, the dissenting judges rejected the idea that the U.S. should look to world opinion or practice in interpreting the Constitution. The summer of 2005 saw continuing anxiety over the longevity of this decision, given the nature of the political response and recent vacancies on the court.

In the view of social work researcher James Garbarino, however, public attention to these civil rights comes not a moment too soon. U.S. attention and questions are being raised despite the anger of the Bush administration, which is committed to a completely independent U.S. that should never be in a position "to ask for a permission slip from the United Nations" (State of the Union Address, 2003). However, abolishing the death penalty for juveniles has reached its own national momentum, including Oprah Winfrey's recent documentary series involving juveniles on death row. The interviews speak to the suffering of the more than seventy young inmates incarcerated with the ultimate penalty hanging over them (Goodwin, 2005). On a more formal, scholarly level, Garbarino (1999) has documented his interviews with boys in adult prisons, including those on death row, and speaks powerfully of the destruction of their spirits and of "the light going out in their eyes." In every case Garbarino describes, the boys had role models of violence and in some instances had watched unspeakable crimes against family members, including coercion and manipulation. In many countries, children are thought to be born innocent and thrive through the attachment and nurturing of the adults and community surrounding them. The PBS documentary *Childhood* vividly portrays the positive results for children in the Japanese culture, which expects that "children live with the Gods until seven years of age," meaning that they are treated as honored and central to the family's well-being (Public Broadcasting System [PBS], 1998).

FAMILY ENVIRONMENT AND ALTERNATIVE CARE

The fourth cluster of articles in the Declaration relates to family environment and alternative care, which includes international adoptions. Article 18 concerns the recognition of parental responsibility, Article 20 concerns children "without family," and Article 21 concerns adoption.

Most agencies are involved in global issues relating to families, but agencies offering international adoptions are particularly at risk if their staff is not globally aware and educated to use international policy instruments, including the Convention on the Rights of the Child. In 2003 the Seattle International Adoption agency was closed, as noted above, because of concerns about protocols with their partners and questions of money laundering and exploitive exchange. The agency would have benefited from knowledge of the articles relating, for example, to the drive to give refugee and migrant children their full rights to identity and natural family participation in finding a home. As reported by Shukovsky, some of the infants offered for adoption as "orphans" had inadequate identification, and in some cases lived in extreme poverty with parents desperate to find ways for their children to survive during economic migration.

Some people in the U.S. are criticizing adoption agencies for their lack of knowledge of the social and economic development of the countries they are working with (Trenka, 2003, p. 138; Traylor, 2002). Also of concern is that agencies' decision-making process on their choice of partner countries is based on political and market availability criteria rather then on social need—moving from Korea to Columbia and then China for reasons of expedience rather than human concern. This search at any price for infants for infertile American couples has taken on a troubling image of exploitation. In a touching and assertive presentation to students at Augsburg College in Minneapolis, Jane Jeongh Trenka (2003, pp. 188, 199) explains her journey as a Korean adoptee in a European American family and community: "The way I think about myself these days is with the word that best describes me: "exile." I hadn't thought of myself as an exile or immigrant before—just a lucky adoptee. But now, I see that "exile" is the word that fits me best." Trenka also developed a list of questions for social workers involved in adoptions:

1. Was there advertising for Korean adoption in rural Minnesota in the 1970s?

2. What was the nature of the advertising?

3. What kind of training was provided for the adoption social workers who placed children?

4. What kind of information did the agency provide adoptive parents about international/interracial adoption?

5. Were there mandatory classes for prospective parents?

6. What kind of follow-up took place in the adoptive families?

7. How are agency records used?

8. What is the logic of having a law that records must be kept if they're not accessible to those who need them? (Trenka 2003)

Traditional pressures to place babies for adoption quickly, partly because the crucial periods of attachment are in the early years, undermine a complex reality. Adoption and correctional agencies for years have focused on facilitating early placement of infants with the presumption of thorough search and due rights for parents. Recently a student intern was alarmed by the rapid placement of children born to women incarcerated at the Shakopee Correctional Facility for Women. She found that it is legal policy for women with more than a year to serve to be encouraged in this way if they have no immediate family to care for the child (Samar, 2005). Professionals have avoided the tough long-term questions of the repercussions for children placed without the fullest possible resolution of obstacles for the birth parent(s) to raise the child. In her vivid memoir as a Korean-American, Trenka speaks to the isolation, self-doubt, and loneliness for children who are uncertain of their natural parentage. There is a persistent undercurrent of questioning: "Why" was I given up, "mothers are supposed to love their children, aren't they?" (Trenka, 2003). Now children are finding their voice as young adults and have high expectations of support for researching and resolving their full identify.

In addition to the common human need to be with family and culture of origin and to have an identity and medical history, the Declaration of Human Rights is a reminder of the way we agree to treat each other respectfully. This particularly applies to people who may be in crisis, transition, status change, or incarcerated. Social work students could choose a group of people who seem vulnerable in terms of their human rights, such as migrant workers, and identify the tension between their rights and their reality. Then they would pay special attention to the inclusion of children in this picture: Are their rights attended to or ignored? The fifth cluster of rights relates to these basic questions of health and welfare.

BASIC HEALTH AND WELFARE

Although some countries have been slow to implement the Convention on the Rights of the Child, others have streaked ahead and given us examples of how conditions for children can improve. One example is the "child friendly" city of Postoia discussed above, the decision of the Jamaican government to pattern its child welfare services on the Convention and the Norwegian decision to make physical punishment illegal under all circumstances, including parental discipline. This continues to be controversial in many nations, including the U.S., where parents see their freedoms as preeminent and superior to those of children (Germain, 1995).

The Convention provides incentives to consider major social policy legislation, such as "welfare reform," from a wider global perspective. For example, Link, Bibus, and O'Neal (2005) developed their research during exchanges between students and faculty in Slovenia, India, Mexico, and the U.S., which produced the idea that children, together with their families and caregivers, regardless of their current plight, have a right to identify how services affect them and how these services can be improved. Children, by far, comprise the greatest number of people receiving welfare in the U.S., and the impact of welfare reform is therefore mostly visited on children. Focus group questions were developed with this in mind; even though researchers later learned that parents did all they could to shield their children from the harsh impacts of sanctions, still they were aware that they could not always "buffer" them. In an introduction to Article 27 concerned with children's living standards, the IFSW manual for social work and the rights of the child states:

> Many people with whom social workers work suffer social exclusion as a result of poverty. They have no realistic hope of securing paid employment and their life chances are blighted by a subsistence existence characterized by malnutrition, poor education and destitution. Breaking into the cycle of poverty requires concerted action at international, national, regional and local levels using the resources of people themselves in self-help initiatives such as cooperatives. It requires resource commitment from national governments and a shift from those policies of structural adjustment that pay little regard to human consequences." (IFSW 2007)

As a result of the debate surrounding implementation of the Convention, the structural adjustment policies of the international monetary fund are recognized as pressuring already poor communities to focus on exports rather than food, on repaying national debt rather than building schools, and on restricting social welfare payments, particularly in the U.S. through sanctions, rather than expanding supports. Welfare Reform in the U.S. is another form of structural adjustment as the country juggles a massive increase in its military budget at the expense of social programs and health coverage.

In Britain, legislation requiring health care visits to every infant born in the country is an example of universal access. Families neither have to prove their need nor go through lengthy admission procedures to be assigned a health care visitor. Ease of access is considered one of the determining factors in high rates of immunization in the U.K. Even in areas of high mobility and population density, the well-being of children is central to budget allocation with regard to health care and social service policy.

It is encouraging that rights to "well-being" were reinforced in the 2003 State of the World's Children report, which identified goals that were since translated into UNICEF millennium development goals for 2015 for all UN member states:

> United Nations Member States have pledged to eradicate extreme poverty and hunger, achieve universal primary education, promote gender equality, empower women, improve maternal health, reduce child mortality, combat HIV/AIDS, malaria and other diseases, ensure environmental sustainability and develop a global partnership for development. (UNICEF, 2003)

According to Bibus, Link, and O'Neal (2005): "Lest these goals seem less relevant to the affluent U.S., families in the Phillips neighborhood of Minneapolis have low rates of health insurance, an outbreak of measles recently threatened the lives of immigrant children, and hunger is the main reason agencies such as Southside Family Nurturing Center offers meals at regular family night."

EDUCATION, LEISURE, AND CULTURE

Article 31 rather poignantly includes the right to rest: "State Parties recognize the right of the child to rest and leisure, to engage in play and recreational activities appropriate to the age of the child and to participate freely in cultural life and the arts." One of the most striking problems of the twenty-first century is the sharp divide between countries of the global north, with plentiful resources, and those of the global south, where there is scarcity, famine, and child labor.

In a passionate plea to students his own age, the Canadian child labor activist and author Craig Kielburger called students to educate themselves about "two worlds"—one of lavish material goods and waste, and the other of the constant struggle to keep food on the table (Kielburger & Kielburger, 2004). Kielburger became interested in child labor when he first read of the assassination of a boy of twelve who was organizing protests in Pakistan. The protests concerned exploitative employers, and the practices of chaining children to looms and forcing them to work long hours without breaks, nutrition, or education. His work has focused on educating people in the global north to realize that they depend on the whole world—rubber, coffee, or tea does not grow in North America, and yet these are daily staples there. Kielburger's work assists the process of recognizing how vital global interdependence is, namely, that none of us can survive without collective action and cooperation.

SPECIAL PROTECTIONS

The seventh cluster relates to special protections, including protection from acute poverty and the trap of being born into whole geographical regions of devastation, famine, or structural unemployment. In addition to disparities between regions, this cluster draws attention to risks for children across national borders who are exposed to the aftermath of political and social upheaval or war. Continuing the discussion of social exclusion defined earlier, the focus here is the common human conditions and geographic realities surrounding children rather than their individual assets or deficits.

An example of practice that is attentive to geography is the English "patch system" instituted with the Seebohm Report in the 1970s. In this system social work teams were located in neighborhoods, which the social workers studied and came to know well. They walked the streets and mapped resources, meeting the local police and leaders, getting to know the family groups, and working to empower communities as well as working with individual cases. This "patch" concept has been adopted in Australia and in Iowa (Adams and Nelson, 1992). As a school social worker in North London at the time of the implementation of the "patch" system, this author took very seriously the expectation that every child on the streets during school time, every runaway or laboring minor, should be invited to hear about opportunities for support, and offered time to discuss their safety and their family supports. Relationships were established with the police department's "juvenile bureau," and troubled children were discussed at monthly reviews but without the children's participation. In retrospect, social work has strengthened its practice in terms of focusing on solutions and participation, and at times these encounters may have seemed paternalistic. These services were available prior to the Convention. Since the 1980s the U.K. has ratified children's rights, an ombudsman for children has been established, and "social exclusion" units of the Blair administration have focused on the well-being of children and families in poverty.

These goals are now part of British policy to expand family centers and ensure the "inclusion" of children and their families in community development and decision making.

Connected to the awareness of children in terms of geography is the question of national borders and human trafficking, particularly of minors, across borders. Under the convention, Article 35 states: "States Parties shall take all appropriate national, bilateral and multilateral measures to prevent the abduction of, the sale of or traffic in children for any purpose or in any form (United Nations, 1989). In some parts of Europe, countries may be classified as places of *origin* for trafficking in human beings (THB), especially children, places of *transit,* and places of *destination:*

> For example Slovenia is classified as belonging to all the three categories. In its role as a country of destination, Slovenia provides a market mainly for adult females and females who are legally still minors, who come from Eastern European Countries and the Balkans. (Kljuc, 2007)

Now that the Convention exists and countries are asking question about the vulnerability of minors and methods for preventing abductions, recognition of the universality of this problem has emerged. Trafficking in human beings is not limited to a few countries but is worldwide and lacks the widespread human awareness that could impede its growth (Free the Children, 2007). The Kljuc organization speaks to the levels of work involved which includes fostering international cooperation, raising awareness of the risk population, increasing knowledge of both the expert community and lay public, and increasing creativity in working with vulnerable groups. One of their innovative projects stood out in a presentation in Ljubljana in the summer of 2005. The project is to circulate a small "dictionary" to victims and young people in bars and vulnerable circumstances. The book begins with translations of words from Slovenian to English, and states, on page 15:

> If you are a victim of human traffickers you can get help and protection now. . . . Traffickers in human beings are often part of criminal gangs that operate in several countries. They work by gaining your trust in your home country, before you leave, and later, once you are in a foreign country, they begin to threaten and abuse you so that you are so frightened

and confused you feel you have no choices . . . [Here is] how you can get help. (United Nations Human Rights Commission [UNHCR], 2004)

The UN Human Rights Commission has coordinated work in implementing the Convention on the Rights of the Child and has supported such publications relating to human trafficking in a number of countries including Afghanistan (Samar, 2005).

IMPLEMENTATION

Regarding implementation, the eighth cluster of articles of the Convention recognizes that no society has a monopoly on solutions and that all share to some degree the challenges and goals identified in the Convention. Articles 42 and 43 are explicit in the macro level approach of each state and its administration:

States Parties undertake to make the principles and provisions off the Convention widely known, by appropriate and active means, to adults and children alike. For the purpose of examining the progress made by States Parties in achieving the realization of the obligations undertaken in the present Convention, there shall be established a Committee on the Rights of the Child, which shall carry out the functions hereinafter provided.

As we note the progress in implementing the Convention in various countries we can see from the UNICEF State of the World's Children reports that children's supports are widely acknowledged as crucial (UNICEF, 2004). Infant mortality is decreasing in countries with access to immunizations, and where national health and children's ombudsman services give voice to a wide variety of needs from Norway to Costa Rica (IFSW, 2007; Human Rights Ombudsman's Report, 2007). The Committee for implementation has encouraged a holistic approach to legislation that affects children, and examples include the policy in Jamaica and Slovenia to utilize the Convention as a template for all child welfare services (Human Rights Ombudsman Report, 2005). At a visit of U.S. social workers to the children's crisis center in Celije, the staff presented their ideas about empowerment and youth participation. One U.S. student asked, "Do you use the Convention on the Rights of the Child in your work?" The instant response, "Of course," surprised the listeners, and they then detailed their approach to having children participate in planning their own futures, described the group norms, and told of seeking permission from youth when approaching parents (Human Rights Ombudsman Report, 2007).

In New Zealand a central office of coordination has established a children's commissioner and overseen major progress in sustaining indigenous Maori culture. Following adverse international reaction to the treatment of two ten-year-old boys who committed murder in the UK in 1999, that country has also now established the office of Ombudsman for Children. Also, the Blair administration has established social exclusion units that identify whole areas of economic deprivation, where families are trapped in cycles of poverty, school dropouts have few opportunities, and rates of teenage pregnancy are high. Additional government funds are made available for community initiatives that benefit children and their families, and are often delivered through the extensive network of family centers and NEWPIN (New Parent Infant Network) services (Stone, 1999).

The International Labor Organization (ILO) continues to deliberate on the concept of social exclusion in implementing policies, referring to it as "multi-dimensional, focusing on exclusionary forces . . . both who and what is responsible for processes of impoverishment and marginalization" (Figueiredo & de Haan, 1998). For many children experiencing poverty, the sense that society has excluded them rather than their having chosen to drop out themselves haunts their ability to survive (Face-to-Face, 1999). This social exclusion invites discussion of how to include children and seek their participation. One example of participation is the practice of "children's parliaments" now spreading in Europe and welcomed by the United Nations (Slovenian Association of Friends of Youth, 2007).

Certainly, for some countries, a natural extension of their non-punitive approach to poverty has been to expand their policies to nurture and protect, and offer opportunities for children to participate. Norway, Jamaica, New Zealand, and Slovenia are some of the countries referred to in this chapter that join others in their detailed attention to the Convention. The recently increased opportunities for participation affect social work in many ways.

This chapter has identified practices that incorporate the Convention on the Rights of the Child as a tool to guide social development and social work at all systems levels: from macro (largest systems of global relationships), to exo (national organizations), to mezzo (local community action), to micro (individual relationships that implement larger ideals). The mechanisms of implementation identified in the Convention assist the actual application of the concepts through channels that include expert committees, support for research, community encouragement, and national and international dialogue. The example of Poistoia illustrates a combination of the community or mezzo and macro approaches to children's rights (GPN media, 2002). In New Zealand the Maori tribal languages are now being cherished and strengthened through the development of language "nests" in schools and communities across the nation. This idea of "nesting" to preserve language and culture has reverberations in different parts of the world, including Native American communities, Wales, and Italy. Similarly, in Slovenia, the concern is to coordinate children's services in dialogue with neighboring countries and to "lay new foundations for its child and family policy" which meet the standards of international research in the Convention (Slovenian Committee for UNICEF, 1995). These examples of implementation are opportunities for social workers worldwide to bring their practice into the luminous expectations of the Convention—expectations that speak to making our commitment to children real.

Summary and Conclusions

In recent years the UN Convention on the Rights of the Child has been implemented across the globe and is now recognized for the dynamic instrument it offers us in coping with the complex needs of children. Carol Bellamy (1998) states that this is a "giant step" since the harsh labor and exploitive conditions for young people at the beginning of the twentieth century, and the current documentation and ratification of a wide array of rights that children need in order to thrive. When we pause to value this remarkable living document, we realize that it offers many layers of support to human service. The following list was generated in an undergraduate course at Augsburg College in Minneapolis in the spring of 2005:

- Countries have a goal to strive for in their services and welfare policies
- The various elements of children's well-being that need attention are identified

- Wide-ranging elements offer a framework and checklist for service development
- Information and examples are given to legislatures so that they can argue and lobby for change in their own countries
- Dialogue is provoked between countries, raising standards and expectations
- Particularly regarding U.S. "welfare reform," we are reminded of the narrow interpretation and restrictions placed on services that increasingly emphasize the marketplace in their programs and delivery of services
- Questions are raised about who is most at risk when economic supports are restricted: when adults experience poverty, children are the first to suffer
- Demands are made that children be allowed their childhood and not be pressed into premature roles as earners, soldiers, or adult prisoners
- Attention is drawn to the overrepresentation of children in all poverty statistics, especially in the U.S. and U.K., and for children of color (list generated in SWK 230 undergraduate course Augsburg College, spring 2005).

Thus the Convention on the Rights of the Child has become the template in social work for meeting the human rights of people eighteen years of age or younger. Although countries openly acknowledge that they have policies to debate and amend in order to meet the best interests of the child as stated by the Convention, progress has obviously been made. For the U.S., this progress led to the federal Supreme Court ruling that no child can be put to death for crimes committed, and that the focus of U.S. policy and practice is the rehabilitation of children back into society. In many countries, there is renewed awareness among social workers regarding concerns about children's identity and the processes of adoption and of incarcerating pregnant women (IFSW, 2007). The UN has led the way in helping children participate in their futures and has celebrated their abilities to speak and be heard. In its summary of the Convention, the International Federation of Social Workers challenges social workers worldwide to understand that, even if their country is still working on ratifying the document, we are global citizens and global practitioners: "Rights are meaningless if citizens do not know they have them. Article 42 requires States Parties to widely disseminate information about the Convention to children and to adults" (IFSW, 2007). As of 2007 the Convention has been ratified by 193 countries; "only two countries have not ratified: the United States and Somalia, [but] have signaled their intention to ratify by formally signing the Convention" (United Nations Children's Fund, 2007).

The Rights of Children are no longer a pipedream. Certainly there are children this morning, today and tomorrow, who are picking through garbage in Mexico and sweating over a loom in California and India. However, the picture on the 1997 State of the World's Children of a small child of six or seven asleep over the softballs he is sewing, has been replaced by images of young girls in the 2004 version who are telling the stories of their part in education, in village public life, and in health projects across the globe (UNICEF 1997, 2004). Social workers have a key role to play in supporting children's rights and keeping society attuned to who is hungry and who is suffering. The Convention on the Rights of the Child demands that we keep our practices focused on a better journey for all children, where they not only survive but thrive in an atmosphere of peace without discrimination. These are real goals, and UNICEF's call for us to accomplish them in the next ten years is within our grasp.

As soon as people have rights enshrined in law, however, these rights seem to be absorbed into the fabric of society (such as the right to vote for women and people over the age of eighteen). Because certain rights seem always to have existed, the enfranchised risk taking them for granted, or ignoring them, especially with regard to children. Even as children's voices are accepted at the adult table, social workers, in particular, are in a position to ensure that they maintain their place and are not only represented adequately but are offered expanded opportunities to participate. Thus the role of social work practice in relation to the Convention on the Rights of the Child is multidimensional and requires that social workers meet the following responsibilities:

- Educate themselves in the goals and expectations of international policy instruments
- Alert social work organizations and agencies to the implementation requirements of these policies
- Question practices that do not meet the principles, in this instance of the Convention on the Rights of the child
- Make the articles of the Convention a priority within the social

work profession in accordance with the agreements of the IFSW and the IASSW

We are all responsible to meet the 2015 UN commitment to eradicate absolute poverty. Living as we do in this period of rapidly changing technology and economic growth, there may be some equalizing of opportunity in terms of access to information through the outsourcing of jobs and the emergence of Internet cafes in isolated neighborhoods. Yet we are still beset with the simple task of making sure children everywhere have enough food to eat, loving adults around them, schools to attend, and a promising future. The Convention on the Rights of the Child helps social workers address this task.

References

Adams, P., & Nelson, K. (1992). *Reinventing human services: Community and family-centered practice.* Hawthorne, NY: Aldine de Gruyter-Bloom.

Bellamy, C. (1998). Quoted, by J. Csete, in *Challenges to children's well-being in a globalizing world.* Fedele & Fauri Memorial Lecture, University of Michigan School of Social Work.

Bibus, A., Link, R., & O'Neal, M. (2005). The impact of welfare reform on children's well-being. In J. Scott & H. Ward (Eds.). *Safeguarding and promoting the well-being of children, families and communities* (pp. 34–52). London: Jessica Kingsley.

European Network of Ombudsmen for Children (ENOC). (2005, July 5). *European Network of Ombudsmen for Children—Submission to the Europe and Central Asia Regional Consultation Conference.* Ljubljana.

Face-to-Face. (1999). Case Study 6.2. In C. Ramanathan & R. Link, *All our futures.* Pacific Grove, CA: Thomsen.

Figueiredo, J., & de Haan, A. (1998). *Social exclusion: An ILO perspective.* Geneva: International Institute for Labor Studies.

Financial Times. (2005, May 10). Supreme Court rejects death penalty for juveniles (p. 17). Editorial.

Free the Children. (2007). An international network of children helping children. Retrieved February, 3, 2007, from www.freethechildren.com.

Garbarino, J. (1999). *Lost boys: Why our sons turn violent and how we can save them.* New York: Free Press.

Germain, J. (1995, April 1). To reduce U.S. domestic abuse, outlaw spanking, as in Sweden. *Minneapolis Star Tribune.*

GPN Media. (2002). Children of the World: Society of the children of Italy. Program No. 1. 1800 North 33rd Street, PO Box 80669, Lincoln, NE 68501–0669.

Human Rights Ombudsman Report. (2007). Ljubljana, Slovenia. Retrieved February 2, 2007, from www.varuh-rs.si.

International Federation of Social Workers (IFSW). (2007). *Social work and the rights of the child*. Berne, Switzerland: IFSW. Retrieved February 3, 2007, from www .ifsw.org.

Goodwin, J. (2005, July). *Too young to kill*. *Oprah* magazine, pp. 188–208.

Kielburger, C., & Kielburger, M. (2004). *Me to we: Turning self-help on its head*. Toronto: Wiley.

Kljuc. (2007). Fairfund. Center for the Fight against Trafficking in Human Beings. Retrieved February 3, 2007, from http://www.fairfund.org/subpage .asp?P=about&s=who_we_are&T=shelters.

Link, R., & Cacinovic Vogrincic, G. (2000). *Models of international collaboration* (chap. 4). Alexandria: Council on Social Work Education.

Mandela, Nelson. (2000, May 6). *Building a global partnership for children*. Johannesburg Conference on the Convention on the Rights of the Child.

Oxfam. (1996). *Answering back testimonies from people living in poverty around the world*. Oxford: Oxfam.

Public Broadcasting System (PBS). (1998). *Childhood*. Film series, part 1 of 7.

Samar, S. (2005). *The history of the Commission for Human Rights in Afghanistan*. Presentation to Peace Prize Forum, Augsburg College, Minneapolis.

Scott, J., & Ward, H. (2005). Safeguarding and promoting the well-being of children, families and communities. London: Jessica Kingsley.

Shukovsky, P. (2003, December 17). Feds claim adopted orphans had parents; U.S. agents break up local agency dealing in Cambodia. *Seattle Post-Intelligencer*, p. A1.

Slovenian Association of Friends of Youth. (2002). Human Rights Ombudsman of the Republic of Slovenia: Who Is the Ombudsman? Retrieved January 13, 2007, from http://en.zpms.si/home/.

Slovenian Committee for UNICEF. (1995). *Situation analysis of the position of children and families in Slovenia*. Ljubljana: UNICEF.

Stearns, P. N. (Ed.). (1998). *Encyclopedia of World History* (5th ed.). New York: Houghton Mifflin.

Traylor, G. (2002, February 16). Closed records leave those who were adopted at risk. *Star Tribune* (Minneapolis, MN).

Trenka, J.J. (2003). *The language of blood*. St Paul: Minnesota Historical Society.

United Nations. (1989). UN Convention on the Rights of the Child. Human Rights Resource Center, University of Minnesota. Retrieved January 13, 2007, from http://www.umn.edu/humanrts/instree/auok.htm.

United Nations Children's Fund (UNICEF). (1997). *The state of the world's children.* Cover image. New York: UNICEF.

United Nations Children's Fund. (2003). *The state of the world's children* (p. 1). New York: UNICEF.

United Nations Children's Fund. (2004). *The state of the world's children.* New York: UNICEF.

United Nations Human Rights Commission (UNHCR). (2004). Representation in Slovenia, Asylum Section of the Ministry of Interior of the Republic of Slovenia Association Kljuc. *Dictionary.* Ljubljana: UNHCR.

Waldmeir, P. (2005, March 2). Top court abolishes U.S. death penalty for juveniles. *Financial Times* (UK).

11

Globalization, Democratization, and Human Rights

Human-Made Disasters and a Call for Universal Social Justice

BRIJ MOHAN

The design, structure, and function of the *global community* are enshrined in a Vedic motif, *Vasudhaiva kutambh kum* (The universe is a family). Indeed, it does take a *village* to raise the human animal. This metaphorical allusion involves a symbiotic relationship between a village and the child "who is father to the man." The implicit reference to the child-community relationship on a global level involves an elemental truth that has become a victim of civilization's own success. My premise is that human development and social development are inseparable; social development bereft of human development, and the reverse, is a body without a soul (Mohan, 2005a).

"The cold war is over, but a strange war has begun. Alienation is widespread; all the more reason for writers to build brides," writes Salman Rushdie (2005, p. 31). The streak of catastrophic events with which the twenty-first century began—9/11, the Iraq and Afghanistan wars, revelations of torture at Abu Ghraib, and the massacres in Darfur—are discouraging about the future of humankind, yet our hopes tend to reflect both our fears and our aspirations. Apparently, the free market, the global economy, new democracies, and the demise of communism auger well for globalization and civility. A new free world of old and nascent democracies should foster freedom, equality, and justice. The twenty-first century may well be called the *Age of Human Rights*.

As a strategic fulcrum of human emancipation, universal human rights are a unifying theme that embraces human and social development as a single, holistic process; globalization and democracy in a world of largely oppressive regimes; and human rights, social justice, and social development as a three-dimensional shield against oppression.

Human rights are conceptualized as inalienable rights of all peoples required for the survival, security, and dignity of each individual, group, and community without prejudice or discrimination. The sole justification of the modern state is its universal, democratic institutions that combat injustices and promote equality and justice. This formulation is in harmony with the values and principles of a free world. However, the gap between ideals and practices presents challenges that the citizens of a free world must confront with courage and conviction.

Are we truly citizens of a free world? This question is fraught with a self-fulfilling prophecy. It is not difficult to argue that social and political oppression abounds in the modern world. The twenty-five European nations struggling to transcend their national identities and the fifty-two countries in Africa are an oppressor/oppressed dyad, as Robert Samuelson points out:

> Ever since 1498, after Vasco da Gama rounded the Cape of Good Hope and opened trade to the Far East, Europe has shaped global history, for good or ill. It invented modern science, led the Industrial Revolution, oversaw the slave trade, created huge colonial empires and unleashed the world's two most destructive world wars. (Samuelson, 2005, p. 7B)

There is no universally accepted theory of human rights. However, the Universal Declaration of Human Rights (United Nations, 1948) may help construct principles for the formulation and implementation of a manifesto. A detailed discussion would have to include five elements:

1. A clear definition and rationale for human rights
2. Criteria for enlisting legitimate rights, which flow from the boundaries just established
3. A taxonomy of rights grounded in an axiomatic constitutional foundation

4. A legal apparatus that ensures the provision of rights

5. A system that sustains and promotes a culture of human rights

One can argue that a pluralist democracy can never fully define absolute, unambiguous criteria for human rights. In other words, even though human rights are "unconditional" by their nature, skepticism will always present insurmountable difficulties in a combustive climate of conflicting moral values. But can we reframe the discussion on human rights so that it considers the current elements of hope and despair? The underlying assumption is that a culture of human rights is crucial for a comprehensive social transformation. What follows is a critique of global aspects of human rights in three different contexts.

Globalization and Democracy

Globalization is in essence the world-wide extension of principles originating in western civilization: the science emerging from the Renaissance. The ideals of democracy and human rights developed in the Enlightenment, and the technology ushered in by the Industrial Revolution. India and China are examples of the application of native industry to these templates. (Wald, 2005, p. 3)

The above quotation, captioned "West Is Best" (Wald, 2005, p. 3), perhaps explains the power and limitations of both globalization and democracy in an increasingly complex world. Indeed, there are "many globalizations" (Berger & Huntington, 2002). "We now have a picture of a cultural earthquake affecting virtually every part of the world," writes Peter Berger in his analysis of the cultural dynamics of globalization (p. 9).

A cultural tsunami may occur if cultural pluralism and a hegemonic global economy strictly remain within the realms of two elite schools that dominate the globalization discourse. The "Devos culture," Samuel Huntington's description of an international culture of political and business leaders, and the Western "faculty club culture" are dangerously oblivious of the spheres of cultural meltdown in an increasingly global world. Beyond the "clash of civilizations" theory propounded by Huntington (1996), there are good reasons to rethink the myth and reality of globalization, given that human rights and equality are crucial for establishing universal social justice (Khor, 2001; Shipman, 2002; Mohan, 2005b).

Because democratization is both a euphemism and synonym for Westernization, varied versions and templates of non-Western ideologies and models of change are usually overlooked. On the one hand we have the New Age synthesizers and, on the other, systems of faith violently hostile to all modern (Western) models and deeply suspicious of U.S. motives, motifs, and movements. A war based on lies and intervention (Afghanistan) augmented by self-defeating foreign policy (Iraq) exemplifies the *perfect storm* in question. The impotence, acquiescence, and indifference of people in general represent the other aspect of the same *storm*. The following illustrations may help to unravel the limits, dangers, and holes in the so-called global democracy fantasia. Ubiquitous lack of a global consciousness and respect for human rights pervades these vastly different views of human reality:

- The limits of globalization are usually underestimated. "Among the reasons cited for the decline [of the nation-state] were the end of the Cold War and the end of history, according to Francis Fukuyama and his acolytes and the accelerating technological revolution that shrank the world and made all sorts of boundaries more elastic. . . . In his 1992 book, *The Twilight of Sovereignty,* Walter Wriston [and Kenichi Ohmae in his influential book, *The End of the Nation State: The Rise of Regional Economies* (1995)] asserted that the rest of world would soon follow the examples of Europe. . . . The nation-state has made quite a comeback, as illustrated by the growing reluctance of Europe's electorates to surrender more sovereignty to Brussels. In the U.S., the same backlash against globalization is stalling efforts to liberalize immigration policy and enact more free trade pacts. . . . Sept. 11 was the ultimate blow to globalization's promise . . . the U.S. retreated into full national-interest-first mode."
- It is only in the context of war against terrorism that US talks about cross-border cooperation (Martinez, 2005, p. B13).
- Amnesty International recently compared and characterized the condition of the detainees at Guantánamo Bay as the "Gulag of our times." The same sentiment was echoed by a U.S. Senator who lat-

er, after taking much criticism from the Establishment, apologized (*The Advocate*, June 22, 2005).

- "China sells what it can produce [at prices the communist government controls] . . . India produces what it can sell. . . . China may win the sprint, but India will win the marathon," says Kamal Nath, India's minister for commerce and industry (cited by Hogland, 2005b, p. 7B).

- The new China presents a puzzling paradox from an egalitarian point of view. In addition to China's disregard for human rights, the only viable communist state in the world is feverishly preoccupied with its military and economic growth creating two Chinas, the very poor and the rising one. Shanghai's Babylonian shining towers look less promising from the eyes of an alienated worker who "sits amid the rubbles an old neighborhood" (*Time*, 2005, pp. 28–29).

- "Gender apartheid" has been in existence for centuries. It continues to be a source of conflict between host societies and immigrants, where ethnic identities forbid integration, and parallel cultures tend to violate the human rights of the younger generation, especially in the case of women in Muslim countries. A case in point is Ayaan Hirsi Ali's passionate fight against Islamist oppression against women. As a champion of free speech and human rights, the Somali-born legislator has demanded that the Dutch intelligence service investigate the honor killings of Muslim girls. Hege Storhaug, the author of *Human Visas*, whose group, Human Rights Service, is awarding her "Bellwether of Europe," says of Hirsi Ali: "I think she is doing a great service to democracy and the future, because Islamism is the biggest threat to democracy and to Europe" (Scroggins, 2005, p. 25).

- The use of rape as a weapon of war is perhaps one of the most heinous violation of human rights.[1] Yet certain nations perpetuate

---

1. "Abducted two years ago when she was sixteen, Ombeni was kept as a concubine in the forests of eastern Congo. She became pregnant and near birth, her captors cut her vagina with a machete, leaving the baby dead . . . 'I laid there for one week . . . until insects came out of my body'" (Mealer, 2005, p. 13A).

misogynist barbarity in the name of religious and traditional piety. Darfur and Congo may be the epicenters of a civil meltdown, but Pakistan, where victims of rape are killed for family honor, seems no better.[2,3,4] A "policy of rape" is an abominable indictment of the state as a political institution.[5]

- Child marriages in India still continue to dehumanize young women in the world's most populous democracy. Any resistance to change is met with feudal authority, including violence. This is evident from the recent attack on an anganwadi (welfare centre) supervisor in Madhya Pradesh who tried to prevent three young girls from being married off in a mass ceremony. Shakuntala Verma, the official, went to Bhangarh village in Dhar district on May 11 after being told that a family there was planning to marry off its

2. See Kristof, 2005a. In June 2002, Mai was raped by four men. She would have been murdered by her family as a matter of "honor" but she went to court and secured the conviction of her rapists (Cf. Hogland, 2005a, p. 9B.)

3. Then there are Pakistan's hudood laws, which have been used to imprison thousands of women who report rapes. If rape victims cannot provide four male witnesses to the crime, they risk being whipped for adultery, since they acknowledge illicit sex and cannot prove rape. When a group of middle-class Pakistani women demonstrated last month for equal rights in Lahore, police clubbed them and dragged them to police stations. They particularly targeted Asma Jahangir, a UN special reporter who is also the head of Pakistan's Human Rights Commission. Ms. Jahangir reports that the directions given to the police about her, coming from an intelligence official close to General Musharraf, were to "teach the [expletive] a lesson. Strip her in public." Sure enough, the police ripped her shirt off and tried to pull off her trousers. If that is how General Musharraf's government treats one of the country's most distinguished lawyers, imagine what happens to a peasant challenging injustice. Kristof's report on human rights violations in Pakistan is instructive (Kristof, 2005a). And yet the United States rewards this country with F-16 bombers capable of carrying nuclear bombs meant to be used against India.

4. Human rights warrant a social climate conducive to those rights, which is a human possibility.

5. "Gang rape is terrifying anywhere, but particularly here. . . . In addition, most girls in Darfur undergo an extreme form of genital cutting called infubilation that often ends with a midwife stitching the vagina shut with thread made of wild thorns. . . . Sometimes the women simply vanish. . . . The attacks are sometimes purely about humiliation. Some women are raped with sticks that tear apart their insides, leaving them constantly trickling urine. One Sudanese woman working for a European aid organization was raped with a bayonet" (Kristof, 2005b, p. 14).

young daughters. As instructed by the Sub-Divisional Magistrate, she asked for proof of the girls' ages, but was forced to leave after members of the family threatened her. Later that evening a person armed with a sword came to her house and began slashing at her. As she tried to protect herself, one hand was severed and the other severely cut. Even as Shakuntala was fighting for her life in an Indore hospital after a nine-hour operation to reattach her hand, the Madhya Pradesh Chief Minister Babulal Gaur announced that "no serious action" would be taken against those who conduct child marriages. "Social customs are stronger than laws," he said (Krishnakumar & Rajlakshami, 2005; see also Sagade, 2005).

- The demise of communism should be no comfort to the functional free market—a system which will not devour its own children. "Rigid ideology is a threat, not an asset" (Garson, 2005, p. B17). The failures of such policies have played havoc with the lives of poor all over the world: "Cholera is an extreme result of a development scheme. But then, privatizing water in Africa is an extreme application of the World Bank's private investment theory. . . . Even in the First World, it's often more profitable to siphon off than to 'develop.' . . . A quarter of a century day-in and day-out asset stripping sponsored by the IMF [International Monetary Fund] and the World Bank left millions of poor people poorer. Meanwhile, unregulated capital flows—another tenet of Washington Consensus—lead to speculative booms and currency crashes that pushed hundreds of millions of people down into dollar-a-day poverty" (Garson, 2005, p. B17).

- In NYC, the rate of syphilis has increased by more than 400 percent in the past five years. Gay men account for virtually the entire rise. . . . Over the past several years, nearly every indicator of risky sexual activity has risen in the gay community. Twenty million people have died of AIDS, most of them in Africa, where the epidemic grows more devastating every year, as it does in places like China, Russia, and India (Specter, 2005, pp. 38–45).

- "London, July 7: Bomb explosions tore through three London subway trains and a red double-decker bus in a deadly terror attack today, killing at least 37 people in coordinated rush hour carnage that left the city stunned, bloodied but stoic" (Cowell, 2005).

Isolated vignettes reflect a wider and deeper malaise. Fundamentalism embodies the evils of a pernicious ideology. However, the archeology of global injustice and the notion of human rights are embedded in the ethics of Western political thought. Political liberation and democratization of Africa calls for institutional deconstruction through postcolonial, bottom-up constitutionalism (Ihonvbere & Mbaku, 2003). This may well be a model for much of the non-Western world. Bride burning is not merely a lust for dowry; it is a heinous nexus of evils that continues to bedevil a "wounded civilization." The above illustrations vividly portray the scope and banality of human-made tragedies. A hapless victim of gang rape in Pakistan and the alarming rise of syphilis rates among gay men in New York City are only the tips of two isolated icebergs separated by an ocean but joined by mutual alienation and despair.

Violation of human rights is a pervasive global reality, especially in regional sectors still engulfed in the vicissitudes of postcolonial decadence. But the historical social movement is irreversible; we cannot rewind the past or amend reality. Nor is it prudent to blame all maladies on the unchangeable le past while ignoring the necessities and obligations of the present. A post-ideological duality of hope—economic growth in Ireland, China, India, and Chile—and despair—human rights violations and communist statism in China; rampant communalism in India; new oligarchies in Russia; and increasing inequality in the U.S.—do not spell global well-being.

The G-8 response to global poverty, especially in Africa, although belated is still encouraging.[6] Buried under the deposits of time is a history of colonial violence and cruelty that dehumanized Africa. African nations by and large present the horrors of age-old oppression and tribal factionalism that

---

6. Finance ministers from the eight industrialized nations that comprise the G-8 agreed to a historic deal canceling at least $40 billion worth of debt owed by the world's poorest nations. The British Treasury chief Gordon Brown said that eighteen countries, many in sub-Saharan Africa, will benefit immediately from the deal to scrap 100 percent of the debt they owe to the World Bank, the International Monetary Fund, and the African Development Bank. As many as twenty other countries could be eligible if they meet strict targets for good governance and tackling corruption, leading to a total debt relief package of more than $55 billion. Aid agencies welcomed the deal, saying that it would save the eighteen countries a total of $1.5 billion a year in debt repayments that could now be used for health care, education and infrastructure development (Associated Press, 2005).

continue to perpetuate the world's most deplorable human conditions. No amount of money can establish peace, security, and human rights without functioning states in Africa. Oppressed people become the worst oppressors, a paradox that only the peoples of Africa can resolve for themselves. Good governance has the potential for achieving a semblance of justice by guaranteeing human rights.

It may not be an exaggeration to say that the evolution and devolution of the state's role in human and civil affairs has significantly changed how people, especially in the marginalized zones, are treated by institutions of authority. Societies and cultures react differently in response to politico-ideological tipping points. We are a civilization that has lost is balance in the dogmas and doctrines that shaped the triumphs and horrors of the twentieth century.

Human Rights and Human Unfreedom

"Human oppression and social development serve antithetical cross-purposes. The unfortunate outcome is global illfare and continuing dehumanization. Social development seeks to enhance human freedom through social reconstruction which is thwarted by the forces of oppression" (Mohan & Sharma, 1985, p. 12).[7]

More than two decades ago, using the area of "darkness" as *unfreedom*, an argument was made to emphasize human freedom as a vehicle against the forces of global oppression (Mohan, 1985). In a subsequent, comparative analytical framework, the freedom/oppression duality was conceptualized as a way to rethink global linkages that divide the world across nations and in terms of hierarchies (Mohan, 1986). It seems that a more articulate and empirically validated thesis later transformed this formulation into Amartya Sen's (1999) "paradigm-altering" *Development as Freedom*, which has impelled the world to think of economic development in a more humane and rational perspective. The dialectics of individual and social development are intrinsically related to global social welfare (Gil, 1985, p. 15). Contemporary nihilism and the eclipse of civility call for new constructs

---

7. This section is based on my paper delivered to the Fourteenth International Symposium of the Inter-University Consortium for International Social Development (IUCISD), Recife, Brazil, July 18–24, 2005.

and strategies for the establishment of a free and decent international society (Mohan, 1993, 2002b, 2004, 2005c). However, tasteless analyses and rampant political corruption have impeded a clearer understanding of global freedom.

The "contours of class have blurred . . . [but] class is still a powerful force in American life" (Scott & Leonhardt, 2005, pp. 1–16). Our globe is once again "flat" (Friedman, 2005). The "imperial hubris" (Scheuer, 2004) may have helped expand hegemonic multinational corporations but "McDonaldization" has not resolved any global issue of consequence. The developmental approach—"a pluralistic and consensual approach to social welfare that transcends the historic welfare statism of the European nations, advocating for the integration of state, market, and community involvement" (Midgley & Tang, 2003, p. 21)—ignores the symbiotic nature of human and social development processes. As all pseudo-materialists pretend, people will behave as they are expected to if income and assets become minimally accessible (Midgley, 2003, 1995). The pseudo-materialist premise has a simplistic quality for easy acceptance in a globalized economy. However, it subtly avoids the forces that affect the quality of "development." This is particularly important as the welfare state seems to transition into a welfare society. A mere residual-institutional hybrid is hardly a model for a postindustrial society still in search of its historical significance in the process of social evolution.

We need a new social development that would universalize the basic tenets of universal justice and human rights. A *universal model of human-social development* is an imperative for promoting minimally acceptable human conditions. The rationale for the holistic approach is grounded in the monumental failures of the twentieth century's reductionist-deterministic ideologies that have failed to achieve a civil and free society. *We have achieved an unfree world in a hopelessly ill-defined culture of freedom* (Mohan 2005a).

The vicissitudes of the state at a time when globalization and democratization require a civil rule of law, present three main areas of global concern that merit our attention: individual freedom, social democracy, and global economy. Each is subject to ideological interpretation. Democracy and freedom are universal fundamental rights of individuals and societies. However, the combination of hegemonic power, corporate interests, and neglect of democratic values has resulted in myriad events and experiences that are counterproductive at best. The following examples illustrate this point in different fields: massive tax cuts and budget deficits endanger economic stability;[8] the post–9/11 war against terrorism has seriously curtailed civil and human rights at home and abroad;[9] the Bush doctrine of preemptive war has resulted in "the 'Salvadorization' of Iraq"[10] (Maass, 2005, p. 38). The interdependence of foreign and domestic policies is an undeniable reality of our times. From Vietnam to Iraq we find this interface impacting the calculus of national and international relationships.

Globalization of free-market enterprise presumably is conducive to both democracy and freedom. The economic growth in China, India, Ireland, Thailand, and Taiwan has been phenomenal. By outsourcing various industrial operations, multinational corporations have enhanced their profits at the expense of millions of Americans' jobs, labor unions, and indigenous industries. American capitalism, on the other hand, has enriched China, which has no intention of developing a multiparty democratic system. Meanwhile, the tidal middle-class growth and consumerist avarice in India has only inflamed an unregulated class war.

The nature of governmental behaviors is a determinant usually neglected in academic policy discourse. The result is that *development* seems to have become a charade to protect new oligarchies with no commitment to public welfare and basic human rights. In response to dwindling public faith, all governments must exhibit transparency, accountability and civility to insure that the state does not become a superstructure of torture, abuse, and neglect. A state's exclusive monopoly over the use of violence as a means of absolute control legitimates dehumanization at the expense of fundamental human rights.

8. Of all industrialized nations, the U.S. has the widest income gap between the rich and poor. "All across America, the rich have their hands out. . . . America's biggest welfare queens are the wealthy," so reported ABC's consumer rights correspondent and co-anchor of the TV series 20/20 Jon Strossle, adding that this is "outrageous" (*Reader's Digest*, April 2004, pp. 37–39).

9. Examples are the criticism of the Patriot Act and the treatment of prisoners and detainees at Abu Ghraib and Guantánamo Bay, which was an embarrassment to the U.S. government. The contradiction is further highlighted by the U.S. attitude toward a Cuban terrorist named Luis Posada Carriles. If Posada is "good terrorist," as President George W. Bush said, then, by implication, terrorism is condoned when it suits U.S. interests (see Anderson, 2005, p. 2A).

10. This also alludes to "Iraqification."

The denial of human rights—a universal and pervasive evil—is the genesis of all social exclusions. The matrix of social exclusions involves a complex array of cultural, economic, political, religious, and ethnic injustices practiced on various levels in different degrees. Social hierarchies, accepted as functional—caste and slavery, for example—serve as the incubators of social exclusions.

We live in a world of massive exclusions that procreate and inflame the passions of destruction. Manufactured misinterpretations become facts, and lies become didactic lessons. The invasion and occupation of a weaker country is sold to people as liberation. The doctrines of human rights do not usually specify, classify, and clarify the instrumentality involved in achieving these rights for all. Human rights are creatures of ethical, philosophical, and historical explanations that signify their need. We know, of course, that societies exist that do not provide, let alone guarantee, human rights. The "terrible twins of the 20th century, Communism and Nazism," Roger Cohen argues, proved the greatest murderers of all times (2005, p. 16). An apogee of Stalinist terror and Hitler's concentration camps and pogroms of extinction have killed more than ninety million people. Ethnic cleansing in East Europe, Rwanda, and Sudan remind us that the legacy of statist evil is still alive and well.

Social hierarchies, economic status, ethnic origins, politico-ideological differences, and historical religious disputes continue to heighten and perpetuate a dangerously dysfunctional culture of oppression. We live in an age of enigmatic paradox: heightened neurosis marked by fear and terror, on the one hand, and arrogance and self-righteousness, on the other. This dissonance is hardly conducive to fulfilling universal human needs. Unless we redefine the nature of the "axes of evil"—terrorism and war, inequality and poverty, and the abuse of human dignity—in its true colors, it is surely impossible to cultivate a climate conducive to human rights. Nurturing such a climate, as Tony Blair succinctly put it, is "the fundamental moral challenge of our generation" (*New York Times*, 2005, 9wk).[11]

---

11. Prime Minister Tony Blair's Commission on Africa underscores his unflinching support: "There can be no excuse, no defense, no justification for the plight of millions of our fellow human beings in Africa today. And there should be nothing that stands in our way in changing it" (*New York Times*, 2005, p. 9).

Human-Social Development:
A Holistic Social Work Approach to Human Rights

America's fiscal mess may be even harder to write about engagingly than Darfur, because the victims of our fiscal recklessness aren't weeping widows whose children were heaved onto bonfires. But if you need to visualize the victims, think of your child's face, or your grandchild's. President Bush has excoriated the "death tax," as he calls the estate tax. But his profligacy will leave every American child facing a "birth tax" of about $150,000. (Kristof, 2005c)

A professional culture such as social work reflects societal institutions, policies, and vicissitudes. The post-Reagan years have transformed an otherwise noble profession into a mediocre discipline engaged in survivalist therapies without adequate substance and subtlety. Social justice and human rights issues have become casualties of this anti-developmental professional culture.

Ideally social work should be seen as a human-rights profession. The "banality of evil"—to use Hannah Arendt's phrase—ranges from sexual exploitation of children to war zones, and is a vast universe where dehumanization occurs with impunity. It is a legitimate domain of social work intervention. This, however, calls for a brutally critical, open-minded approach. George W. Bush's main political adviser, Karl Rove, has accused liberals of unpatriotic "therapism" in the wake of 9/11, viciously demeaning people dedicated to human rights.[12] Therapism (Sommers & Satel, 2005) and commodification of human misery by "grief gurus" basically validates a call for the reinvention of social work (Mohan, 2005d). Social developmentalism deriving its strengths from contemporary social work is a misguided endeavor in pursuit of a flawed ideal. As Shanti Khinduka observes:

It is unfortunate that despite its lofty rhetoric that exalts human interdependence and international cooperation, social work in the United States has largely remained an American-centered profession. Social Work edu-

12. Karl Rove, White House adviser, in a speech at a Republican Party fund raiser in Manhattan: "Conservatives saw the savagery of 9/11 in the attacks and prepared for war. Liberals saw the savagery of the 9/11 attacks and wanted to prepare indictments and offer therapy and understanding for our attackers" (*Time*, 2005, p. 15).

cation, too, has failed to make serious strides to learn or teach about the rest of the world. (Khinduka, 2004, p. 3)

An unfortunate reality of our time is that civilizations indulge in mass murder under religious pretexts. Humankind remains paralyzed under the yoke of centuries-old prejudices and doctrines of bigotry and hate. We still unleash crusades against our enemies under dubious pretexts (Suskind, 2004). Programs of social reconstruction must therefore precede strategic planning. In a multipolar, increasingly globalized world, it is imperative that social change and transformation are conceived and achieved within a universalistic approach. The premature demise of the welfare state is not the end of welfare development. As "human-social" development evolves in due course, social arrangements across the nation will readjust and adopt new developmental strategies without resorting to minimalist programs of individualized assets, de-contextualized micro-tragedies, and ill-conceived "clientization." Once human rights are universalized and implemented, a new culture of work, production, and distribution will emerge where global human needs will warrant alternatives far better than personalized modalities of a therapeutic state.

Progressive social work offers a fertile ground for a wholesome growth of human and communal behaviors. However, today's ideological constraints and contradictions thwart the symbiosis of "human-social" development. Liberating the basic human condition without soulless social engineering requires the deconstruction of a global culture based on human dignity and creative development. The social contract that glued together the fabric of human society since the dawn of civilization seems to be faltering. The metaphorical human family has become a dysfunctional unit. In order to ensure that all members of that family receive dignified status, human rights must be universalized.

The idea of a renewed social contract is a romantic fantasy in light of the realities surrounding us. From Guantánamo Bay to Darfur, one finds the blatant abuse of human rights. In civil life human rights are violated routinely. From the silent sexual abuse of children within churches to the naked brutality of slave camps, evidence of human rights violations is worldwide.[13]

---

13. The U.S. State Department identified ten countries that practice human slavery in some form (June 4, 2005). This includes some of the richest (Saudi Arabia and Kuwait) as well as the poorest (Sudan) countries of the world.

Social work, a quintessentially human rights approach to most of the human-made tragedies, may well reequip itself, both pragmatically and epistemologically, if its smorgasbord is focused on universal, indivisible, and inalienable areas of the evolving structure of human rights. From AIDS, poverty, and hunger to ethnic cleansing and war, it is the ennobling spirit of basic rights that makes the human animal social. It is time to expand horizons in professional discourse beyond the occasional editorial (Witkin, 1998); it is heartening to see the emerging interaction between policy and practice (Reichert, 2003). As a profession, however, we are still mired in our intra-professional conundrums without breaking away from the traditional model which is fraught with the duality of functional-reductionism (Mohan, 1999; 2002a; 2004; 2005c).

Globalization, unless wedded to fundamental democratization, appears to be a false messiah. Robert Merry (2005), in his *Sands of Empire*, remind us of the rise and fall of Rome. The world may be "flattening," but the equality gulf is widening, especially between the North and the South. In the words of Hugo Bedeau (1982, p. 289): "It seems natural to suggest that a society that lacks rights is morally inferior to a society that has rights." What we are witnessing is the rise of new social hierarchies that are changing the contours of inequality without alleviating injustices. Human rights and social exclusions logically fit the "comparative-analytic" framework that unraveled the dialectics of freedom and oppression as two inalienable dimensions of human-social development (Mohan, 1985, 1986). If societies across nations aspire to achieve freedom, democracy, and social justice, they will have to embrace human rights as the fulcrum of comprehensive development—programs, policies, and people—or else the chimeras of hope and delusions will continue to sap resources and energies in a tautological design that may breed atavistic horrors. The world would have been a better—perhaps more peaceful and less violent—place had the three sons of Abraham better understood one another. The synthesis of cultural, psychosocial, and economic factors is helpful, but it is the symbiotic relationship between humans and society that shapes the outcome of the developmental process. As Nelson Mandela forcefully reminded today's world leaders: "It is within your power to prevent genocide."[14] And, as stated at

---

14. "History and the generations to come will judge our leaders by the decisions they make in the coming weeks," stated Nelson Mandela (*Lawless*, 2005, p. 1A).

the Live Aid concert where musicians and fans gathered in numerous cities to pressure the world's leaders to take action: "All of that promise will be made concrete in nine cities, four continents, one culture, [and among one thousand] artists—all because too many people are dying on one continent.[15]

References

Anderson, C. (2005, May 19). Cuban militant case challenges Bush. *The Advocate,* p. 2A.

Associated Press. (2005, June 11). Leaders agree on debt relief for poor nations. *The Advocate,* p. 7A.

Bedau, H. A. (1982). International human rights. In T. Regan & D. Van de Veer (Eds.), *And justice for all: New introductory essays in ethics and public policy.* Totowa, NJ: Rowman & Allanheld.

Berger, P. L., & Huntington, S. P. (Eds.). (2002). *Many globalizations: Cultural diversity in the contemporary world.* New York: Oxford University Press.

Cohen, R. (2005, May 15). 1945's legacy: A terror defeated, another arrives. *New York Times,* 16.

Cowell, A. (2005, July 7). After coordinated bombs, London is stunned, bloodied and stoic. *New York Times.* Retrieved July 7, 2005, from http://www.nytimes.com/2005/07/07/international/europe/07cnd-explosion.html.

Friedman, T. L. (2005). *The world is flat: A brief history of the twenty-first century.* New York: Farrer, Straus & Giroux.

Garson, B. (2005, May 30). True believers at the World Bank. *Los Angeles Times,* p. B17.

Gil, D. G. (1985). Dialectics of individual development and global social welfare. In B. Mohan (Ed.), *New horizon of social welfare and policy* (pp. 15–46). Cambridge, MA: Schenkman.

Hogland, J. (2005a, June 23). Woman's truth rattles Musharraf. *The Advocate,* p. 9B.

Hogland, J. (2005b, June 6). Asia's rise no reason to panic. *The Advocate,* p. 7B.

15. A thunderous Live Aid concert opened in London and eight other cities of the world. Musicians and fans were gathering in ten cities for a global music marathon to raise awareness of African poverty and pressure the world's most powerful leaders to do something about it at the G-8 summit in Scotland (*New York Times,* July 3, 2005).

Huntington, S. P. (1996). *The clash of civilizations and the remaking of world order.* New York: Simon & Schuster.

Ihonvbere, J. O., & Mbaku, J. M. (Eds.). (2003). *Political liberation and democratization in Africa.* Westport, CT: Praeger.

Khinduka, S. K. (2004, fall). Musings on social work and social work education. *Social Development Issues*, 26, 2/3, pp. 1–6.

Khor, M. (2001). *Rethinking globalization: Critical issues and policy choices.* New York: Zed Books.

Krishnakumar, A., & Rajalaksmi, T.K. (2005, July). Child brides of India. *Frontline*, 22(14), pp. 2–15. Retrieved July 2005 from http://www.frontlineonnet.com/fl2214/fl221400.htm.

Kristof, N. D. (2005a, June 21). The 11-year-old wife. *New York Times*, p. 13.

Kristof, N. D. (2005b, June 5). A policy of rape. *New York Times*, p. 14.

Kristof, N. D. (2005c, June 26). A glide path to ruin. *New York Times.*

Lawless, J. (2005, July 3). Live 8 rocks for the poor. *The Advocate*, p. 1A.

Maass, P. (2005, May 1). The way of the commandos. Is the war getting dirtier? *New York Times Magazine*, pp. 38–47.

Martinez, A. (2005, June 1). The borders are closing. *Los Angeles Times*, p. B13.

Mealer, B. (2005, June 23). Rape used as a weapon of war in Congo. *The Advocate*, p. 13A.

Merry, R. W. (2005). *Sands of empire: Missionary zeal, American foreign policy, and the hazards of global ambition.* New York: Simon & Schuster.

Midgley, J. (1995). *Social development: The developmental perspective in social welfare.* Thousand Oaks, CA: Sage.

Midgley, J. (2003, spring/fall). Assets in the context of welfare theory: A developementalist interpretation. *Social Development Issues*, 25(1/2), 12–28.

Midgley, J., & Kwong-leung Tang. (2003). East Asian welfare: Theoretical perspectives. *Social Development Issues*, 25(3), 6–26.

Mohan, B. (Ed.). (1985). *New horizons of social welfare policy.* Cambridge, MA: Schenkman.

Mohan, B. (Ed.) (1986). *Toward comparative social welfare.* Cambridge, MA: Schenkman.

Mohan, B. (1992). *Global development: Post-material values and social praxis.* New York: Praeger.

Mohan, B. (1993). *Eclipse of freedom.* Westport, CT: Praeger.

Mohan, B. (1997). Toward new global development. *International Social Work*, 40(4), 433–450.

Mohan, B. (1999). *Unification of social work: Rethinking social transformation.* Westport, CT: Praeger.

Mohan, B. (2002a). *Social Work Revisited*. Philadelphia, PA: Xlibris/Random House.

Mohan, B. (2002b, July 15–18). Toward an international society: Social work education for world citizenship. Congress of the International Association of Schools of Social Work, *Social Work Education and Citizenship in a Globalizing World*. Montpellier, France.

Mohan, B. (2003). *The Practice of Hope: Diversity, Discontent and Discourse*. Philadelphia, PA: Xlibris/Random House.

Mohan, B. (2004, October 2–5). Demise of civility: The future of human society. Paper delivered to Global Social Work 2004 Congress (Ref. 2089; Session 18 Exclusion/Diversity: Dynamics of Inclusion), Adelaide, Australia.

Mohan, B. (2005a, July 24–28). Social exclusions: Challenges for new social development. Paper delivered to the Fourteenth International Symposium of the Inter-University Consortium of International Social Development (IUCISD), Recife, Brazil.

Mohan, B. (2005b). New internationalism: Social work's dilemmas, dreams and delusion. *International Social Work, 48*(3), 237–246.

Mohan, B. (2005c, February 27). Social practice and the archeology of evil: Ideology, dystopia, and new challenges. Paper delivered at the Fifty-first Annual Program Meeting, "One World, Many Cultures, and New Challenges," Council on Social Work, New York.

Mohan, B. (2005d). *Reinventing Social Work: The Metaphysics of Social Practice*. Lewiston, NY: The Edwin and Mellen Press (forthcoming).

Mohan, B., & Sharma, P. (1985, spring). On human oppression and social development. *Social Development Issues, 9*(1), 12–24.

New York Times. (2005, July 3). Africa at the summit (Editorial), p. 9. Retrieved July 3, 2005, from http://www.nytimes.com/aponline/arts/AP-Live-8.html?hp=&pagewanted=print.

Reichert, E. (2003). *Social work and human rights: A foundation for policy and action*. New York: Columbia University Press.

Rushdie, S. (2005). The PEN and the sword. *New York Times Book Review*, p. 31.

Sagade, J. (2005). *Child marriages in India*. New Delhi: Oxford University Press.

Samuelson, R. J. (2005, June 15). Status quo endangering Europe. *The Advocate*, p. 7B.

Scheuer, M. (2004). *Imperial hubris: Why the West is losing the war on terror?* Dulles, VA: Brassey's.

Scott, J., & Leonhardt, D. (2005, May 15). Class in America: Shadowy lines that still divide. *New York Times*, pp. 1–16.

Scroggins, D. (2005, June 27). The Dutch-Muslim culture war. *The Nation, 280*, 21–25.

Sen, A. (1999). *Development as freedom.* New York: Anchor Books.

Shipman, A. (2002). *The globalization myth.* London: Icon Books.

Sommers, C. H., & Satel, S. (2005). *One nation under therapy: How the helping culture is eroding self-reliance.* New York: St. Martin's.

Specter, M. (2005, May 23). Higher risk. *New Yorker,* pp. 38–45.

Strossel, J. (2004). *Give me a break.* New York: HarperCollins.

Suskind, R. (2004, October 17). What makes Bush's presidency so radical. *New York Times Magazine,* pp. 44–51, 64.

Time. (2005, June 27). China rising (Cover), pp. 28–29.

Time. (2005, July 4). China rising, p. 15.

United Nations. (1948). United Nations Resolution 217A (III).

Wald, G. (2005). *Columbia.* New York: Columbia University Press.

Witkin, S. (1998). Human rights and social work (Editorial). *Social Work, 43,* 197–201.

12

Law and Social Work

Not-So-Odd Bedfellows in Promoting Human Rights

ROBERT J. MCCORMICK

Many lawyers, at some point in their work, will cooperate with social workers, usually regarding child abuse or neglect, or child custody hearing, with social workers investigating and making recommendations for a court proceeding. Lawyers, in these cases, often defer to the expertise of social workers and readily acknowledge the importance of the social workers' contribution.

Although many issues in court involve the human rights of parents and children, rarely does the term *human rights* itself enter court proceedings, at least within the United States. The vague legal concept of "best interests of the child" generally prevails (e.g., Illinois Domestic Relations Act, 1976), with lawyers and social workers tailoring their approaches to the realization of this elusive goal. Yet, unknowingly in many cases, both professions are tackling human rights issues together. Lawyers may not always agree with social workers' recommendations, and social workers may find the legalistic language and procedures cumbersome and ineffective. However, the courtroom is a forum where law and social work come together to jointly promote human rights activities.

Outside court, however, lawyers and social workers seem to part ways on promoting human rights. Lawyers often appear to determine the agenda of human rights, even though human rights seem to form the basis for social work itself. How is it possible that in one area of human rights, child advocacy, lawyers and social workers merge their expertise to further human rights, but in almost every other area remain apart? This makes little sense, but perhaps some analysis can help answer this question.

If human rights merely consisted of concepts surrounding political and civil rights, then lawyers would naturally dominate these areas. After all, guarantees of free speech, due process, and religious freedom require adherence to and interpretation of laws, the work of lawyers. The reluctance of social workers to more fully embrace human rights most likely has something to do with this legalistic view of human rights (Reichert, 2003). Social workers are not lawyers and can do little to promote the legal entitlements that are the basis for many human rights. The word *rights* is not a social work concept. Whether one has the *right* to do this, or the *right* to do that, are legal concepts. Yet the reality is quite different.

The exercise of human rights goes far beyond notions of government clashes with individuals who simply want their day in court to obtain a right. Human rights encompass many components directly relevant to social work policy statements and ethical standards, especially within economic, social, and cultural areas (United Nations, 1948, 1976). Why, for instance, in the United States, should the human right to adequate medical care be more a topic for lawyers than for social workers? The legal profession struggles with the promotion of economic and social human rights, assuming that these precepts are too messy or not as important as political and civil rights. Also, if the law has not recognized a human right as law, then lawyers stumble. They can argue for laws to recognize human rights, but will not win cases if they cannot support their arguments with the ever important legal precedent.

On the other hand, social work has everything to do with the economic and social well-being of all (or at least most) individuals (NASW, 1999, 2003). Where lawyers stand aside because there is no law to enforce an economic human right, social workers can come forward to promote that right, regardless of whether a law exists for its enforcement. In this sense, social workers are even better positioned to promote human rights than lawyers.

Lawyers and social workers seem to take different approaches to human rights, but both should actively work together in promoting human rights. The societal roles of social workers and lawyers may differ, but they can and often do share a common goal: the promotion of human rights.

Legal Approach to Human Rights

When lawyers address a human rights issue, they naturally rely on their training as to how they will proceed. Lawyers typically approach a situation or case by referring to established laws, court opinions, and other binding legal precedents. This method of analysis requires reference to documents, especially those with legal effect. The lawyer views a set of circumstances through a prism of legal principles, rather than what he or she believes is correct. The presumption is that if courts and legislatures have addressed an issue, then the positions of those institutions generally must prevail.

Certainly, though, with sufficient resources, a lawyer may challenge an established precedent. This challenge often does not succeed, given the overriding force of existing laws and court decisions. Yet challenging established precedents, especially those that appear inherently wrong, can result in a more enlightened and just social policy. For instance, successful legal challenges to egregious human rights violations concerning racial segregation have occurred within the United States, although the challenges took many years to bear fruit. A short history of how lawyers attacked racial segregation within the U.S. legal system points up an approach which social workers may view as unnecessarily legalistic, even illogical or counterproductive.

Social workers might believe that the forced segregation of races is a gross violation of human rights that should require no elaborate, legalistic proceedings to fix the problem. Not so from a legal perspective. Without legally binding precedent, a lawyer has an uphill battle to address human rights violations. If a law exists that appears to violate a human right, then the lawyer must find a court decision or some legal document that will allow the lawyer to argue against the validity of the existing law.

Historical events surrounding racial segregation in the United States often defy belief, particularly within the lengthy legal process required to overturn what most people would simply describe as abominable. How could any decent person believe that separate schools, drinking fountains, seats on buses and trains, should be legal? Sadly, this situation existed in many parts of the United States for more than a century, with the blessings of the U.S. Supreme Court. While courts and laws cannot directly change attitudes, legal precedents can entrench and aggravate social ills. In the context of racial segregation, the Supreme Court played a significant role in allowing this egregious practice to continue until recent times.

U.S. Supreme Court Views on Racial Segregation

After the Civil War ended in 1865, two key amendments to the U.S. Constitution came into play addressing racial segregation (U.S. Constitution, 1787, as amended). In 1865 Congress ratified the Thirteenth Amendment, which abolished slavery and involuntary servitude except as punishment for a crime. Three years later Congress approved the Fourteenth Amendment, which contained crucial protections against racial and other discrimination, with many of these concepts subsequently incorporated into current human rights documents:

- Citizenship was bestowed to all persons born or naturalized in the United States. The significance of this citizenship benefit is clear when viewing the Supreme Court's infamous *Dred Scott* decision (*Scott v. Sandford*, 1857), which denied U.S. citizenship rights to slaves even if they were born in the U.S.
- States were prohibited from making or enforcing any law that infringed upon the privileges or immunities of U.S. citizens. The apparent purpose of this provision was to prohibit states from restricting the established freedoms of U.S. citizens.
- States were prohibited from depriving any person of life, liberty, or property, without due process of law. This clause was to prevent states from arbitrarily punishing former slaves and others without concepts of fairness, including the right to be heard.
- States were prohibited from denying to any person the equal protection of the laws. In other words, states were not to interpret or make laws that would benefit one group to the detriment of another. Today this legal concept of equal protection is one of the most significant components of political and civil human rights.

By putting faith in these two amendments, the casual observer might have believed that the U.S. was well on its way to overcoming the egregious practices and results of its slavery past. As events unfolded, especially through decisions of the U.S. Supreme Court, the legal process illustrated the difficulty of overturning entrenched violations of human rights.

Soon after the enactment of the Thirteenth and Fourteenth Amendments to the U.S. Constitution, the Supreme Court began interpreting their provisions and how they applied to the states. In 1873 the Court ruled that basic civil rights and liberties of citizens remained under state control (*Slaughterhouse Cases*, 1873). Although this particular decision did not directly involve the civil rights of black Americans, the decision may have effectively impeded progress at removing discriminatory practices by states (Hall, 1992). If, under the Fourteenth Amendment, states could enact discriminatory legislation without federal intervention, then black Americans had little recourse against that legislation. The Court did not want the federal government to impinge on states' rights, a debate that continues today.

Ten years after the *Slaughter House* decision, the Court held that private individuals operating facilities open to the public could discriminate against various individuals, as the Fourteenth Amendment only prohibited state action and not purely private action (*Civil Rights Cases*, 1883). As stated by the Court:

> Innkeepers and public carriers, by the laws of all States, so far as we are aware, are bound, to the extent of their facilities, to furnish proper accommodation to all unobjectionable persons who in good faith apply for them. If the laws themselves make any unjust discrimination, amenable to the prohibitions of the Fourteenth Amendment, Congress has full power to afford a remedy under that amendment and in accordance with it (p.25).

This language assumed that states would not pass laws that unfairly discriminated. However, if states passed such laws, then Congress could intercede under its authority in the Fourteenth Amendment. This assumption of goodwill on the part of states seems incredible considering recent historical events like the Civil War.

In addition to restricting the power of the Fourteenth Amendment to limiting discrimination, the *Civil Rights Cases* decision included language that clearly showed how courts viewed the slavery issue:

> When a man has emerged from slavery, and by the aid of beneficent legislation has shaken off the inseparable concomitants of that state, there must be some stage in the progress of his elevation when he takes the rank of a mere citizen, and ceases to be the special favorite of the laws, and when his rights as a citizen, or a man, are to be protected in the ordinary modes by which other men's rights are protected. There were thousands of free colored people in this country before the abolition of

slavery, enjoying all the essential rights of life, liberty, and property the same as white citizens; yet no one, at that time, thought that it was any invasion of his personal status as a free man because he was not admitted to all the privileges enjoyed by white citizens, or because he was subjected to discriminations in the enjoyment of accommodations in inns, public conveyances and places of amusement. Mere discriminations on account of race or color were not regarded as badges of slavery. (p. 25)

Unquestionably no black American confronting the above judicial authority had any chance of overcoming entrenched discriminatory practices. The key sentiment couched in these statements is that discrimination based on skin color can be acceptable.

Perhaps, however, in respect to racial segregation, the most forceful wallop against equal protection of blacks in a predominantly white society came with the Court's 1896 decision to uphold a Louisiana state law requiring railways to provide separate cars for the "white and colored races" (*Plessy v. Ferguson*, 1896). The two races also were not to commingle in the same car. The plaintiff, Plessy, agreed to challenge the law, even though he was only one-eighth black. Louisiana laws classified Plessy as "colored," and he was therefore required to travel in the train car allocated to the "colored" race.

The Court held that the Thirteenth Amendment could not apply in this case, as that amendment only applied to actions whose purpose was to reintroduce slavery itself. According to the Court, that amendment did not address distinctions based on color, many of which were acceptable. The Court further held that the equal protection clause of the Fourteenth Amendment did not apply because requiring separation of the races did not suggest that one race was inferior. Inferiority arose only because one race chose to perceive the laws in such a way:

We consider the underlying fallacy of the plaintiff's argument to consist in the assumption that the enforced separation of the two races stamps the colored race with a badge of inferiority. If this be so, it is not by reason of anything found in the [law], but solely because the colored race chooses to put that construction upon it. . . . The argument also assumes that social prejudices may be overcome by legislation, and that equal rights cannot be secured to the Negro except by an enforced commingling of the two races. We cannot accept this proposition. If the two races are to meet upon terms of social equality, it must be the result of natural affinities, a mutual appreciation of each other's merits and a voluntary consent of individuals. (p. 551).

The Court also referred to separate educational facilities on the basis of color as being just as acceptable as separate public transport facilities. The Court indirectly validated separate educational facilities by stating that the "constitutionality" of these facilities does not appear to have been questioned (p. 551). This seeming approval of separate educational facilities essentially opened the door to a widespread system of racial discrimination under the phrase "separate but equal." As long as states separated whites and blacks under an obvious fiction of equal facilities, the federal government would not attempt to substitute its judgment for that of the states.

For almost sixty years this separate but equal doctrine formed the central basis of the U.S. Supreme Court's judicial expressions regarding racial discrimination. Finally, after a persuasive and lengthy legal challenge by the National Association for the Advancement of Colored People (NAACP), the Supreme Court ruled in 1954 that the separate but equal doctrine no longer applied to education (*Brown v. Board of Education*, 1954). As stated by a unanimous Court:

In approaching this problem [of separate educational facilities based on color], we cannot turn the clock back to 1868 when the [Fourteenth] Amendment was adopted, even to 1896 when *Plessy v. Ferguson* was written. We must consider public education in the light of its full development and its present place in American life throughout the Nation. Only in this way can it be determined if segregation in public schools deprives these plaintiffs of the equal protection of the laws.

Today education is perhaps the most important function of state and local governments. Compulsory school attendance laws and the great expenditures for education both demonstrate our recognition of the importance of education to our democratic society. It is required in the performance of our most basic public responsibilities, even service in the armed forces. It is the very foundation of good citizenship. Today it is a principal instrument in awakening the child to cultural values, in preparing him for later professional training, and in helping him to adjust normally to his environment. In these days, it is doubtful that any child may reasonably be expected to succeed in life if he is denied the opportunity of an education. Such an opportunity, where the state has undertaken to provide it, is a right which must be made available to all on equal terms. (p. 493)

After stressing the importance of education, the Court then decided that segregation of children in public schools solely on the basis of race, even though physical and other facilities may be equal, was "inherently unequal" (p. 495). Therefore plaintiffs and others similarly situated had been deprived of the "equal protection of the laws guaranteed by the Fourteenth Amendment" (p. 495). States had to take steps to end the egregious practice of racial segregation in schools.

Subsequent Court decisions and federal laws (e.g., the Civil Rights Act of 1964) finally began to chip away at remaining vestiges of legal racial segregation. Although southern states played the most overt role in promoting racial segregation, other states also promoted policies that inhibited a more integrated society. The simple fact of whites moving away from city centers all over the country to escape negative perceptions of lower-income residents, many of whom were black, can only be described as informal, but legal, racial segregation. A primary lesson from racial segregation in the U.S. is that reliance on a legal approach to promote a human right or correct a human rights violation can be extremely difficult and cumbersome. And where the legal process closes its eyes to the violation, public attitudes can even harden against taking steps to correct the violation.

In reviewing U.S. Supreme Court decisions addressing issues of racial segregation, social workers can see that lawyers and courts rely on past decisions to make their arguments. If the Court has previously ruled that states may pass laws that separate blacks and whites, overcoming that decision becomes extraordinarily difficult. Waiting for legal action to overcome human rights violations can be futile. Yet, without laws to enforce human rights, violations can continue with impunity.

Social Work Approach to Human Rights

Outside of their contact with social workers in court, many lawyers may have little association with social work in a professional setting. In a human rights setting, this absence of contact is unfortunate, as social workers could contribute crucial information and practical recommendations to the legal process of enforcing human rights.

Provisions within various codes of ethics, policy statements, and educational standards, identify and define the social work profession. In the U.S., the National Association of Social Workers (NASW, 1999) has approved a Code of Ethics that should place social workers at the forefront of social welfare policies. For instance, the following ethical principles reflect the core values of the social work profession:

- *Social workers' primary goal is to help people in need and to address social problems.* Social workers are expected to use their knowledge and skills to address social problems (p. 5).
- *Social workers challenge social injustice.* Social workers are to pursue social change, particularly with and on behalf of vulnerable and oppressed individuals and groups. Social workers' efforts in this respect are focused primarily on poverty, unemployment, discrimination, and other forms of social injustice (p. 5).
- *Social workers respect the inherent dignity and worth of the person.* Social workers should treat each person in a caring and respectful fashion, mindful of individual differences and cultural and ethnic diversity (p. 5).

These ethical principles extend the mission of the social work profession directly into the area of human rights.

The NASW (2003) also publishes a number of policy statements that advocate human rights. One particular policy statement discusses the strong connection between human rights and social work (pp. 209–217). The organization that accredits schools of social work in the United States also mandates that social work education include the study of human rights and social justice (Council on Social Work Education, 2003).

The Code of Ethics approved by the International Federation of Social Workers, in 2004, also highlights the need to incorporate human rights into social work policies and practices. This code specifically refers to human rights as the basis of the social work mission.

Compared to lawyers who often address human rights issues from a distant perspective, social workers should be on the front lines, at least from an ethical and educational position. The social work approach to human rights would be one of advocacy and direct involvement in human rights issues. Lawyers, and particularly courts, generally must wait until a human rights issue comes to them. They do not actively walk the streets looking for human rights violations. In this respect, social workers have the unique capacity to identify and address human rights violations.

How would social workers have addressed the egregious practice of racial segregation after the Civil War? This question is difficult to answer, because social work as a clearly defined profession did not exist in 1865. Social work as a profession is more a feature of the twentieth century, with the first social work Code of Ethics in the U.S. having been developed in 1920 (Reichert, 2003).

In studying the activities of early social workers like Jane Addams, however, racism was abhorrent to the budding social work profession at the time of the "separate but equal" doctrine. Possibly some social workers simply would have closed their eyes to the obviously inequitable practices of segregation. But many did protest the legal division of blacks and whites in the South, although within the context of perceiving themselves as part of the "better element" of society:

One thing . . . is clear to all of us, that not only in the South, but everywhere in America, a strong race antagonism is asserting itself, which has various modes of lawless and insolent expression. The contemptuous attitude of the so-called superior race toward the inferior results in a social segregation of each race, and puts the one race group thus segregated quite outside the influences of social control represented by the other. Those inherited resources of the race embodied in custom and kindly intercourse which makes much more for social restraint than does legal enactment itself are thus made operative only upon the group which has inherited them, and the newer group which needs them most is practically left without. (Addams, 1911, pp. 22–23, quote at p. 22)

This objection to racial segregation by a foremost social worker in 1911 indicates opposition to racial segregation but within Addams's position of being part of a societal upper crust, or the "better element":

The "better element" was a synonym for a group of the educated and enlightened, for the most part upper middle class in origin. This elite felt it had civic, humanitarian, and moral responsibilities to mediate between the upper and lower classes, create mutual understanding and sympathy,

268

Robert J. McCormick

and secure through social reforms the stability and progress needed for social order. (Lissak, 1989, p. 17)

Although it is easy to criticize the "better element" notion based on contemporary cultural and societal standards, this movement certainly provided more impetus and support for abolishing racial segregation than U.S. Supreme Court decisions. Addams (1911, p. 23) also encouraged the NAACP to "soberly take up every flagrant case of lawbreaking, and if it allow no withdrawal of constitutional rights to pass unchallenged, it will perform a most useful service to America and for the advancement of all its citizens."

The social work approach to racial segregation and other human rights issues does not rest upon legal precedents or what the U.S. Supreme Court has decided. Social workers would view these issues more from their mission as a profession: *The primary mission of the social work profession is to enhance human well-being and help meet the basic human needs of all people, with particular attention to the needs and empowerment of all people who are vulnerable, oppressed, and living in poverty* (NASW, 1999, p. 1).

A more contemporary example in which to contrast the legal and social work approaches to human rights issues might be the aftermath of a hurricane such as Katrina, which devastated New Orleans in 2005. The goal of social workers would be to immediately provide counseling and other direct assistance to those in need of help. The legal approach would be to interview victims and determine which laws might apply to assist them. For instance, if an insurance company refuses to pay a claim, lawyers would then review policy guidelines and existing circumstances to determine the correctness of the insurer's denial of coverage. Essentially social workers would be the first responders, with lawyers playing a more technical support role.

Advantages and Disadvantages

Neither the legal profession nor the social work profession can claim to play a superior role in addressing human rights issues. The approaches are simply different. However, a better understanding by both professions as to how they address human rights could result in a better coordinated effort to reach a common goal.

The Legal Approach

A primary advantage to the legal approach in promoting human rights issues is that lawyers have concrete tools to address these issues if laws exist prohibiting the human rights violations or granting the human right. If necessary, lawyers can take action in court to assist individuals in obtaining access to their human rights.

Without legal enforcement, actual enjoyment of rights may depend too much on cultural and societal norms. Cultural relativism certainly plays a key role within the concept of human rights (Reichert, 2003, 2006a, 2006b). But, in some instances, established human rights should prevail over cultural traditions. Thus cultural norms should not excuse racial segregation or domestic violence. The legal approach, although cumbersome and heavy-handed, may result in an outcome that social workers find incomplete or ineffective. Without the option of legal enforcement, however, many human rights may never be realized. For that reason, laws promoting human rights are important tools, no matter how cumbersome the legal process.

A primary disadvantage of the legal approach to human rights, on the other hand, is the focus on existing laws. If a law or court opinion does not exist with which to address a particular human rights issue, the lawyer's hands will generally be tied. This was the case in the U.S. legal fight against racial segregation, which seemed so clearly wrong. Because decisions by the U.S. Supreme Court continued to allow segregation to exist, lawyers found it difficult to overcome this gross human rights violation. This reliance on past court decisions, which may have appeared socially acceptable at the time of the decision but which no longer apply to current circumstances, can create a societal logjam. What if the Court had never overruled the "separate but equal" doctrine in 1954? How many more years would it have taken to allow blacks and whites to attend the same schools in the South? Would racial segregation still exist today if Supreme Court justices had believed in or accepted segregation as many previous justices did? Sadly, that was a distinct possibility.

Clearly the primary disadvantage to the legal approach is the opposite of its advantage: laws can work against realizing human rights just as they can promote human rights. Bringing human rights issues to court can also be expensive, leaving many individuals outside the legal process.

Robert J. McCormick

The Social Work Approach

The primary advantage of the social work approach to human rights clearly consists of its direct intervention into a human rights issue. Social workers, in their dealing with human rights, do not have to wait for laws to be passed. They have the unique advantage of experiencing circumstances firsthand, as many are positioned with agencies whose specific duties encompass the well-being of society.

In times of crisis, social workers would be instrumental in meeting the needs of those without food, medical care, mental health counseling, and shelter. The lawyer could only refer these individuals to agencies for assistance, whereas the social worker can directly intervene in order to help.

The disadvantage, however, is that, compared to the legal approach in promoting human rights, the social work approach can go only as far as the laws will allow. Certainly it is not advisable for social workers to violate existing laws in order to assist those in need. Thus, although social workers are in a position to more readily assist those in need, legal guidelines place limits on that assistance. For example, a social worker employed to evaluate individuals for government medical care, housing assistance, or food subsidies, should not falsify evaluations to include individuals who do not meet legal guidelines. Although the inclination of social workers might be to include those individuals, especially where the need for assistance is obvious, the law forbids this action.

A primary disadvantage of the social work approach rests upon its limitations in bringing about change without legal approval. In that sense, social workers can only assist lawyers who can represent clients seeking the enforcement of human rights laws.

Merging Law and Social Work to Promote Human Rights

The overwhelming logic mandates that lawyers and social workers pool their efforts to promote human rights. This cooperation could resemble the juvenile court situation. Social workers would provide lawyers with information as to actual conditions and make recommendations without regard to restrictive legal procedures. Lawyers would then take this information and tailor it to existing laws or take action to change laws if necessary.

The "second Bill of Rights" is an excellent example of how lawyers and social workers could work together. On January 11, 1944, before the end of World War II, the U.S. president Franklin D. Roosevelt made a speech before the Congress in which he listed a number of rights to which every citizen is entitled (Sunstein, 2004, p. 243):

- The right to a useful and remunerative job in the industries or shops or farms or mines of the nation;
- The right to earn enough to provide adequate food and clothing and recreation;
- The right of every farmer to raise and sell his products at a return which will give him and his family a decent living;
- The right of every businessman, large and small, to trade in an atmosphere of freedom from unfair competition and domination by monopolies at home or abroad;
- The right of every family to a decent home;
- The right to adequate medical care and the opportunity to achieve and enjoy good health;
- The right to adequate protection from the economic fears of old age, sickness, accident, and unemployment; and
- The right to a good education.

By contemporary standards, most of these rights still seem desirable to share with all individuals. Many of these rights were incorporated in the Universal Declaration of Human Rights adopted by the United Nations several years later. Most countries (but not the U.S.) have also bound themselves to promote similar rights by adopting the UN Covenant on Economic, Social, and Cultural Rights, which requires countries to at least make efforts to promote these rights, according to their resources (United Nations, 1976). Clearly the focus of this second Bill of Rights is to ensure an economic and social fabric that benefits all.

Even with the above legal precedents for incorporating a second Bill of Rights into U.S. legislation, existing laws and court opinions inhibit the United States in promoting these human rights. As noted, unlike European countries, the U.S. has failed to adopt the UN Covenant on Economic, Social, and Cultural Rights. By adopting this covenant, a country agrees to recognize the "right of everyone to an adequate standard of living for himself and his family, including adequate food, clothing, and housing, and to the continuous improvement of living conditions" (Article 11). The covenant also requires countries to recognize the right of everyone to the "enjoyment of the highest attainable standard of physical and mental health" and requires countries to create "conditions which would assure all medical service and medical attention in the event of sickness" (Article 12). In other words, the UN Covenant on Economic, Social, and Cultural Rights contains many provisions similar to President Roosevelt's second Bill of Rights.

What went wrong? Why has the U.S. lagged behind in promoting economic and social human rights? Some of the resistance to economic rights might be cultural: "America's underlying individualism, its belief that poverty can be escaped through sheer effort, and its caution about strong efforts to redistribute resources from the wealthy to the poor" (Sunstein, 2004, p. 134) probably reflects the best version of the cultural account. In one poll 70 percent of Americans said that people are poor because of laziness, not because of society, whereas 70 percent of West Germans said that people are poor because of society rather than laziness (ibid.). However, an additional, noteworthy point stems from the earlier discussion of racial segregation. "In the United States, racial issues have played a large role in determining the shape and nature of redistributive programs" (ibid.). Compared to Europeans, Americans are especially likely to think of poor people as coming from a different racial group. The absence of a European-style social welfare state in the United States is certainly connected with the widespread perception among the white majority that the relevant programs would disproportionately benefit African Americans (and, more recently, Hispanics) (ibid.).

Although the U.S. has not embraced economic and social human rights, this does not mean that the redistribution of income is absent. In fact, large-scale government programs to redistribute income to large corporations, wealthy or upper-middle-class individuals through tax cuts and other benefits are common in the United States (Reichert, 2003). The problem of lagging in the promotion of economic human rights seems to be a result of historical and cultural motivations rather than lack of resources.

Considering the historical and arguably contemporary reluctance of the United States to address racial segregation and societal ills that have resulted from this egregious practice, what right does the United States have to hold itself out as a beacon of human rights? A leading human rights author, Michael Ignatieff, posed this question in a contorted essay entitled "Who are Americans to Think That Freedom Is Theirs to Spread?" (Ignatieff, 2005). Ignatieff notes that Thomas Jefferson and other founding fathers believed that the American experiment of freedom would spread to the whole world. Although Ignatieff does not miss the irony of such an idea from Jefferson, a slave owner, he gives this idea of American exceptionalism too much leeway.

Ignatieff is most likely correct in presenting the premise that most people want freedom to decide for themselves how they wish to be governed. However, Ignatieff takes this further and proposes that Americans are special in their desire to spread freedom elsewhere. He uses this exceptionalism to argue that Americans have earned the right to spread freedom, just as the early founders thought might happen. The problem with Ignatieff's proposition is that freedom has many meanings and shades of gray. Freedom is not simply something that can be packaged American style and exported. Americans themselves struggle with economic and social conditions within the United States that others find repulsive. Nowhere is this more evident than in U.S. Supreme Court decisions on racial segregation.

Promoting the United States as the enforcer or disseminator of human rights on a global scale creates enormous problems, especially as the U.S. itself does not even recognize many international human rights treaties and guidelines. From a legal perspective, the best approach for the United States is that of promoting human rights within its own borders and working with other countries to realize human rights. Claiming U.S. exceptionalism in the area of human rights runs the danger of hypocrisy and a dilution of the actual attributes the U.S. has established in this area.

Promoting Economic, Social, and Cultural Human Rights: The Role of Social Workers and Lawyers

After Hurricane Katrina devastated parts of New Orleans in 2005, news media from all over the world exposed not simply the physical damage of the hurricane but also a racial and economic divide that raised obvious questions about U.S. social conditions. Poverty afflicts all races and communities within the United States, but the starkness of the economic and social conditions in New Orleans after Katrina made it difficult for people to close their eyes to reality.

The purpose of economic, social, and cultural human rights is to alleviate and respond to situations that exist in New Orleans, in other parts of the U.S., and in the world beyond. To downplay these human rights while trumpeting political and civil rights is unreasonable, punitive, and insensitive.

Social workers are uniquely positioned to assist in promoting economic, social, and cultural human rights. By the very nature of their work, many social workers see firsthand the economic and social deprivations so highly visible after Katrina. If the social work mission is truly to "enhance human well-being and help meet the basic human needs of all people, with particular attention to the needs and empowerment of all people who are vulnerable, oppressed, and living in poverty," then social workers should be at the forefront of promoting economic human rights. Their role should be to assist the needy, informing the public about these conditions, and advocating laws that promote educational and economic opportunities for the impoverished. No other group has an equivalent firsthand knowledge to play this role.

Lawyers, too, have a role to play in promoting economic, social, and cultural human rights. Too often, the legal profession has succumbed to greed while ignoring its own role of assisting those in need. During the civil rights movement in the 1960s, lawyers often donated time and effort to bring about a more just society. Legal aid societies often represented low-income individuals in efforts to change inequitable societal conditions. However, a seemingly inevitable backlash appears to have halted the legal profession's zeal to undertake issues that promote economic, social, and human rights. Yet, as Katrina and other global events have shown, the need for these human rights worldwide has never been greater.

The experiences of social workers and their knowledge concerning human rights could arouse the legal profession to once again take on causes to promote these rights. The outcome would be that, as with the juvenile court system, social workers would supply information and recommendations, and lawyers would place that information in legal arguments promoting human rights. Together the two professions could advocate for changes in laws, supporting their advocacy with actual case studies and legal theories based on human rights law. Although courts may initially reject these types of cases, the importance of the issues would ultimately overcome the resistance. Education, health care, living wages, housing—the list of human rights issues is lengthy. Social workers and lawyers could do much to help by devoting at least a part of their time in promoting these worthy causes.

Conclusion

The legal and social work professions may seem odd bedfellows in the advocacy of human rights. Too much emphasis on the legal side of human rights may turn social workers away from a more profound embrace of this area of need. By working together, however, both professions have much to offer in promoting human rights; by doing so, lawyers and social workers could bring about a fundamental shift in contemporary approaches to such rights. No longer would human rights be left to politicians posturing for election; instead, human rights would truly become a key component of everyday society.

References

Addams, J. (1911, January). Social control. *Crisis*, 22–23.

Brown v. Board of Education. (1954). 347 US 483.

Civil Rights Act, as amended. (1964). 42 USC sec. 1971, 1975a-d, 2000a-h-6.

Civil Rights Cases. (1883). 109 US 3.

Council on Social Work Education. (2003). Handbook of accreditation standards and procedures (5th ed.). Alexandira, VA: CSWE Press.

Hall, K. (Ed.). (1992). *The Oxford companion to the Supreme Court of the United States*. Oxford and New York: Oxford University Press.

Ignatieff, M. (2005), June 26). Who are Americans to think that freedom is theirs to spread ? New York time Magazine.

Illinois Domestic Relations Act. (1976). 750 ILCS 5/602.

International Federation of Social Workers (IFSW). (2004).Code of ethics. Retrieved, November 192005 from www.ifsw.org/enp38000324.html

Lissak, R. (1989). *Pluralism and progressives: Hull house and the new immigrants, 1890–1919.* Chicago: University of Chicago Press.

National Association of Social Workers (NASW). (1999). Code of Ethics. (Rev. ed). Washington DC: NASW Press.

National Association of Social Workers. (2003). *Social work speaks: National Association of Social Workers policy statements, 2003–2006* (6th ed.). Washington, DC: NASW Press.

Plessy v. Fergusson. (1896).163 US 537.

Reichert, E. (2003). *Social work and human rights: A foundation for policy and practice.* New York: Columbia University Press.

Reichert, E. (2006 a). Understanding Human Rights: An Exercise Book. Sage, Thousand Oaks,

Reichert, E. (2006 b). An Examination of Universalism and Cultural Relativism. Journal of Comparative social Welfare, 22 (1) 23-36.

Scott v. Sandford. (1857). 60 US 393.

Slaughterhouse Cases. (1873). 83 US 36.

Sunstein, C. (2004). *The second Bill of Rights: FDR's unfinished revolution and Why We Need It More Than Ever.* New York: Basic Books.

United Nations. (1948). Universal Declaration of Human Rights. Adopted December 10, 1948. GA.Res. 217 AIII. United Nations Document a/810. New York: United Nations.

United Nations. (1976). International Covenant on Economic, Social, and Cultural Rights. United States Constitution, 1787.

Contributors

Silvia Staub Bernasconi has been a professor of social work and human rights at the Zurich School of Social Work (1967–1997) and at the Technical University of Berlin (1997–2003). Since 2002, she has been director of the Master of Social Work (Social Work as Human Rights Profession) in Berlin and is currently vice president of the German Society of Social Work. Dr. Bernasconi has special interests in theory of social problems and social work; social work and human/social rights; poverty, gender, migration, and intercultural conflicts, and racism.

Mary Bricker-Jenkins is a member of the National Staff of the Poor People's Economic Human Rights Campaign (PPEHRC) and co-convener of the School of Social Work and Social Transformation of the University of the Poor, PPEHRC's educational arm. She began her career over forty years ago as a New York City welfare worker and has practiced, taught, and published in the areas of child welfare, feminist social work, community organizing, social welfare history, and economic human rights. Recently retired from Temple University, she has returned to her home at WIT's End Farm in Tennessee, where she continues her work with PPEHRC, teaches part-time at Dalton State College and the University of Tennessee-Chattanooga, and spends as much time as possible on the Tennessee River.

Lena Dominelli is professor of applied social studies and head of Social, Community and Youth Work at the University of Durham in the UK. She is an educator, researcher, and practitioner with many years' experience and has written widely in the fields of social work. Her most important books are *Revitalising Communities in a Globalising World*; *Social Work: Theory and Practice for a Changing Profession; Women and Community Action* (2nd ed.); *Anti-Racist Social Work* (3rd ed.); *Anti-Oppressive Social Work Theory and Practice*; and *Feminist Social Work Theory and Practice*.

Cheri Honkala is the national coordinator and co-founder of the Poor People's Economic Human Rights Campaign. A formerly homeless mother, she founded the Kensington Welfare Rights Union in 1991 and helped pioneer an economic human rights movement in this country. She has organized massive marches, freedom bus tours, and projects of survival led by the poor themselves. In 2003, Cheri became the national coordinator for the PPEHRC, and she continues speaking, writing, demonstrating, and organizing toward building a nonviolent movement, led by the poor, for economic human rights for all.

Jim Ife has been professor of social work and social policy, and head of the School of Social Work and Social Policy, at the University of Western Australia, and at Curtin University, Perth. He was foundation professor of human rights education and head of the Centre for Human Rights Education at Curtin University until his retirement in 2006. He is a former president of Amnesty International Australia, and former secretary of the Human Rights Commission of the International Federation of Social Workers. His books include *Human Rights and Social Work: Towards Rights-Based Practice* (Cambridge University Press, 2001).

Rosemary Link is a professor in the Department of Social Work, Augsburg College, Minneapolis, and chair of the board of Southside Family Nurturing Center. Dr. Link has a special interest in children's rights and family well-being and has published studies in the United States and United Kingdom relating to children, poverty, and the impact of U.S. welfare on people in poverty. As a commissioner for the CSWE Global Commission, she is also participating in developing curriculum and pedagogy that expands global cooperation, increases reciprocal exchange of ideas, and builds international partnerships for social workers and educators. This work includes a Department of State grant to develop video Internet classrooms in Slovenia and Singapore.

Robert McCormick is a lawyer who, through his work in family law and other areas of the law, has experienced firsthand the deficiencies in social welfare within this country. He has previously published with Elisabeth Reichert, including articles on human rights of immigrants, role of social workers in criminal prosecution of child sex abuse, and child welfare in the United States and Germany.

James Midgley is Harry and Riva Specht Professor of Public Social Services and former dean of the School of Social Welfare, University of California, Berkeley. He has published widely on social development and international social welfare. His most recent books include *Social Policy for Development* (with Anthony Hall; Sage Publications, 2004); *Lessons from Abroad: Adapting International Social Welfare Innovations* (with M. C. Hokenstad; NASW Press, 2004); *International Encyclopedia of Social Policy* (edited with Tony Fitzpatrick, Huk-ju Kwong, Nick Manning, and Gail Pascall; Routledge, 2006) and *International Perspectives on Welfare to Work Policy* (edited with Richard Hoefer; Haworth Press, 2006).

Brij Mohan is professor and former dean of the School of Social Work at Louisiana State University, Baton Rouge. Recent works include *Fallacies of Development* (2007), *Reinventing Social Work* (2005), *The Practice of Hope* (2003), *Social Work Revisited* (2002), *Unification of Social Work* (1999), and *Eclipse of Freedom* (1993). He is founding editor-in-chief of the *Journal of Comparative Social Welfare*. During nearly a half century of academic voyage, he has contributed to the understanding of complex social systems, problems, and phenomena with critical reasoning, uncanny analytic thinking, and passionate humanism.

Elisabeth Reichert is professor in the School of Social Work at Southern Illinois University at Carbondale. She received her degree in social work from the University of Tennessee with the aid of a Fulbright Scholarship. She also holds an equivalent degree in Germany. She practiced clinical social work until 1994, when she began teaching social work policy and practice. She has published extensively on social work practice and human rights, including: *Social Work and Human Rights: A Foundation for Policy and Practice* (Columbia University Press, 2003) and *Understanding Human Rights: An Exercise Book* (Sage Publications, 2006).

Katherine van Wormer, M.S.S.W., Ph.D., is professor of social work at the University of Northern Iowa. She has written twelve books in the fields of social work and criminal justice, most recently *Human Behavior and the Social Environment, Micro Level,* and coauthored *HBSE, Macro Level, Women and the Criminal Justice System* and *Addiction Treatment: A Strengths Perspective,* 2nd ed.

Janice Wood Wetzel is a former dean and professor emerita of Social Work at Adelphi University. She is the main United Nations NGO Representative for the International Association of Schools of Social Work and serves as chair of the UN Committee on Mental Health. Dr. Wetzel has published extensively, with a focus on women's international human rights, advancement, and mental health.

Joseph Wronka is professor of social work, Springfield College, Springfield, MA and principal investigator of The Universal Declaration of Human Rights Project, originating in the Center for Social Change of the Heller School for Social Policy and Management, Brandeis University. He has extensive practice, research, and teaching experience in a variety of settings, such as New York City, Alaska, and Europe. He has published extensively in a variety of scholarly and popular fora, having presented his work in fourteen countries.

Carrie Young is a member of the national staff of the Poor People's Economic Human Rights Campaign (PPEHRC). She is a social worker and has participated in developing models of social work practice based on economic human rights. Carrie is a member of the Kensington Welfare Rights Union (KWRU) and the School of Social Work and Social Transformation of the University of the Poor, the educational arm of PPEHRC. She is an adjunct faculty member at the School of Social Administration at Temple University and is parenting two young children.

Index